DEVON AND CORNWALL RECORD SOCIETY

New Series, Volume 53

Issued to members of the society for the year 2010

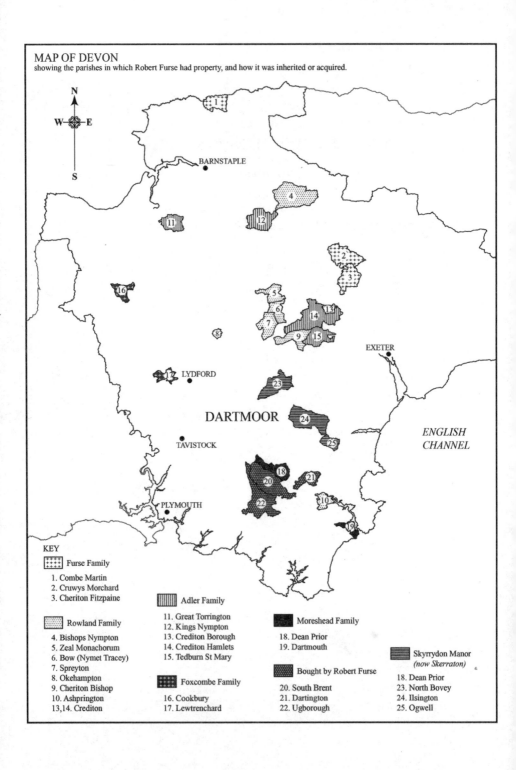

MAP OF DEVON
showing the parishes in which Robert Furse had property, and how it was inherited or acquired.

N
W—E
S

BARNSTAPLE

4
12
11
2
3
16
5
6
13
7
14
8
9
15
EXETER
17 LYDFORD
23
DARTMOOR
24
TAVISTOCK
25
ENGLISH
CHANNEL
18
20 21
PLYMOUTH 22
10
19

KEY

▦ Furse Family
1. Combe Martin
2. Cruwys Morchard
3. Cheriton Fitzpaine

▦ Rowland Family
4. Bishops Nympton
5. Zeal Monachorum
6. Bow (Nymet Tracey)
7. Spreyton
8. Okehampton
9. Cheriton Bishop
10. Ashprington
13,14. Crediton

▦ Foxcombe Family
16. Cookbury
17. Lewtrenchard

▦ Adler Family
11. Great Torrington
12. Kings Nympton
13. Crediton Borough
14. Crediton Hamlets
15. Tedburn St Mary

▦ Moreshead Family
18. Dean Prior
19. Dartmouth

▦ Bought by Robert Furse
20. South Brent
21. Dartington
22. Ugborough

▦ Skyrrydon Manor
(now Skerraton)
18. Dean Prior
23. North Bovey
24. Ilsington
25. Ogwell

DEVON AND CORNWALL RECORD SOCIETY

New Series, Volume 53

ROBERT FURSE

A DEVON FAMILY MEMOIR OF 1593

Edited by

Anita Travers

Exeter

2012

ISBN 978-0-901853-53-0

Typeset by Kestrel Data, Exeter, Devon.

Printed and bound in Great Britain by
Short Run Press Ltd, Exeter, Devon.

CONTENTS

LIST OF ILLUSTRATIONS
AND TEXT FIGURES

PREFACE AND ACKNOWLEDGEMENTS

When Keystone Historic Buildings Consultants of Exeter surveyed the sixteenth century farmhouse Broomham, in Kings Nympton, in 1995, and I assisted with documentary research, we became aware of the remarkable description of it by Robert Furse (c.1530–1593), in the book of information he compiled for his fledgling son, when he himself knew he had not long to live. In particular we thought the information about buildings notable, and that it was well worth transcription, and that the Devon Buildings Group might be interested in publishing it in some form. When the Devon and Cornwall Record Society expressed an interest, we were pleased at the prospect of wider distribution. This is not merely a Devon text; it has a wider interest for historians of Tudor England.

Dr Jo Cox and John Thorp of Keystone have been unfailingly helpful and supportive of the project with travel, photographs and advice, and I am deeply grateful to Sandi Ellison for assistance with typing, formatting and general technology beyond my capacity. I have had help thoughout from the staff of the Devon Record Office, the Westcountry Studies Library and the Devon and Exeter Institution. Bevan Ashford, solicitors, Tiverton, successors to Penny and Harward who deposited the document in Devon Record Office in 1975 (D2507), confirm they have no record of ownership of the document.

Thanks are due to Mr and Mrs David Smith, the current owners of Moorshead, for making both the ruins of Furse's house, and their collection of historic material, available to us. Mrs Phoebe Woollcombe kindly allowed us to photograph the watercolour of Furse's house, Moorshead, in her family possession, and the *Western Morning News* agreed that we might use the drawing which appeared in the newspaper in 1937. The Revd D. J. Rowland, whose ministry includes Dean Prior, gave permission for the photograph of Furse's tombstone. The map of Devon showing the whereabouts of Robert Furse's properties has been prepared by Brett Humphries.

Finally, I would like to thank Dr Oliver Padel for his patient help and guidance in steering me through the final stages of preparing this volume for publication.

INTRODUCTION

Robert Furse of Moreshead in Dean Prior (d. 1593) was a proud man. By his own sagacity and that of his ancestors he had acquired a sizeable estate in Devon. By 1620 his son bore arms and was included in the herald's visitation. He was proud of the arms borne by the Trunchard family, his grandmother being Mary Foxsecombe alias Trunchard. Robert was not ashamed of his humble origins and gave credit to ancestors who, although some were 'but sympell and unlernede', had nevertheless bettered themselves, acquiring and passing on land. He was proud of relatives who had been in royal service, or that of the Marquess of Exeter, or had been at the inns of court. He inherited Moreshead, now Moorshead, in 1557, and probably married then or soon after, and had nine daughters, and at last, in 1584 what must have been a longed-for son. When the boy was only nine, however, Furse realised he was ill and had not long to live. He refers to having 'plage', but it cannot have been bubonic plague, for that is a quick death and Furse had time to put his affairs in order. Because his son was too young to be taught all the background to his inheritance, and how to manage it, Furse wrote it all down for him in a book. Although sometimes referred to as his memorandum book it is much more systematic than the jottings which that might suggest. It introduces each known line of ancestry, and then details the lands which that family had and passed on to their heirs. He used 'evidences', which must have been a considerable collection of deeds, no longer extant, as well as reports of older men and his own experience, particularly in courts of law, and he refers to documents of the Courtenays, to which he appears to have had access.

He was proud of his public offices as constable of Stanborough hundred and juror, and of his high subsidy payment and the substantial quantity of armour and weaponry required of him for a muster.[1] He was proud of the dowries he provided for his daughters.[2] He defended his title at law when provoked to do so and was proud of his legal victories, refused to pay dues not properly authenticated,[3] and defended his seating in church.[4] He seems to approve of his forebears who kept a good house and entertained generously, but not those who were over-lavish, spending too much of the wealth which should have descended to him. A revealing remark concerns Walter Furse, who played 'an instrument', then apparently came to his senses, set it aside and married a rich widow.[5] One of Furse's proudest achievements was to purchase 'Skyrrydon', or Skerraton, a whole manor with an impressive history.[6] His character and aspirations are most fully revealed in the homily with which he begins, addressed 'to the Reder and to all his Sequelle', that is to his son and descendants. It is full of advice on moral conduct, husbandry, maintaining a household, treatment of servants and tenants, choosing a wife and bringing up children. His advice is packed with obscure proverbs, and quotations from philosophers and from scripture.

He took pride in the renovation of the house he inherited, Moreshead.[7] Sadly it does not survive, although it was sufficently intact in the first half of the twentieth century for some sketches and photographs to be made. Some ruined walls remain in the grounds of the present house, which is a barn conversion. The house was already empty in 1878, and Lord Churston removed the linenfold wainscotting for preservation at Lupton House, in Brixham, which was gutted by fire in 1926.[8] It was being farmed at the time of the tithe award, when the farm comprised 149 acres as to Furse's 68. The house and courtlage are tithe no. 614. Some field names are recognisable as those given by Furse.

1. p. 75; Howard and Stoate, *The Devon Muster Roll for 1569*, p. 208.
2. Below, pp. 76–7.
3. For example, for Rowdon mills, below, pp. 81–4.
4. Below, pp. 78–9.
5. Below, p. 31.
6. Below, pp. 93–126.
7. Below, pp. 72–3; its remains are at SX713634.
8. *Western Morning News*, 1 May 1937; Keane, *Herrick's Parish: Dean Prior*, p. 17; Pevsner, *Buildings of Devon*, p. 833.

G. W. Copeland described it in his notebooks in 1934, using his own idiosyncratic architectural abbreviations. These have been expanded in square brackets as far as possible, but some remain obscure.

Morshead

A derelict mass[ive] farmho[use]. Main front, S., 2 proj[ecting] wings N + later timber and sl[ate] h[un]g: gabled addn between. S. porch has a low pyr[amidal] roof, a dep[ressed] crude c. clef. outer d[oor]w[ay] + mono[lithic] jambs, 2 steps to, + rem[ain]s of m[oun]t[in]g bl[ock], E., st[one] slats, a pebble floor, and a c. clef. obt. gran[ite] inner d[oor]w[ay]. W. of porch a lofty and boldly proj[ecting] chim[ney] which diminished considerably upwards. Over porch and to E of it a row of nest holes bel[ow] eaves. St[one] steps at end, E. all W[indow] frames gone. Farm bldgs W[est]. Rect[angular] st[one] trough at rear. The main room on the ground floor behind and to W of porch has the remains of a g[oo]d flat timbered roof + m[ou]l[de]d principals on corbels, & mld. rafters stopped at ends. The roof to E, or ceiling, is pl[aine]r, lower, and sagging. The firepl[ace] to the chim[ney] is rect[angular] and of gran[ite] + ch[am]f[ered] jambs and a mono[lithic] rect[angular] gran[ite] lintel. N is a w[oo]d fr[a]m[ed]d. dec. + a dep[ressed] [drawing: triangle] – ar. bd. [*possibly arch braced, though usually of a roof*], c. clef. In a room NW is a rect. firepl. + w[oo]d rect. lintel and gran. jambs & cr. caps. Nothing of interest upstairs, but app[arent] rems. of an inner st. staircase at rear.

He draws three mouldings from the ceiling: rafter and stop, principal, and corbel.[9]

The exact nature of Furse's book appears to be unique, but it is related to a number of genres. First and foremost it is a family record for posterity, and in particular a record of landholding. It is not, however, a secular cartulary, as it does not transcribe deeds in full. It acts rather as a sort of index or guide to Furse's

---

9. Copeland notes (Plymouth and WDRO, 712/1/3). Gustave Wilfred Copeland (1893–1967) was a Plymouth schoolmaster, and Hon. Secretary of the Devonshire Association 1957–66 (*TDA* 100, 1967).

collection of deeds, which he envisaged remaining intact. This was disingenuous of him, since he himself referred to instances of documents stolen or eaten by mice. No doubt he kept his records safely and carefully in a good strong chest and expected his 'sequel' to do the same, but somewhere along the way they were scattered or lost, and only his remarkable book survives. He had already passed Crediton deeds to Sir Richard Prideaux of Thuborough when he sold him most of his Crediton lands in 1580 at the time of purchase of Skyrrydon (some going to his cousin Kingwill).[10] Prideaux's deeds eventually descended to the Shelley family, baronets, of Shobrooke, and are in Devon Record Office as Z1/10. These are the only known originals to have passed through Furse's hands. He must have kept informal copies or a detailed abstract in order to write so precisely about these properties a dozen years later. The other very striking difference from a cartulary is the wealth of human incident, anecdote, character and downright gossip which he interpolates, much no doubt from his long-lived grandmother Nicole Moreshead.

The book is also sometimes referred to as a 'diary', but it is far from a day-to-day or even intermittent account of Furse's life. Contemporary or near-contemporary diarists often included births and deaths of immediate family, and land transactions as they happened, but the writers do not explore and record ancestry in the way Furse does, anticipating the modern enthusiasm for family history.[11] If Furse had kept a diary it would have complemented this book and clarified obscure points, but if he did, it is not known to be extant. Diaries might include elements of the commonplace book such as favourite prayers, poems,

---

10. Below, p. 42.
11. For example, Dr John Dee, writing 1577–1601, noted births and baptisms of his children, hiring of servants, their wages, weather, his travels, astronomical phenomena and professional exchanges of information (Halliwell, *The private diary of Dr John Dee*). Henry Machyn of London, writing 1550–63, was more concerned with public events, producing more of a chronicle than a diary (Nicholls, *Henry Machyn, Diary 1550–63*). In Devon, William Honnywell, in the 1590s to early 1600s, records the property acquired with his wife, land and stock transactions, expenditure, annual visits to London, losses at play, the loan of a book (Apperson, *Gleanings after time*). Philip Wyott, town clerk of Barnstaple, writing 1586–1608, like Machyn made a more public than personal record, with the deaths of notables, weather and harvest, musters, assizes and shipping activity (Chanter, *Sketches of the literary history of Barnstaple*).

recipes and cures, but this is not Furse's intention either. The only prayer included is one of his own, composed for practical family use.

Furse was anxious that his young son should have not only a handy record of his ancestors and landholding, but good sound advice on moral conduct and in practical matters, but the morality informs the practicality. There were plenty of precedents. Peter Idley of Gloucestershire did it in the fifteenth century,[12] Lord Burghley did it in the sixteenth.[13] An elderly Parisian wrote advice for his child-bride in the fourteenth century, the Knight de la Tour Landry wrote advice for women, the generic goodwife advised her daughter and the wise man his son.[14] Few of these were available in print in Furse's lifetime, and similarities between them probably come down to common sense, handed-down wisdom, and conventional preaching. What were becoming popular in print were self-help books on etiquette, health, housekeeping, husbandry and child-rearing and it is possible Furse was aquainted with Boorde on health, or Ascham or Elyot on education and upbringing,[15] but he does not quote any contemporaries, only classical philosophers and the Bible.

This fondness for quotation raises interesting questions about Robert Furse's education and the books to which he did have access. He was born about 1530, in Great Torrington. He was thus educated in a turbulent period of the Reformation: during his schooldays the Bible in English went from being banned to

12. C. D'Evelyn, *Peter Idley's instructions to his son.* Idley was an Oxfordshire landowner and minor courtier who died in 1473. In her introduction (p. 36) D'Evelyn remarks on the Old English tradition of *fæder larcwidas*, apparently referring to the type of wisdom literature in which an older man advises a younger, exemplified by the Old English *Precepts*.

13. William Cecil, Lord Burghley, *Precepts, or the direction for the well ordering and carriage of a man's life.* Burghley chooses 'Precepts' as his title.

14. Power, *The Goodman of Paris*; Wright, *The Book of the Knight of La Tour-Landry*; Furnivall, *Caxton's Book of Curtesye*. F. J. Furnivall edited a large collection of books on child-rearing and manners as *Early English Meals and Manners.* It includes books of nurture by Hugh Rhodes and John Russell, 'The Babees Book', 'How the goodwife taught her daughter, 'How the wise man taught his son, 'Stans puer ad mensam', and many more.

15. For example, Andrew Boorde, *Introduction of Knowledge, 1547, Dyetary of Helth, 1542*; Roger Ascham, *The Scholemaster*; Sir Thomas Elyot, *The Book named the Governor.*

being state-sponsored. At the same time the Renaissance had influenced and changed the textbooks used for teaching. Printing had been in use in England for only 50 years, one book had been printed in Devon (Boethius, at Tavistock Abbey in 1525),[16] and the availability of particular books in the provinces is uncertain. Exeter Cathedral had a well-stocked library of course,[17] and by the end of the century parish libraries were not uncommon, and the surviving collections of four of them are preserved in Exeter University Library.[18]

Furse may have been educated at Torrington, where there was a school: a widow is recorded as holding part of the 'scolehouse' in 1486,[19] and Thomas Bennet, who taught in Exeter in 1525–30, had previously taught in Torrington, but this does not prove a continuity of schoolmasters.[20] He may have been educated at Exeter, where relatives had connections with the cathedral, or at Barnstaple, which is much nearer Torrington, and had a reputable school. Bishop Jewel, Furse's contemporary, was at school in South Molton in the 1530s.[21] Furse's uncle Edward, apparently not much older than he, was at school in Tavistock in the 1530s. This is a considerable distance from Torrington, but Edward's father was steward to Tavistock Abbey.[22] It is just possible that Furse accompanied his young uncle, but his schooling remains conjecture. Although his father had come up in the world, a private tutor seems unlikely.

Furse does not come across as a bookish man: a man of action, a man of law, but not one to read for pleasure. His will does not survive, so we cannot know if he left any books. He certainly had enough Latin to keep manor court rolls, which he quotes a few times, but his classical quotations are all in translation. As his reaction to the need to educate his son was to compile a notebook, it may well be that he had other notebooks, such as a commonplace book, maybe from his schooldays, in which he noted the improving platitudes he draws on to illustrate

---

16. Kingdon, 'Tavistock Library'; Finberg, *Tavistock Abbey*, Appendix D.
17. Lloyd and Erskine, *The Library of Exeter Cathedral*.
18. Crediton, Barnstaple, Totnes and Ottery St Mary.
19. Orme, *Education in the West of England 1066–1548*, p. 100.
20. *ibid.*, p. 46.
21. *ibid.*, p. 104.
22. *ibid.*, p. 106.

his points. They may reflect his own translation exercises. 'Those who worked in schools did copying themselves, and, as the manuscripts show, they could produce a comprehensive miscellany of texts by their own efforts.'[23] Just so may the pupils have come away with a useful miscellany. It is a telling point that where Furse writes 'Isaiah liij'[24] he should have written 'li:j', the inference being that he was copying from not the Bible itself, but some handwritten source easily misread. Furse's English spelling is highly idiosyncratic and obviously reflects how he heard and said words. It can be tempting to wonder if he dictated from his sickbed, but the sheer narrative drive, and the recourse to documents, makes that unlikely. The original spelling has been retained for the benefit of dialect research.

Most of Furse's biblical quotations can be traced, although not to one single translation. His classical quotations are much more obscure, partly because they are so bland and platitudinous as to be hardly worth attributing. The editor of Peter Idley's advice says he had before him 'the familiar stock of medieval didactic material, the precepts made common by "Cato" and by Solomon before him, and the moral teachings set for them by every parish priest.'[25] Furse's sources do not seem to be the *Distichs of Cato,* or the *Vulgarias* of Stanbridge or Whittinton.[26] Newly popular were Horace, Livy, Terence, Virgil and Ovid,[27] but of these Furse cites only Ovid, and only once. It is no surprise that he should cite Socrates, Seneca, Marcus Aurelius or Aristotle, but the surprising two are 'Cleob' and 'Pyream', apparently Cleobulus and Periander, two of the Seven Sages of Greece, their names again perhaps distorted by transcription from a manuscript. It is possible that they were quoted in turn by the later philosophers. Unlike the Bible, Furse never gives the title of a book for classical authors, and this seems to have been common to published anthologies of adages and proverbs in the sixteenth century. Erasmus published quotations from the Seven

---

23. Orme, 'Schools and Schoolbooks', in *The Cambridge History of the Book in Britain*, III, p. 455.
24. Below, p. 12.
25. D'Evelyn, *Peter Idley*, p. 36.
26. White, *The Vulgaria of John Stanbridge and the Vulgaria of Robert Whittinton.*
27. Hellinga and Trapp, *Cambridge History of the Book in Britain*, Introduction, p. 26. Byrne, *The Elizabethan Home*, p. 4.

Sages, and Richard Taverner translated and published them in
1540, but they do not match Furse's quotations.[28] Neither do
they match Erasmus's Adages published by Taverner or Udall.[29]
If he did keep a school notebook Furse's English translations may
be his own, which further lessens the likelihood of pinpointing
them in such classical concordances as exist, in the original
Latin or Greek. Whatever his source, Furse clearly felt that the
quotations gave his words gravity and authority.

Towards the latter part of the book Furse was running out of
time. In his descriptions of properties acreages and values are
often left blank for filling at a later date, which never came. It was
his intention that the book should be added to by his successors.
Certainly his son John filled in information on marriages of
his sisters after their father's death, but John died quite young.
There is also a ghostly 'sould' alongside some properties, which
may be the hand of John, or his stepfather, or a descendant.
Furse's widow, Wilmot, remarried within a few years, to Arthur
Hart, of Plympton St Mary, and it was probably he who oversaw
the young man's upbringing. What recourse he had to Furse's
book can only be conjecture. Although Furse had proposed a
marriage for John to Susan Alford, probably a relation although
the connection is untraced, he in fact married Welthian Snelling
of Plympton, who brought a property, Chaddlewood, with her,
and was possibly a better prospect. Their son John used the end
pages to record details of his Chaddlewood inheritance. When
the last Furse heiress, Elizabeth, married John Worth of Worth
in 1705 the book went with her and was used to record births of
her children up to 1717.

When H. J. Carpenter wrote about the book, with extracts,
in 1894, it was in a 'West Country house.'[30] Unfortunately he
does not name the house, nor is this necessarily the date at
which he saw it. The book was also used by C. J. Perry Keene
in his *Herricks's Parish: Dean Prior, with stories and songs of
the Dean Burn* (Plymouth, 1926), but he was working from

---

28. Richard Taverner, *Flores aliquot sententiarum ex variis collecti scriptoribus: the
    Flowers of Sencies Englished by R. Taverner* (1540).
29. Richard Taverner, *Proverbs or Adages by Desiderius Erasmus* (1569); Nicholas
    Udall, *Apothegms first gathered by Erasmus* (1564: Boston 1877).
30. H. J. Carpenter, 'Furse of Moreshead. A family record of the sixteenth century',
    TDA 26 (1894), pp. 193–209.

transcripts made for certain members of the Morshead and Skardon families 'of which their solicitors have kindly lent copies'. There is no means of telling whether these were complete transcripts, or sections relating only to those families (Skardon scarcely features as a family), or what has become of them since. Keene's quotations are riddled with inaccurate spellings, and even the date he ascribes to it, '25 Elizabeth, 1582' is wrong. Mildred Campbell cites Furse in her *The English Yeoman under Elizabeth and the Early Stuarts* (Yale, New Haven 1942), but only drawing on Carpenter's article and extracts. Carpenter's article was also used by W. G. Hoskins in a chapter on 'The estates of the Caroline gentry' (1952); he compared the estates described by Furse with those registered by the Court of Wards (National Archives, Wards 5/10, no. 1813) after the deaths of Robert Furse (1594), his widow Wilmot (1600), and John Furse (1627). Lyn Collins and Elizabeth Collins made a transcript in modernised English in 1988, and privately published a revision of this in 2000 for circulation to existing Moorsheads, who held a family convention in that year. Although some might welcome Furse's English modernised, much of the flavour would be lost, as well as the interest of the Devon vernacular and pronunciation of his time. This transcript retains the original; a glossary is provided.

Part of the Worth estate was sold in 1873. Reginald Worth, last of the line, died in 1880. He was rector of Newton Poppleford, and died in Wiltshire. His sister, Henrica Duntze, completed the sale of the estate in 1888. Carpenter might have seen and used the book before Reginald Worth's death and published his extracts later, the book may have stayed in the house, or he may have seen it in another house. Henrica married the Rector, William Lloyd Jones, who assumed the name Worth in 1882. They lived at Worth House; he died in 1882 and it was in 1887/8 that Mrs Lloyd-Worth sold it and moved to Beauchamp, an old family property in the same parish. This might have been the house where Carpenter saw the book.

The book was amongst a group of totally unrelated documents deposited in Devon Record Office by Penny and Harward, solicitors, of Tiverton, on 23 April 1975, and given the deposit number D2507. Successors Bevan Ashcroft of Tiverton have no record of its provenance or ownership. It is possible that

Carpenter, himself a solicitor, acted for the family, and borrowed the book or took it into safe-keeping. Although the name of the practice has altered many times over the years, Carpenter's address in Hamnett Square remains the same as that of the present solicitors.

Furse refers to his 'book', and appears to have acquired a book ready bound in leather rather than writing on loose pages with the intention of binding later. The incidence of blank pages after his own preliminary indexes, and at the end of the book, would tend to suggest this, although he might have deliberately inserted blank pages for the intended continuation of the volume by his descendants. Had he done so the blanks would be expected to occur at the beginnings or ends of gatherings, but this is not the case. However, he does write extremely close to the outside edge of the righthand pages, which would be less comfortable in a bound volume than loose sheets, and occasional words appear as if possibly cropped in binding. The volume was handsomely rebound at Devon Record Office in *c.* 1990, without any cropping, and the original cover retained with it, along with a few paper scraps presumably used as page markers. It is 8 inches by nearly 12 inches in size, and thus approximate to the modern A4 paper size. It begins with twelve unnumbered leaves including some genealogical notes and Furse's own indexes and introductory matter. This is followed apparently by 140 numbered folios, although in fact Furse misses two numbers and a few numbered folios are blank. There are seven unnumbered leaves at the end.

EDITORIAL PRACTICE

Robert Furse's text has been transcribed in his original spelling, because it comes across as a true 'voice', conveying much of Devon vernacular dialect and pronunciation in his time. A glossary is appended. However, where sense requires it, 'u' has been substituted for 'v', so that *vpon* becomes *upon*, and conversely, 'v' for 'u', so that *conueyans* becomes *conveyans*. Capitals have been applied to personal and place names where he is inconsistent, and some capitals he occasionally uses at the beginning of words, particularly 'R', changed to lower case to avoid undue emphasis. His use of lower case for 'god' has been retained, as it may be indicative of a sixteenth century righteous man's confident familiarity with his maker. Some additional punctuation has been introduced to his breathless headlong sentences for the comfort of the reader. Although he does not indent in modern fashion, he does introduce a kind of paragraph break by using bold letters in a broader pen for a new subject, or a fresh aspect of his subject. He frequently omits letters and these have been supplied in square brackets when particularly needed; similarly a few emendations of letters incorrectly written. Furse was inconsistent in his use of a flourish at the end of a word, using it for both *-es* and *-s*, so it has had to be inconsistently expanded. All matter in square brackets in the main text may be taken as insertions by the editor, in particular the expansion of regnal years. Furse's use of roman numerals has been retained, because it is all the more striking when he suddenly uses arabic. He lived in a period of transition, perhaps was conscious that his young son was going to conform to new styles, and that he should make a nod towards this. Similarly, his practice with pounds, shillings and pence has been retained, with no attempt to standardise to modern form. His abbreviations of personal names have been retained as illustrative of personal style, and of the pressure he felt to work at speed. Different typefaces have been employed to indicate later additions to the book in other hands, for example where his son adds to the information on his sister's marriages, and the whole section at the end where a grandson describes Chaddlewood, not a property owned by Furse. Furse's own numbering of the folios, starting at the beginning of his main text (p. 24), is given in the margins.

The following abbreviations are used:

DRO	Devon Record Office, Exeter
IPM	inquisition post mortem
PNDevon	*The Place-Names of Devon*, ed. J. E. B. Gover, A. Mawer and F. M. Stenton, English Place-Name Society 8, 9 (1931, 1932)
TDA	*Transactions of the Devonshire Association*
TNA	The National Archives
WSL	Westcountry Studies Library, Exeter

[ROBERT FURSE'S BOOK]

Anno Dno [*sic*] 1593

[*Robert Furse's opening for the whole book. The remainder of the page contains incomplete and damaged notes inside the front cover, including a quantity of numbers of no obvious meaning. The following relate to John Furse's children.*]

Elizabeth Furse was boren the 19 of March & cristned the 24th day of March Anno 1604 & the on Mayde that was boren to sune

Robert Furse was borne the 14th day of September and Crystened the 21st of Sep tember in Anno 1606

[The following page relates to a later generation.]

Mary Furse daughter of John Furse was borne
the tenth day of December & was baptized
the Twenty ninth day 1686 ... ... died [*torn*]

Elizabeth Furse daughter of John Furse was borne the two and
twentieth of January & baptize[d] the twentieth of February 1688.

[New hand]

Elizabeth Furse sole daughter and heir of John Furse Esq. married
John Worth of Worth Esq. in Devon June 11th 1705 and had [*torn*] by
him in Jany 1713/14 six children, one son dead, viz:

Mary Worth, John Worth, Elizabeth, Reginald (dyed), Henry, Bridgett,
Bamfylde.

[The following list has been added later.]

Mary Worth born Dec 15th 1706
John Worth born March 12 1707/8
Eliz: Worth born March 5 17[0]8/9
Reginald Worth born March 9 1709/10 (dead)
Henry Worth born June 13 1711
Bridgett Worth born Aug. 1712
Bampfylde Worth born Jan. 7 1713
Simon Worth born March 10th 1714/15
Reginald Worth June 11 1716
Furse Worth born J. 1717

[ROBERT FURSE'S INDEXES]

A plene and brefe note
howe hathe bynne cooheres
with us

John Chechester fo. 29
Nicolas Toker fo. 29
for John Foxsecombes londes
Benett Kyngewill fo. 21
for John Addeleres londes *sold*
John Honychurche fo. [117]
Johan Hoyell fo. [117]
for Edmonde Rolondes londes

The name and porsyon
the londes departed from us
by partision

Chechester hadde Weke fo. [29]
and Axseworthye fo. 29
Kyngewill hadde Morepytte
one tenement in Certon and
Chollacome and more he hade
the halfe of Erygge fo. 22
Tokyr hadde Foxsecome and
Kyttehyll fo. 29

A brefe note howe
of our awnsetores have
solde londe or otherwyse
alyenatde anye londes

Wyllyam Moreshed
solde londes fo. 33
Richarde Moresed fo. 33
Robert Furse fo. 18. 27. 111

Howe of our aunsetores
did purchas anye londes
and of whom

John Moreshede fo. 35
John Moresede fo. 38
John Furse fo. 7
John Furse fo. 21
John Furse fo. 31
Roberte Furse fo. 34. 71. 67. 65.
59. 110. 111. 113
Edmonde Rolond fo. 121. 122. 123.
125. 129. 133. 134. 135. 136

A Brefe note of the names of all those persones by whom we do inyoye their londes and from whom we are lyneally dyssended

Rolonde de Comba vide fo. 1
Willyam de la Furse fo. 1
Thomas Furse fo. 1
John Furse fo. 1
Willyam Furse fo. 1
Willyam Furse fo.1
Roberte Furse fo. 2
John Furse fo. 7
John Furse fo. 21
John Furse fo. 30
Roberte Furse fo. 34
John Furse fo.
John Adler als Atheler fo. 15. 16
Robert Hoper fo. 16
Rafe Dabernon fo. 16
Ellezabethe Dabernon fo. 15. 16
Thomas Harpeforde fo. 15
Elles Att More fo. 15
John Foxcombe fo. 29
Axseworthy fo. 29
Willm Foxcombe fo. 29
John de la Wall fo. 29
Willm Foxsecome fo. 29
John Foxcombe fo. 29
John Foxcombe fo. 29
Marye Foxcombe fo. 29. 21
Annes Addeler fo. 9. .7. 16
Walken le Bonde fo. 33
Marten le Bonde fo. 33
Rafe le Bonde fo. 33
Ame de Nuston fo. 33
[*torn*] illm Moreshede fo. 33
Symon Moreshede fo. 33
Simon Moreshedde fo. 34
Richard Moreshede fo. 34
Richard Sympeston fo. 33
Ellezabethe Sympeston fo. 33

John Moresede fo. 34
John Moresehede fo. 35
Robert Moreshede fo. 35
John Moresehede fo. 35. 36
John Moresehede fo. 38. 39
Johan Moreshede fo. 39. 30
Edmonde Rolonde fo. 117
Willmot Rolonde fo. 34. 117
. . . Furses petygrew fo. 1 [*torn*]
. . . deleres petygrewe fo. 15
. . . xsecombes petygrew fo. 29
. . . Morsehedes petegrew fo.
. . . Rolondes petegr . . fo. 117
. . . illiam . . . . fo. 40
For John Furses issue de Yggeruge fo. 8
for his sones issue fo. 25
John Furse of Toryton his issue fo. 32
Roberte Furses issue fo. 49
Edmonde Rolondes issue fo. 117
John Alfordes issue 120
Johan Drewe our good frynd 119
Necolle Moresehed 39
John Foxsecomes issue fo. 29

A Brefe note what londes hathe cume to us by disente and the
perticuler names therof or by purchase or other wyse viz

Furse fo. 1. 2. 3. 4
Westewaye fo. 1. 2. 3. 4
Bromeham fo. 7. 11
West Kynstere fo. 7. 11. 12
Harforde. fo 7. 9. 18. 22
Scorehyll. fo 7. 9. 18
Henbere fo. 7. 9. 18
burgo de Crediton fo. 7. 9. 18
Torryton fo. 7. 9. 18
More fo. 7. 9. 18. 22
Comemarten fo. 21. 26
Chydyngebroke fo 7. 9. 18. 22
Eggerudege fo. 7. 9. 19
Holstrom fo. 22. 27
Wallonde fo. 22. 27
Moresehede fo. 33. 34. 51
Nuston fo 33. 38. 61. 62. 63
Rowdon fo. 33. 53
Peneton fo.33. 36. 69
Dartemowthe fo. 36. 65
Thenecome fo [*smudge*] 67. 43
Lydforde fo. 28
Dertyngeton fo. 110
Cuttewyll fo. 111
Skyrrydon barton fo. 78
Hollagrepe fo. 78
Skyrrydon wode fo. 80
Skyrrydon waste fo. 79
Redeclefe fo. 91
Hethefylde fo. 90
Horreton downe fo. 89
Horreton fo. 83
Morewull fo. 107
Denecome fo. 84. 85. 88
Tynneren mede fo. 90
Shuttaclefe fo 90
Hockeneye fo. 102. 103

Lytell Kynedon fo. 106
Grett Kynedon fo. 106
Churchebere fo. 98
Stancombe fo 93. 95. 96
Fostardes parkes fo. 99
Ocke fo. 122
Hethe fo. 121
Cobbadowne fo. 134
Rocke fo. 123
Est Cadworthye fo. 123
Har . . . eston fo. 125
Hyllersedon fo. 124
. . . ckehamton fo. 136
Cornedon smythe fo. 28
Sempeston fo. 58
[*few entries lost*]
the Tynne Mylles fo. 28
the Greste Myll fo. 53. 55
the Tokenmyles fo. 53. 57
Skyrrydon maner 71
the Chantery londes fo. 129
Overdene fo. 108

[*3 blank pages but ruled as for more 'index'.*]

[ADDRESS TO HIS READERS]

Robert Furse to hys heres wysshethe to them and to there sequele [*fo. A*]
that they maye leve yn all thynges dewtyfullye accordynge to
there vocasyon. And God blesse them all and grante them longe
lyfe and prosperytye accordynge to hys good wyll and plesure.
Amen.

MOSTE DEREBELOVED consederynge your tytell and interres of
your londes ys lynually dyssended from dyvers persones I have
thofte hit good to make and provyde this lytell bocke where yn
my purpose and intente ys in the beste and pleneste sorte that I
can for your better understondynge to declare and sette furthe
what our proyenytors have bynne of them selves and spesyally
those that have bynne w^{th}yn this seven score yeres. I do mynde
bryfely to speke of all and everyche of them in ther callynge.
That ys what there names were, wythe whom they marryed,
whatt issue theye hadde, where the dewelled, where the dyed,
what londes they hadde and by whatt tytell and where the londes
lyethe and the valye thereof, of whom hyt ys holden and by what
rente, sute and serves and all other charges dewe for any parcell
thereof and howe yt hathe dissended, and the perfytt names of
the londs and howe and by whom hyt hathe bynne lesed, what
yeres our aunsettores leved, what welthe or existimasion they
were of, what plesure for there recreasyon and pastym they
moste delyted of what stature quallytes and personage they were
of and what wylles and testements theye made.

AND I do knowe that this bocke wilbe necessarye and
profytabell for you consederynge our londs lyethe in dyveres
paryshes and come to us from dyvers persons and by dyvers

tyteles for by makynge thys bocke perfytt and kepynge of the
same in good order you shall alwayes be abell to make a perfytt
petygrew and to understonde the ryght name of your londes and
your wrytynges and what you ofte to have and what you ofte to
do.

THEREFORE as I have wyth grette care peaynes and studye
labored to sarche and sette forthe the plenes and perfyttenes of this
nedefull and necessarye worke for your better understondynge of
the foresede premisses yeven soo I do moste instantly desyre you
and everyche of you that at anye tyme hereafter shalbe my heres
or inyoye anye parte of my londs that you and everyche of you
do from tyme to tyme safelye kepe and mentayne this presente
bocke or some other bowcke sette forthe for the same purpose
yn som better order. AND THAT you do cose after my dyssesse
the names of everye person that shall dye sesede of anye parte of
the foresede premisses as my here or here to anye of my sequele
orderly fayethefully and trylye to be wryten in shuche order and
forme as I have donne or after some better order herein in this
presente bocke or yn som other bocke, and that wythyn som
convenyente tyme immedyatelye after the dyssesse of everye here
as longe as anye parte or parsell of the londs here yn contayned
shall happen to come by dyssente to anye of my sequele and
the same beynge so recorded or wryten in this bocke or in som
other bocke hadde and made for that purpose safely to kepe
and preserve as is aforesayed this hopynge you will performe
this my sympell and small requeste consederynge yt maye do
more plesure to your on sequele then to yow nowe presente, the
labor ys not myche nor the charge grett but the worke wilbe to
thos that shall com after you no dowte gret quyettenes perfyt
knowlege and a trewe menes to understond all ther evydenses
& tyteles. In wyttenes [*torn*] this is my only wylle mynde desyre
and requeste to this present I have subscribed my name 28 die
Junii anno xxxv Ellezb^r [1593] by me Roberte Furse.

[*fo. B*]   **Robert Furses prayer**

The lorde o^r omnypotente god be allwayes praysed and to hym
lette us geve moste humbell and hartye thankes for that hyt
hathe plesede hym of his grett mersye and goodnes this from
tyme to tyme to preserve and kepe us and all our proyenytors

lette us nowe therefore allwayes praye unto hym that he will of his accustomede mersye and goodnes geve us and our sequele shuche grase that we all maye remember and conceder o^r deutes towardes hym howe myche we are bownde to geve hym thankes and to confesse all that ever wee have comethe onlye of hym and of his goodnes and not of our selves nor of o^r one deservynges and god moste mersyfull grante that we and o^r sequele maye so geve and mynyster shuche thynges as god shall geve us that hyt maye be to his honer will and plesure and so to rune our curse and paste ou^r tymes here in thys wracched worell that after this lyfe ended we maye inyoye the everlastynge kyngedom of god to whom be all honer lawde and prayse bothe nowe and for ever more.

Amen.

Roberte Furse to the Reder and to all his Sequelle [*fo.* C]

EVEN LEKE AS THE bees delygentelye do labore and gether together substans of dyvers swyte floweres to make ther honye, even so have I gatherede together thys bocke or mater hereyn contayned some of your evydenses, som by reporte off old awnsyente men and som of my on knowlege and experyens. And althoffe hyt be but sympellye and rudely sette forthe yt I praye you to acceppe my goodwyll and intente prayenge you gentellye to correcte and amende the same yn shuche plases where as newde shall requyre for trulye I cane nott sowe better sedes then I have repen; my purpose and intente ys to resyte the names of our awnseters or proyenytores as a thynge verye necessary and profytabell for your knowlege and allthoffe some of them wer but sympell rude unlernede and men off smalle possessyones substanse habillytye or reputasion, yt I do wysshe and exhorte you all that you sholde not be asshamed of them nor mocke dysdayne or spyte them, for I am sure that the gretes oxse was fyrste a lytell calfe and the gretes ocke a smalle branche or lytell tewygge and the grette ryver at the hedde whiche I do accownte the begynnynge ys but a lytell spryng or water but by kypynge of his on curse and wythyn his on bands yt growyethe by lytell and lytell so that at laste yet ys become an excyddynge grette ryver.

EVEN SO you all thoffe our proyenytores and forefatheres were as the hedde I do mene at the begynnynge but plene and sympell

men and wemen and of smalle possessyon and habylyte yt have
theye by lytell and lytell by the helpe and favor of our good
god and by ther wysedom and good governanse so renne ther
curse passede ther tymes and alwayes kepte themselves wytheyn
there on bowndes that by thes menes we ar come to myche more
possessyones credett and reputasyon then ever anye of them
hadde but yt not wythestondynge conseder and remember wythe
yourselves what ys wryten in the liij chapyter of the profytte Esaye
whiche sayithe Remember of what stones ye were hewen owte of
and of what graves you were dygged owte of & c.¹ Surelye yf you
remember and conseder welle thes words then shall you plenelye
understonde and confesse that we are come of ther sedes and by
the grete worke of god we indede are become fleshe of ther fleshe
and bludde of ther blude. Remember also what an excydynge
good wille favor love and mynde they all hadde of us and of our
sequele for theye made ther goods to be our goods, ther londs to
be our londs. Surelye thes be prynsypall and grett cawses that we
sholde thynke well of them and to reyoyse and be gladde to here
of them and to geve unto god moste hartye thankes that he dyd
so from tyme to tyme defende and preserve them. Therefore be
not asshamed to rede or here of them nor yt do nott mocke geste
dysdayne or spyte them, but lette ther honeste good and godlye

[fo. D]   acts and lyves be a scolemaster to you and to yours for ever for
of ther smalle porsyones they did increse and that was to them a
grette credett and a prefermente to you and you and your sequele
do inyoye the frute there of yeven so yf you do the lyke you
shall have the lyke commendasyon of your sequele and increse
your on credett and the credett off your howse. And as you will
judege in our proyenyt[ors] to be a shame and a fowle fame and
ignorante poynte or thynge for them to consume ther levynges
that never coste them anye thynge, so no dowte the worell ye
and your one sequele will judege a gretter fawte in you yf you
do the leke becose you are better provyd for then ever anye of
them were, therefore spende not your tyme idelly wantonlye or
leke a brute beste, but remember your one credet and what you
ofte to do in dede and be as wyllynge to here and rede what
our proyenytores have bynne as you are contente to inyoye the
benyfytte and commodytye of there levynge, and wythe all here
note and followe thos wyse menes saynges: the wyse felosopher

---

1. Isaiah chapter 'liij' should be lj:j.

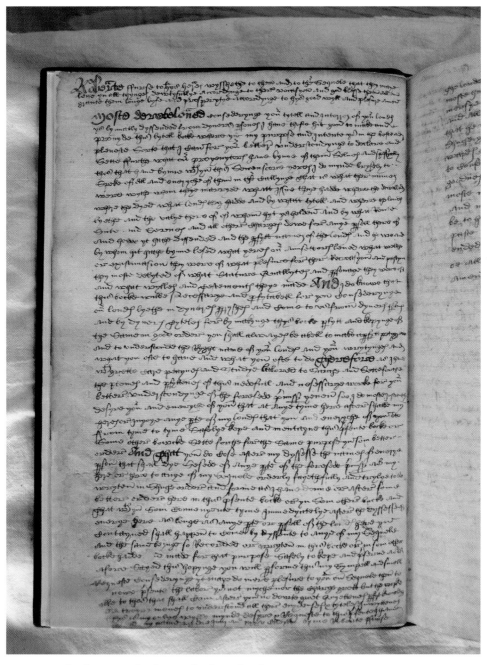

First page of Robert Furse's advice to his heirs (p. 9).
Photograph by John Thorp.

The old cover of Robert Furse's book before rebinding.
Photograph by John Thorp.

A sample of Robert Furse's text detailing properties (fo. 18, pp. 40–2).
Photograph by John Thorp.

Robert Furse's tombstone in the floor of Dean Prior church.
Photograph by Nigel Cheffers-Head, by permission of the Revd. D. J. Rowland.

Cleob' sayethe Remember thos that have donne the good and forgette not ther benyfets; the wyse phelosypher Pyream sayethe mocke not nor lye or saye falselye on thos that be dede and paste, for the wyse phelosypher Arestottell sayethe loke whatt thankes thow doste render to thye one parens, loke thowe to have the lycke of thy one chyldern. Pytagrophus an other wyse man sayethe yf god have geven or indued thee wythe more ryches and possessyones then he hathe otheres be not prowde there of for as toychynge our creasyon god hathe made all men lycke, therefore be not dysseved.[2] The holye man Jobe sayethe the lorde geveth the lorde takethe[3] and in the seconde bocke of Kynges yt is wryten god makethe ryche and god makethe powre.[4] Therefore I do exhorte you all consederynge that god ys onlye the awtor and gever of all good gyftes as wyttenyssethe Sente James, whyche sayethe everye good and perfytte gyfte comethe from god,[5] therefore abowve all thynges fere god, geve all honer lawde and prayse unto hym, praye to god onlye for mersye grase and forgevenes of all your synnes and wyckedenes. Calle only to god onlye for helthe helpe and soccor, putt all your hole hope tryste and fayethe onlye in hym and yn his mersye for surely the lorde hathe sayede by his holye profytte Davyd, I will not sayethe the lord fayle nor forsake them that putt there truste in me, but wilbe alwayes to them a helper.[6] Then geve yere to his lawes and followe his lawes and preseptes. Bere no malles or hatrede in your hartes but moderate your anger, recompense to no man yevell for evell but forgeve all men as god shall forgeve you. Remember hyt ys wryten vayngeanes ys myne sayethe the lorde god and I will rewarde hyt accustome not your selves to [*torn*].

Reverens your yelderes and betteres mayntayne truthe and [*fo. E*] honestye fleye and abhore synne and vyse, be mersyfulle unto all men, geve almese of thye goods to the powre and nedye and lette alwayes thye hyrede sarvante have hys penye for his payne.

---

2. Cleob' and Pyream: see Introduction p. xix.
3. Job chapter 1 verse 21.
4. 'In the seconde bocke of Kynges . . .' appears to be 1 Samuel chapter 2, verse 7, 'the Lord maketh poor, and maketh rich.' [Tyndale, and *Authorised Version*] The first and second books of Samuel were formerly known as 1–2 Kings, and 1–2 Kings as 3–4 Kings.
5. James chapter 1 verse 17.
6. David: 'I will not sayethe the lord fayle not forsake them' etc. This is possibly 1 Chronicles chapter 28 verse 20, although that is not in the first person.

Beware off false docteren be constante yn relygion, abstayne from horedom, dronkenys and peryurye, performe your promyses in all thynges and paye your dewtes to all persones quyettelye. Remember your lege obedyens and dewtye to your prynse and to all ther lawes and mynysteres and in no wyse rebelle not nor transegresse ther lawes for hit ys wryten that the hyer powres arre ordayned of god. Have a delyte in good howse kepynge for so shalte thow have the love of god and man and yt is a thynge worthye to be commended. Beware of userres and borynge of monye upon interres and of surtyschyppe and what bands or wrytynge you sele. Have no delyte to kepe companye with lyers, coseners, whyspereres, flattereres, taletellers, rowleleres, scolders or malycius and vycius persones but kepe companye wythe best wyse and honeste companye for the proverbe ys, the lyke will to the lyke.

When god shall putt into your mynde to marrye then conseder wythe your selves the sayenges of the wyse felosypher Hermes, whyche sayethe gette the a wyse woman and she shall rule well thye howse and that yn good order and brynge the forthe wyse and dyscryte chylderen, and agayne he sayethe marrye wythe thye mache,[7] and to this dothe agree the saynges of the wyse poyett Ovyde whyche sayethe, Sette too oxen to drawe together in one yoke not of equall mache, and surely the one will hurte the other then surelye the beste mache ys the lyke to the lyke in equallytye.[8] So then when you marrye remember all thos sayenges and have also a spessyall care and regarde to whom and wythe whom you do intende to marrye, yn dede, I do not mynde to her fere beawtye favor or goodelye stature or personnage or to her grette ryches or possessyon or to her worshyppefull stocke or kyndered. Yt I do not mene but all thos thynges be good and ar to be desyred as a thynge fytte and convenyente for you so that theye be plased in a dyscryte woman of good and honeste conversasyon. But whate so ever she be inquyre dylygentelye of what nature quallytes or condysyones her mother ys of, for commenly the dofter do lerne the quallytes and maners of ther mother and marke also howe and yn what companye she hathe bynne brofte uppe from her yuthe for the proverbe ys loke

Howe to chuse
a wife

7. Hermes Trismegistos was 'the supposed author or inspirer of a number of books, highly valued by the Alexandrian Greeks, from whom they passed to the Middle Ages and the Renaissance' (Latham, *Poems of Sir Walter Raleigh,* p. 182).
8. Ovid used oxen in many metaphors, but this one has not been identified.

what lycor ys fyrste brofte or putte ynto an newe vessell the
vessell shall ever savor thereof.[9] Beware that she be not of more
abyllytye then you are, for then surelye she wylbe chargeabell for
you to mentayne. See that shee be of a good name and fame and
of a good and honest kyndered and inclynede and exersysede
in good quallytes and condysyones. Lette here be sober wyse   [*fo. F*]
dyscryte gentylle and shamefaste. Beware that she be not a fowle
nor geven to horedom, drunkenes, a comen scole a gyggehalter,
or one that ys ignorante howe to use and governe thos thynges
appertenynge and belongen to her charge for althoffe that there
be no grette newde for them to do the thynges them selves, yt no
dowte yt ys nesessarye and newdefull for them to knowe howe to
do hyt inded, and to see ther sarvantes to do hyt in good order,
whiche no dowte wilbe myche for your profytt. A wyse woman
can play the partes of a gentyllewoman and of a good hussewyfe,
but ther be some clene fyngerede gentyllewoman that can do no
thynge but sytte at home and pycke in a clowte or shuchelyke
serves, whiche surely do myche plesure yn the common welthe.
Beware of shuche for the wyse phelosypher Seneca sayethe,
nor gorgyus apparell nor exelente plentye of golde and ryches
or possessyones dothe not become a womane so well as sylenes
sobernys feathefullnes chastytye and wysedom dothe. The wyse
man Socrates sayethe there ys no greter ancombranse that maye
happen to a man then to have an ignorante wyfe. Ecclesiastycus
sayethe I wyll rather dewell wythe a lyon or dragon then wythe a
wyckede woman.[10] Sallamon sayethe a feayre woman wytheowte
dyscryte to maners ys lycke a rynge of golde upon a swynes
snowte.[11] Agayne he sayethe favor ys dyssettefull and beawtye ys
but a vayne thynge, but Ecclesyasticus sayethe happye ys the man
that hathe a wyfe that is wyse and off understondynge.[12] For hyt

9. The proverb about liquor in a new vessel was a popular saying which Furse felt no
   need to attribute. Sixteenth century authors who use it include Richard Taverner
   in his version of Erasmus's *Adages*, p. 26, which in turn cites Horace: 'Quo semel
   est imbuta recens seruabit odorem testa diu. A vessel will kepe long the savour
   wherewith it is firste seasoned' (Epistles I.2, 69–70). Whittinton used it in his
   Vulgaria (Tilley, *Dictionary of Proverbs*, p. 110); 'A pytcher wyll have a snatche
   longe after of the lyquoure that was fyrst put in it', and Richard Whytford 'For
   it is an olde sayenge. The pot or vessell shall euer sauour or smell of that thynge
   wherwith it is fyrst seasoned' (*A Werke for Householders*, ed. Hogg).
10. Ecclesiasticus, or the Book of Jesus Son of Syrach, in the Apocrypha, chapter 25
    verse 16.
11. Proverbs chapter 11 verse 22.
12. Ecclesiasticus chapter 25 verse 8.

ys wryten wythe her wysedom and travell she shall brynge her hussebonde to worshyppe and grette exystymasyon. To shuche a one and yn shuche a one I praye god you maye affyxse your myndes and take for your one, for surelye in my oppynyon yt is better to marye a woman wytheowte goodes then to marye goodes wythe owte a woman, but yt is but badde for a man to marrye a fowle and a begger bothe. You know what I do mene but by wysedom and good advyse yn the begynnynge all this ys to be remedyed.

BE CAREFULL for your householde use mesure yn all thynges, so spende to daye as you maye to-morrowe be not an negarde nor yt to lyberall. Be fere speched unto all men and do inhawnte myche wyseme[n]s companye be famylyer wythe all men but have fryndeshyppe but wythe serten. Be not heyght mynded, hate pryde ande vayne glorye, and leve alwayes withe yn your one compas and sele uppe secrets in your one hartes. Take not your fryndes for your enymes nor your enymes for your fryndes, and lette your mynde rule your tonge. Fyrste here and then speke. Do thow not that they selfe whyche thowe doste dysprayse in an other, nor be not unthankefull to them that have don the good. Applye your myndes to good lernynge and brynge uppe your chylderen in the feare of gode in obedyens vertue lernynge and yn som good syens or exersyse. Be not leke the bunter that castethe owte the good mele and kepethe the branne. Remember allwayes your one estate and abyllytye and dele at no tyme farder than thowe arte well abell to performe. Be thowe the same man in dede that thowe doste pretende to be nor crave not that that thou canste not optayne, nor yt thynke not thye selfe to be better then thowe arte indede. Geve to the nedye yt so give that thow nede not thyeselfe and lett your gyftes be accordynge to your habyllytye. Yf you do dowte anye thynge then aske you cownsell of them that be wyse and be not angerye wythe them, allthoffe they do reprove you for your welthe. Beware of the companye of idell and wanton wemen, pryde, vayne glorye, kyettusnes, idelness, and dysordered playes, yt hathe bynne the menes of monye menes ruen and decaye. Excesse not yn your apparell nor make your cote alwayes afftter your wyves mynde. Geve yourselves to the redynge and herynge of the holy scryptures and shuche leke good docterene be lerned in the lawes of the realme and have to rede the olde crownenekeles and shuche leke awnshyante

[*fo*. G]

Very good
exersyses

hystoryes rememberynge yt ys a commone saynge yt is a shame for a man to be ignorante of that whyche he ofte to knowe. Be mery at home amongeste your howseholde and use them wythe gentyllenes, have alwayes a respecte to good husebondery and be not to seke to have provysyon and thynges that be nedefulle all wayes in a redynes for you[r] howse and mentenans of the same, for in somer remember that wynter will surely come.

A necessary thynge

Have no delyte in fylthye talke, for surelye thos thynges arre not honeste to be spoken that are vysyus and fylthye to be donn. Beware of evell and noftye companye and off thos that be lyghte and suspected persones for as the olde proverbe ys shuch as a man ys yn shuche shall he delyte. Mocke not nor yt dyspyse the powre sympell and innosente person but geve god thankes that he hathe induede the better. Flatter nor dyssymbell wythe no person nor use not to lye or saye untruthe but speke boldely the truthe unto all men and lett your wordes be your dedes, be not a roler a slonderer or a man of fowle langage have not to do wythe that that dothe not appertayne unto you but let everye man shutt in his one bowe. Be slacke and slowe to wrathe myschyf and wyckekednes and swyfte and hastye to mersye pettye and forgevenes. Be constante and pasyente in trobell and adversytye and lawlye and ware yn prosperytye, geve blameles cownsell to your nyghtebures, have a grete desyre wylle and plesure to make pease, concordes and agrementes betewne your nyghtebures when anye of them be yn varyence, for so shalte thow be called the chylde of god. Yf anye man or woman putt anye truste yn the defrawd nor in any wyse do not dysseve them. Yf thow be putte yn to anye offes or actoryte exersyse thyen thye offes and actoryte wythe mersye equytye justes wysedom and sobernys alwayes havynge a regarde to the truthe of the cawse accordynge to your dewtye and tryste commytted unto you. Take good advyse yn the begynnynge of anye thynge that you intend to do what the yende wilbe there of but when you have begonne to do anye thynge dyspache and fyneshe hit quyckelye. Pretende not to monye thynges att one tyme for fere the one do hynder the other, atende no thynge abowve thy strenthe or thynge that thow canste not brynge to passe, but abowve all thynges remember before what wilbe the yende, beware off hadde I wyste, but as the olde saynge ys knowe or you knytte so maye you well slacke but knytte not before you knowe, for then hyt may be to late.

Bad company

Marke well this

[*fo. H*]

Telle not a brode what thow doste pretend to do, for yf thow spede not, thy enymes shall laght the to scorne, threten no bodye for that ys woman lycke. Dowte them whom thow doste knowe and tryste not them whom thow doste not knowe but remember that Deogynes sayethe Trye and then tryste after good assurans but tryste not or you trye for fere of repentanse.

A good rule observe it

HAVE ALWAYES a spessyall care and mynde to your sarvantes and to shuche as be under you, and see that everyche of them do trulye ther labuor and busynes comytted to there charge, and be som tymes amongeste them, for I have harde saye that the masteres yee or presens amongeste sarvantes ys as good as one that dothe labour. Se that theye do not waste spoyle and consume your goodes more than newde shall requyre, for there be som that will consume spoyell and waste as myche in one daye yf that theye maye have ther one wyll and lybertye as maye well serve them iij dayes. Beware of shuche and brynge not uppe your sarvantes yn idellenes. See that your balyefes and other offyseres do make ther juste and trewe accowntes for all that they have to doo or reseve for you, and always kepe you a perfytte bocke and a trewe invytorye of all your goodes and cattalles, and sonderye tymes call your sevants and by your bocke examen them what thynges there ys loste spoyled consumed lacke or gonne, and howe and whene and by whom and se that your thynges be well mentayned and reperede and that in tyme from tyme to tyme when newde ys for one shyllynge in tyme maye save three shyllynges.

Remember this also

SEE ALSO that your hussebonderye labor and all your other labure and busynes bothe wythe yn dowres and wythe owte be all wayes done yn good seson and yn dewe order, for there ys a tyme for all thynges and the thynge that is ons well donne and yn dewe seson ys too tymes done. Shuche sarvantes as have done you good serves helpe them to be preferred in marrage or to some resonabell levynge and then you shall never be wytheowte a good sarvante. Take no ronnagates roges or suspected person ynto your serves, but have men abowte you and they will do lyke men, but have fowles and theye will do lyke fowles.

Forgete not this beware

SEE ALSO that your tenantes and shuche as dothe holde your londes that theye do not waste spoyle or lette downe ther howses, hagges, gardenes or tymber trees. Se that no man do incroche anye of your londes, kype your churche and lett your sarvantes and famelye do the lyke at all tymes convenyente and se the same

mayntayned. Paye your tythes justely and trulye and lett your
hole famylye faste and praye as gods lawes and the prynses dothe
appoynte them. Yf you mynde to kype a good howse then beware
never grante your barten yn junter or lese from your here nor yt
suffer hyt to be spowlede yf you mynde your here shall leve when
you arre dede, but yf you will kepe a good howse in dede then
muste you kepe and observe thys rule that ys to saye, you muste
kepe and mentayne a good tyllage and have a good rerynge and
make a good provysyon [*torn*] the mentenans of the same.

REMEMBER also that hyt is your parte and dewtye to provyde
appoynte and assure to and for every one of your chylderen as
well shuche resonabell levynges and bargaynes that after your
dyssesse then theye of them selves maye be abell to mentayne
them selves and there famelyes as also resonabelle maches for
them in marrage. Learne of Abraham and Tobyas ande be carefull
for ther marrage,[13] but chefely for your dofters remember when
that an appell ys rype hyt is good to take hym leste he rotte,
so detractynge of tyme and wante of care maye torne to your
farder trobell and inwarde gryffe, for I am sure that men muste
before dyner provyde mete yf theye thynke to fare well, and
agayn yt ys but a vayne thynge to stryve agaynste the streme for
no dowte nature passethe nurtor, there fore followe the felosyfer
whiche sayethe stoppe the begynnynge so maste thow be sure
all dowtefull dysyeses to swage and to cure but yf you be careles
and suffer his barste then commethe plestur to late when all
cure ys paste,[13a] so I mene yf you wilbe owte of dowte of the
yell successe or dawnger of the discredyt of your chylderen then
muste you nedes make provysion for your chylderen as well for
mentenans as for marrage and that in dewe tyme.

BE GOOD AND gentyll to your Tenantes and love them and
have alwayes ther good wylles and reporte. Performe ther leses
and that wythe owte vexsasyon or sute, make them sure and
good wrytynges when they do take or purchase anye thynge of
you, do not to them alwayes that you maye do but do to them
that that dothe appertayne to reson justes and good consyenes.
Burden them not wythe more fynes, rents, or serves more then

[fo. I]

How to use
your chylderen

Howe to use
your tenantes

---

13. Abraham (Genesis) and Tobias (Apocrypha: Tobit). Furse's intention here is
    not clear, although in both cases the couple underwent and survived hardship,
    Abraham and Sarah in conceiving a child, and Tobias's bride Sarah the curse that
    killed her seven previous bridegrooms.

13a. Four lines of verse quoted from William Baldwin, *A Treatise of Morall
    Philosophie* (1547; ed. Palfreyman, 1620, p. 163d).

theye be well abell to paye you. Dysplase not an honeste fryndely tenant for a tryfell or smalle some of moneye. Reyoyse and be gladde to se your tenantes to prosper for then your londes shall prosper and yf they growe in welthe then no dowte when you com to ther howses they will fryndelye intertayne you, and yf you nede anye thynge that theye have they will surelye helpe you and be alwayes at your commondemente and redy to do you and yours good. Therefore esteme an honeste fryndelye tenant more then monye. Seke not all thynge at ther hondes after the most extremeste fassyon but lett them so have hyt at your hondes that they maye be abell to paye ther rentes, mentayn them selves ther famylye and tenemente. Be contente wythe gods blyssynges and the porsyon that you have. We in dede be but mynystares or stuardes thereof fore a tyme, for we brofte no thynge ynto this worell, nor shall we carye anye thynge wythe us, but surely as Sallamon sayethe all ys but vayne and vanytes,[14] therefore whyles you have tyme and spase her in this worell lett us do good unto all men and be mersyfull unto all men and do wronge unto no man. Be not a userer or accownted a covetus person nor gett your welthe by crafte or dyssette, for surely yt wyll not then longe prosper, for goodes wyckedelye goten will sone be spente. The profyt Esaye sayethe woe be to you that june howse to howse londe to londe, shall you alone inhabytt the yearthe.[15] Agayne he sayethe he that pyllethe others shalbe pylled hym selfe.[16] Davyd in the salmes sayethe he hepeth uppe tresure and yt he dothe not knowe howe shall have hytt.[17] Cryste in his gospell sayethe to the covetus man thow fowle this nyght will I take awaye the sowle from the then house goodes are all thos.[18] Agayne he sayethe howe ys that that dothe see his brother hathe nede and shuttethe uppe his compassyon from him howe dewelleth the love of god in hym.[19] Therefore do you remember the seven workes of mersye resyted in Sente Mathewes gospell,[20] and Cryste hym selfe sayethe you shall not geve a cuppe of water to thos that be my bretheren but hyt shalbe rewarded,[21] then

[fo. J]

14. Ecclesiastes chapter 1 verse 2.
15. Isaiah chapter 5 verse 8.
16. Isaiah 'he that pylleth', meaning cheat or plunder, has not been identified.
17. David: 'hepeth uppe tresure' probably alludes to Psalm 49.
18. Luke chapter 12 verse 20.
19. First Epistle General of John chapter 3 verse 17.
20. The seven works of mercy are found at Matthew chapter 25 verses 34 to 45, but there seem only to be six of them, excluding burial of the dead.
21. Matthew chapter 10 verse 42.

use mersye and pyettye and no dowte god will prosper the and
thyne. Marke the storye of kynge Ahabbe and dyvers others in
the olde Testament, what frute comethe of yell goten goddes.[22]
Ther fore be not covetus for covetusnes ys as Sent Pawle sayethe
the rowte of all evell.[23] And what is all the worlye goodes worthe
yf a man lese his one sole. Yt is wryten in the gospel not every one
that sayethe lorde lorde shall enter into the kyngedom of heven,
but he that dothe the wyll of the father whiche ys in heven.[24]
Then this to conclude I praye you to remember this my shorte
exortasion and cunsell taken owte of dyvers good awtores and
to followe the same, wysshynge you all to use all your tenantes
well and all wayes to kepe and mentayne your one credett and
to be carefull and provyde for your chylderen and famylye and
to love and leve wythe your wyfe as a man by the lawe of god
and nature and the lawes of the realme he ofte to do. You bothe
muste be lyke unto the powre turkell dowves that is the one to be
gladde of the otheres companye, and the one fathefullye to love
the other wythe harte mynde and mowthe and that wythe owte
anye kynde of desimulasion or flatterye. Yn no wyse you muste
not hate one the other for your owen flesshe but yf ther be anye
occasyon of stryfe brydell nature and reforme hyt by gentyll
and fryndelye perswasiones and good cunsell, and not wythe
rygor or browlynge leke ignorante persones or brute bestes. But
be of the Emperor Marcus Aurylyus oppynyon, that ys to saye
that yf good fryndelye wyse and grave cownsell, the fere of god
and the shame of her one person can not reforme a wycked or
pervarse woman, surely then browlynge will not serve. Cryste
sayethe that a kyngedom that is devyded muste nedes com to
confusyon[25] then no dowte where the man and his wyfe dothe
not agree that howse can not prosper. The beste waye to have
your wyfe to be quyett and honeste ys to be honeste your selfe,
and to be carefull for your one busynes, and to leve quyettelye
and yn good order wythe her and bewar of gelosye, yt ys a fyre
that never quynchethe. I remember that ther is an olde saynge
a redye hycke doth make a redye kytte[26] [*torn*] even so I maye

*Howe to use
your wyfe*

---

22. The story of King Ahab is in I Kings chapter 21.
23. I Timothy chapter 6 verse 10.
24. Matthew chapter 7 verse 21.
25. Matthew chapter 12 verse 25, Mark chapter 3 verse 24, and Luke chapter 11 verse 17.
26. 'A redye hycke dothe make a redye kytte'. There are so many meanings to the words *hick* and *kit* that it is difficult to know what Furse means. See Glossary.

compare a younge marryed wyfe leke a pese of waxse, whiche beynge made sumpell yt will reseve what sele you lyste or prynte yeven. So your wyfe yf you at begynnynge do dele wyselye wythe her yn dede then [*torn*] dowte so she will contynewe, but

[*fo. K*]   yf you be careles an[d] suffer and geve her to myche her one wyll and lybertye, and flatter wythe her and mantayne her in to myche pryde and vayne glory, surely then hit wilbe harde for you to reforme her for by that menes she wyll forgett bothe you and her selfe. Therefore yt is the beste waye to begynne wythe them as you mynde to contynewe and lett her nowe forgett her chyldys fantassyes and idell toawyes and leve her gaddynge or wanderynge from plase to plase, and now lett her love her own howse and lerne and exersyse to rule and goveren well thos thynges commyttytt to her charge, and not to sytte idell like a careles creature, and as the common saynge ys sett ocke yn hope and lett Tawe go weste and saye we have olde Abraham to our father and here ys yenowe.[27] Yt is moste sertayne and a thynge proved by good experyens that where the wyfe is a fowle and hathe no care to rule her howse, surely that howse doth not beste prosper be the man never so good a hussebonde, for in myn oppynyon yt were better to wante a good hussebond then a good howsewyfe, but no dowt the wante of anye of them wylbe a grett henderans for theye muste bothe drawe togethere yf theye mynde to be wellthye.

OURE AWNSETORES and proyenytores from tyme to tyme and at all tymes before the wrytynge of this present bocke which was in Julye in the yere of our lorde god 1593, they all leved in good credett, ther was never anye of them condemned or attaynted of felonye murder manslafter treson or rebellyon or accessaryes to anye of thos, or any woman proved for a common hore or anye other mysdemener, but in all thynges they usede themselves honestelye, and praye god that our sequele maye from tyme to tyme and at all tymes here after do the lyke & increse ther credett.

REMEMBER that our forefathers dyd not geve and provyde there goodes and levyngs for us to mentayne gluttenye, drunkenys, pryde, unlawfull playe, excesse of apparell, idellenys, and synne,

---

27. No other instance of this 'common saying' has been found: it is presumably native to Devon with its reference to the river Taw, and its gist would seem to be to do the best you can, planting for the future, and trusting to providence.

but to mentayne our selves our famylye and sequele and to releve the powre god grante that we maye so spende hyt that hit maye be to gods honer and the increse of our credytt.

AND THIS I commytt you to gods tuysion and I praye god to geve you grase & wysedom and so to passe and spende your tymes here in this wrached worell that you maye have the love of all your nyghtebores, famylye and tenantes, and to see all your chylderell plased & abell to leve of them selves well and honestelye as our proyenytores and forefatheres have done, that after thys lyfe yended we maye have and inyoye the lyfe everlastynge. God the father the son and the holye goste be mersyfull unto us and to our sequele, blesse us and defende us agaynste the worell the fleshe and the devell &c.

By me Roberte Furse.

[FURSE FAMILY AND THEIR PROPERTIES]

fo. 1   THYS YS THE TRUE and perfytte petygrewe and lyneall successyon off Rolonde de Cumba al^z Furse and of dyvers other persones whiche were lawfullye sesede of dyveres messuages londes and tenementes whych nowe by lawfulle and lyneall dyssente ys the inheritanse of Robert Furse of Moresehede yn the paryshe of Denepryer in the Cowntye of Devon gentylleman in maner and forme folloynge

Furse our
fyrste londes

Furse of Furse

ROLONDE de Cumba had londes in Furse of the grante of one Willyam Downynge, and becose the dede berethe no date I can not judege the tyme serten, but as I do suppose he had a sone callede Willyam de la Furse, for the order of the old wryteres and the use then of the cuntereye was to calle men after the names of ther one howses, and so by dewellynge at Furse the men were called Furse.[28] In the xth yere of Edwarde the thyrde [1336/7] one Vicarye did grante Furse and dyveres other londes to the Person of Caddeleye, & by an other dede the same Person did grante the londes in Furse and iiij akeres of londes in Soulhyll to the same Vicarye for the terme of his lyfe, the remender to one John delafurse & to Mabely his wyfe in fee tayle. But here note that before this laste grant there was one Thom' Myggelacke by a relese wthowte date did grante londes in Furse, Turgeres downe & la Rygge to one Thom' the son of Willyam de la Furse. More in Henry the Vth tyme on Willyam Furse did grante his londes in Furse and Westewaye to too of the Averyes, and at that tyme ther was a dower owte of all the londes. This too Averyes reassured all the londes backe agayne, dyveres conveyeances hathe paste,

Then nexte
Westewaye

---

28. Furze in Cheriton Fitzpaine was extant as a farm in the tithe award *c*.1840, and as a farm in Kelly's *Directory* 1939. It is possibly Furze Park, SS835940.

but I suppose all in truste, but sethenes the xth yere of Edward the Thyrde [1336/7] the men have bynne called Furse and by no other name. All the foresede londes in Furse and Westewaye hathe contynuallye remayned in the possessyon of the Furses and of ther tenantes. So I do mynde to saye that Rolonde hadde issue Wyllyam Wyllyam, Wyllyam hadde issue Thomas, Thomas hadde issue John, w[ch] marryed one Mabelye of what kynderede I do not understonde, but be leke she was Thomas Vycaryes dofter or syster. John and Mabelye hadde issue Willyam which marryede one Engelyshe and they hadde issue one Willyam. I suppose this laste Willyam marryed one Averyes syster of Dolyshe.[29] He dewelled at Cherton,[30] he was an honest man & of good credett. Ther was an olde woman at Cruse Morcharde that was boren and dewelled at Cruse Morcharde in one tenemente called Weste Waye that did reporte that she did remember that Willyam, Roberte Furse his son, John Furse, John Furse, John Furse and Robert Furse all sexse she did see wythe her yee and was tenant to iiij of them.

And this our petigrewe

A rare thynge

ROBERT FURSE the sonne and here of Willyam Furse and Annes his wyfe marryed one Johan, of what kynderede I do not understonde, but theye hadde issue John Furse. This Roberte did dewelle at Colbroke,[31] he was a man of good credytt, he by dyssente did inyoye all the londes called Furse and Westewaye and did homage for the same, and made also dyvers leses of the same. He was a sure man of his promyse but in his later dayes he was blynde. Yt ys reported that by his last wille he did geve one cowe to his here and did wyll his sonne to do the lyke and so everye of his sequell sholde geve a cowe to there here for ever to the intente that the valye of the calfe of the same cowe sholde yerely for ever sholde be geven or bestowyed in som good dedes of charyte, when the lawe did permytte hit for mase and to the powre, but sethenes the mas abbolyshed all was geven to the powere. This Roberte was grettely to be commended for that he trayned uppe his son John Furse to be a lernede mane for by

fo. 2

His dewellynge

A cowe fyrste geven

29. Avery of Dolyshe: although there is a Dolish Farm in Luppitt, and Dolditche Manor in Shaugh, this is most likely to be Dawlish, which has been spelt this way in the past (*PNDevon* II, p. 491). The 1524 tax for Dawlish included John 'Daveryn' (Stoate, *Devon Lay Subsidy Rolls 1524–7*, p. 220).

30. 'Cherton': the 'h' is indistinct and may be a deletion, making it more likely to be Certon, a variant of Crediton, than Cheriton. There is no 'i'.

31. Robert Furse of Colebrooke parish witnessed a deed there in 1465/6 (Plymouth & WDRO 107/471).

that menes our credy.t & levinge ys grettly incressed as here after
hit shall more at large appere. This Robarte leved in Henrye the
VI tyme in all Edwarde the IIII and Edward the fythes tyme

His dethe & Richard the thirds tyme and dyed in Henrye the sevenethes
tyme, no dowte an olde man and he and Johan his wife were
both buryed at Colbroke.

His grants Roberte payed a releve for Furse in an° 28 of Henry the VI
[1449/50]. He made a lese of Furse to one Grantelonde in the 28
of Henry the VI and after to one Hockewaye in an° the 2 of Ric.
the 3 [1484/5] and more londes he had not to my knowlege. And
more I can not saye of Roberte Furse & Johan his wyfe but god
send them a joyefull daye in the Resurrection.

fo. 3 ### Furse in Cheryton Fytzpyne

FURSE ys a tenemente devyded ynto dyvers closes, there names and
quallytes shalbe here under wryten. Yt lyethe w^th^yn the paryshe
of Cheryton Fytzpayne and hit is holden of the lord of the maner
What rente
suite & serves of Stockeleluckecombe, wch nowe is Mr Arundell[32] by knyghtes
serves and vij^d^ rente and sute to the curte, and hit ys nowe in
the tenure of Wyllyam Hoper and ys worthe yerelye abowve all
charges and repryses vij^s^ vj^d^. Ther is also payd for the oxylion
fyftydole rente to the Shryfe yerely ij^d^ and for everye hole fyftyedole xiiij^d^.
Furse lyeth wytheyn the hundred of Westebudeleye.

Note that Robert Furse in the xxxvj yere of Kynge Henry the VI
[1457/8] payed but xxij^d^ for his releve for Furse, but Robert Furse
yn an° xvj of Ellezbt [1573/4] payed vij^s^ for his releve.

A good note Note the reve of the maner doth demonde vij^s^ iiij^d^ rente for Furse,
& in tymes paste no dowte so payed, but this mony yeres we
have payed but vij^s^, and more paye not, for by our dede we be
bownd to paye but vij^s^.

Note that one Hockewaye and Roger Oldynge pretended to have
the grante of a lese of Furse from Roberte Furse of Denepryer.[33]
That sute cost Furse C marke and a thowsante myles rydynge,
yt contynewed in sute longe yt was in the Chancery in the Curte
of Requeste & in the Common Lawe. They folloyed the sute in

---

32. Sir John Arundell of Trerice was seised of the manor of Stockleigh Luccombe
at his death in 1560, as was his grandson John in 1580 (WSL IPM transcripts).
33. See Appendix I, p. 158.

forma pawperis, yt coste Furse viij[li] some termes but yn the yende ther falsehode and connynge myght not prevayell, but Furse styll defended his tytell and in the yend optayned the vyctorye. All ther hole hope was to have the mater to som compremens in hope of som thynge but Furse wold never yelde to that. I am serten that Oldynge spente xxx[li] of his one monye & yt went in forma pawperis. He hadde in the Curte of Requeste vij cownseleres at the barre agaynste me at one tyme & all in vayne. Intruthe I did grante to make a lese to Richard Hockewaye to Alse Cade & to a thyrde person upon condision that one John Langeham & Alse his wyfe wolde relese ther interres, and upon payement of serten somes of mony a daye tyme & plase was appoynted for the makynge of the relese and payemente of the monye & selynge of the newe lese, at whiche tyme & plase Langeham cam not. His wyfe came & ther refusede to make anye shuche relese. Hockewaye was absent, the monye was not payd, and Hockewaye never tendered anye lese made accordynge to Furses grante. Hockewaye did promise to marry Alse Cade & hadde her home vij or viij wyckes & then put her home & he wolde marrye an other. So durynge the sute Hockwaye and his mother dyed, then Oldynge married Alse Cade & having a badde fellow dewelling in the howse when he myght not there dewell no longer for xxxiij[s] iiij[d] he brofte Oldynge in possession, but by forse of an indytemente I was restored to the possessyon, but by amosyon in the Chancerye upon a false surmyse an inusyon was granted, & by that menes he came agayne to the possession the whiche inyunsion was shortely reversed. Yt spyte of me he stylle kepte the halle howse untill the mater was ended and in the yende he moste bytterlye cursed them that sette hym a worke and cosed hym to followe that sute. He was as suttell craftye & prowde mynded fellowe and as wycked & wylfull mynded fellowe as anye in Devon, he wolde scolde and roell leke a beste.

The pertyculer names of all the closes of the tenement called *fo. 4* Furse viz:
The Peacke, on aker, one other close called the Fowerakers of iiij akeres, The Grett Downe xj akeres, the three Brodamores ix akeres, viz. the hyer v akeres, the lower and myddell but iiij akeres, The Rowe lese v akeres, the Sowthe mede v akeres the Sowthedowne iiij akeres, the longe parke iiij akeres, the Lyttel

Parke ij akeres the meddowe the grove the hayes and all the reste iij akers.

Sm^a to. xlviij^{ti} akeres.

Note that ther was and yt is myche good Tymber in the meddowe.

fo. 5

Westewaye in Cruse Morcharde

WESTEWAYE[34] ys also a tenemente yt lyethe wythyn the paryshe off Cruse Morcharde yt is aso devyded yn dyvers closes the names and quantytes shalbe here under wryten. Yt is holden of James Curteneye as of his maner off Langeleye by knyghte serves, the heye rente ys vij^d and sute to the curte. Hyt ys nowe in the tenure of Sybbelye Drake, yt is worthe abowe all charges and repryses xij^s x^d a yere. We paye for one hole fyftyedole for this tenemente viij^d and yt lyethe wythe in the hundred of Wetherygge.

By what rente sute & serves

For fyftydole

Note I payed Mr James Curteneye vij^s for a releve for Westewaye yn an^o xvj Ellezabt [1573/4].

fo. 6

The particular name of all the Closes of the Tenemente called Westewaye

FYRSTE the longe parke ij aker, the Brode Close v aker, The Westerdowne v aker, the Esterdowne v aker, the longe mede one quarter of on aker, Quary close v akeres, the myddell parke too akeres and halfe, the laye too akeres and halfe, the newe mede three quarteres of on aker, the hame mede three quarters of an aker, the parke be este the garden one aker, the croseparke one aker and quarter, the furseparke too aker, the lytell parke one aker, the Whetteparke one quarter of on aker, the Boyshes and the Copes one aker, the wode iij akeres, the too gardenes and curtelage halfe on aker.

Sm^a to. xxxix akeres.

fo. 7

JOHN FURSE [*c.* 1432–1508/9] the flower of our garlonde the sonne and here of Roberte Furse and Johan his wyfe after his fathers dyssesse he by dyssente was possessed of all the foresede londs called Furse and Westewaye he marryede one

---

34. Westway in Cruwys Morchard (SS888101) is a grade II listed farmhouse, described as early seventeenth century, possible remodelling and extension of later medieval. Margaret Cruwys, in *A Cruwys Morchard Notebook 1066–1874* (p. 60), thinks it is fifteenth century. The tithe award gives 51 acres, compared to Furse's 39.

Annes Adler one of the dofteres and cooheres of John Atheler
of Nymettregis by which menes he was possessede of the one
moaytye of all John Addeleres londes that is to saye of londs
in Erygge, More Herpeforde Chydyngebroke Pytte, Torryton.
This John hadde also londs of the grante of John Adeller in
the xv[th] yere of Kynge Edwarde the IIIIth [1475/6] to hym and
to Annes his wyfe and to there heres in Henbere Scorehyll and
one tenemente wytheyn the burrow of Certon. This John Furse
fyrste bofte the fee sympell of Bromham[35] and West Kynstere of
Ser Thomas Cornewall knyght[36] yn xv[th] yere of Kynge Henrye
the Seventhe [1499/1500]. This John Furse and Annes his wyfe
dyd dewell at Erygge[37] in Kynges Nemett they hade issue John
Bowden Willyam Water Phillyppe and one dofter. He kepte a
verye good howse and was of grett welthe he meayntayned his
son and here in lernynge at the yndes of the curte this John Furse
was on M[r] Renayes clerke[38] he payed monye to John Addeler for
his wyfe his exercyse was makynge of wrytynges and kepynge
of curtes, he was ons Collector of the ffytyedole. This John did
make dyvers leses, viz. in an° 22 H 7° [1506/7] he made a lese
of his londes in Furse to one John Hockewaye and others, and
in the fyrste yere of H 7° [1485/6] he made a lese of Scorehyll
to one Thomas Gollocke. This John leved untylle he was lxx
yeres he dyed in the 23 or 24 of Henr' the 7° [1507–09] of the
stronggury. He was buryed at Kyngesnemet in the Churche there
havynge a blew stone upon hym. He made his wyfe executor and
gave to all his chylderen serten legasyes, he also delevered to his
here a cowe accordynge to his fathers mynde, and more I can
not saaye of this John but God sende hym a joyefull daye in his

His marrage to Adleres here

Adleres londes

The purchase of Bromeham and Weste Kynstere

His dewellynge
His issue

His exersyse

His leses

His dethe

The delevery of the cowe

35. Broomham in Kings Nympton (SX709213): (Keystone Historic Buildings
Consultants Report K 443, *Broomham, Kings Nympton, Devon*, June 1995:
Keystone unpublished report). Listed Grade II*.
36. Sir Thomas Cornwall is not identified: a Thomas Cornwall witnessed deeds at
Arlington in the 1490s (Devon RO 50/11/1/3/6, 8, dated 1494, 1497, and temp.
Henry VIII), but inquisitions on a Sir Thomas who died 1501/2, and another
1537/39, concentrate on Herefordshire property with no mention of Devon
(*Calendar of Inquisitions Post Mortem*, Henry VII vol. II (1915); *Lists and
Indexes* XXIII, *Index of Inquisitions post Mortem, Henry VIII to Philip and
Mary* (1907).
37. Eryge, Erydege, Yerndege etc are variant spellings for Highridge in Kings
Nympton (SS714208), almost entirely rebuilt by John Furse.
38. Mr Renaye (or Revaye) is not identified; compare p. 44.

Resurrection, and whatt John Adeler was and where his londes did lye[39] and what becom of John Furses issue[40] yt shalbe more att large appere here after.

John Furses dofter

This John Furses dofter was marryed to one Cowte of Bysshopes Nemet and had dyveres issues.

fo. 8

What ys become of John Furses issue, viz.

Bawdon Furse

What John Furse his son was yt shall apper here after. Bawden Furse diede wth owte issue but he was a verye stronge man and a lusty yn all exercyses of manhode. Willyam, Water and Phillype all were gallant men, but John and Phyllyppe were the grettes and strongeste. They all wolde wraxell, caste the barre, shotte, bowle and were therefore grettelye commended and beloved.[41]

Willyam Furse

Willyam dewelled at Bromeham. He hadde issue John and Willyam and too dofters, the one maryede at Holl to one Richarde Man, and Man had isue iij dofters, the other dofter marryed one Harres of Staverton & they had isue dyvers sones and dofters. John Furse ther brother dyede wythe owte isue, William his brother had issue iij sonnes and one dofter.

Water Furse & the good successe of his issue

Water Furse hade issue John, Willyam, Hewe, Roberte, Water, Antonye and iij dofters. This Water dewelled at Eryge and was a man god be praysed of good welthe worthe V^c li. His wyfe consumed yt wantonly yn brynge uppe of her chylderen in idellenes and plesure but yt here what becom of all them: John was lustye and by good happe marryed a ryche wyddoes dofter in Somersettshere and by thaat menes he be came from a wanton and wylde man to be a carefull man to leve. He purchased for terme of his lyfe the berton of Borryngeton and Eggerudege and was yn the yend a man of good welthe and grett credet and kepte a good howse and hade dyvers sones and dofters. Yt was he that newe bulded all moste all Erydege howses and ther he dewelled monye yeres.

39. See below, pp. 38–42.
40. See below, pp. 49–50.
41. Sports: see Appendix II.

Willyam his brother for his manhode became a sodyer in Captain Furse Irlond[42] where he contynewed in grett credytt and was an excydynge man of welthe he was in Irlond nere fortye yeres he was a valyente sodyer and nere xxx yere a good capten and grelye in the prynses favor and feared of his enymye and dyd monye grette exployts and valyente actetes in Irlonde and ther he in the fylde wonde his armes he did dewell at a Castell that he hadde in Irlond and was marryed and had issue on son or too and one of his sones was a capptayn in Flanders.

Robarte John and Willyam were all iij exelente wraxselers so Yeman of the Garde that Robarte by that menes was on of the yemones of the garde monye yeres, he had dyveres wyves he dewelled nere London and ther he dyed and hadde no issue. Hewe was slayne wythe an arrowe by mysfortune he dyed unmarryed. Water did use to playe upon an instrumente and by good happe he marryed a wyddowe, then he loste his instrumente and becom an exciden good hussebonde. He was too tymes marryed but what isue he hadde I do not understonde. Antonye wente also into Irlonde, I harde he also was a captayne there but what is become of hym or what issue he hadde I am not serten. Ther iij syster were all well marryed but what issue they hadde I do not understonde.

Philyppe Furse was the myghtes man of welthe of all his brotheres Phi' Furse he deweled in Thorverton in a berton called Roddon curte worth vj or vij score powndes a yere. Yt was on Mr Dyggyes londes he bofte the fyeesympell of Kyngewylle parte of Erydege & Pytte. He alonge tyme served a valyent knyght called Ser Thomas Dennes. He was marryed and hade no issue but a base son to whom he procured the foresed barton of Roddon & all his

---

42. Captain William Furse does not occur in *Calendar of the State Papers relating to Ireland of the reigns of Henry VIII, Edward VI, Mary and Elizabeth, 1509–1573* (1860), but possibly because of a change in editorial policy there are many references to Captain William 'Furres' and his band of 100 (or 106) footmen in the recently published *Calendar of State Papers Ireland, Tudor period 1571–75*, ed. Mary O'Dowd (2000). These are mostly references to garrisons, troop movement and pay. The Earl of Essex wrote to the Privy Council on 5 July 1575 'The fort at Blackwater is fully finished and left in the custody of Captain Furres whose band of 100 footmen lie half there and half at the Newry.' On 12 September 1578 Sir Edward Fyton wrote from Dublin to Burghley 'in favour of Captain Furres for his principal and valiant service to be forgiven his debt to the Queen of 700^{li}, occasioned by the naughty falsehood of his clerk, who deceived him, not knowing how to read or write.' (*Calendar of State Papers relating to Ireland, Henry VIII etc., 1574–85*, 1867). Subsequent volumes in the old series do not refer to him.

londes and goodes. This Philyppe before he dyed was blynde. He was by the rebelles longe a prysoner at Samford and very evell intreted & in grett haserde.[43] His base sonne was marryed & had issue and did consume all his fathers goods & londes & yt awyse and a very talle man and well extemed of all peapell & very good fe [*torn*]

fo. 9
Her dewellyng

ANNES Furse late the wyfe of the foresede John Furse contynually did dewell at Erydege. She contynued a wyddo xxx yeres and mentanyed a verye good howse at Erydege and was a woman of grette welthe. She inyoyed the foresede moytye of all her fathers londes and Henbere Scorehyll the tenemente in Certon and Kynstere. Phyllypp Furse and Water Furse was her only joye. This Phillypp was fyrste brofte in credytt and serves by menes of his brother John, yt notwythe stondynge after he came to welthe and credytt yn dede he was contente and dyd practyse wythe foresede Annes his mother to have all her londes, and upon som prevye malles that this Annes hadde unto Margerett John Furses wyfe and that by Phillyppes menes she did pretente in dede to allenate all her londes from John & his heres, yt at laste by menes of good ffryndes and for good wyll she hade to John Furse her sones son and here in the xxij^{ti} yere of Henry the VIII [1530/1] she gave all her londes to one Roger Vessycke and to Water Furse by dede to the use of her selfe for the terme of her lyfe, the remender to John her son for the terme of hys lyfe and after hym to remayne to John Furse the younger & to his heres in fee tayle.[44]

What londes
she did inyoye

Phill Furses
curtyseye

The londes
intaylede

Her yage &
her dethe

This Annes leved lxxx yeres and she dyed the xij^{th} daye of February yn the xxxj yere of Kynge Henry the VIII [1540]. She made Water Furse her hole executor and she ys buryed in the Church of Kyngesnemet. She made dyvers leses as hit shall here after appere. Water Furse survyved Vyssycke, therefore John Furse his son & here in the vj yere of Edward the VI [1552/3] did by wrytynge reassure all the foresed premisses to John Furse

43. The Prayer Book Rebellion, 1549.
44. Agnes Furse's grant to Roger Vesyke the elder of Torrington, and Walter Furse, 1 February 1530/1, is DRO Z1/48/1/3, and is a feoffment in trust of all her lands and messuages in Crediton, Hembeer, Moor, Pitt, Hollacomb, Harford, Skorehill and Chiddenbrook, with Highridge, to her own use for life then John Furse the elder of Swimbridge, and then to John his son, and then brothers Jerome and Edward. Her seal bears a merchant's mark.

the younger of Torryton and to his heres for ever. She was in her lyfe tyme a very wyse and a dyscryte woman and a perfytt good hussewyfe and a carefull woman for her busynes and more I can not saye of Annes but sende her a joyefull daye in her Resurreccyon & joye everlastyng.

Note here that John Furse and Annes hys wyfe were too of the beste laboreres that came ynto our harveste for we inyoyede moste of our londes from them and by there menes therefore we have good cose to have them in memorye for in truthe theye were the fyrst fondasyon of all our credytt prayse god for hit.

What leses Annes Furse made in her lyfe tyme viz.

She made a lese of Mowre to one Holcombe in the vth of Henr' VIII [1513/4] for 26^s 8^d rent

She made a lese of Henbere to one Hamton in the xxij of Henr' VIII [1530/1] 13^s 4^d rente and another lese of the same Henbere to Westyngeton in an^o xxix Henr VIII [1527/8] xj^s

She made a lese of Harpeforde to Ballaman in the ix of Henr' VIII [1517/8] for xj^d rente

She made a lese of Erygge to Water Furse in an^o xxij of Henr' VIII [1530/1] for x^s rent

She made a lese of Chydyngebroke to Gollocke in the xxiiij of Henr' the VIIth [1532] 12^d rent

She made a lese of Scorehill to Gollocke in the xxx of Henry VIII [1538/9] iij^s iiij^d rent

She made a lese of the townehouse in Certon to Phill Furse for x^s rente.

Bromeham in Nymett Regis

BROMEHAM ys a tenement, yt lyethe in Nymett Regis and yt was on tyme copye holte londes and parsell of the maner of Kyngenymton. By our offyses yt is sayed yt is holden of the maner of Nettelcome in free socage but the lorde of the maner of Kyngenemett Mr Pollarde sayeth hit is holde of his maner & we ofte to paye hym x^s rente yerely and sute to his curte & x^s for a releve, truthe yt is this rente was payde certen yeres in dede, but here note Ser Lewse Pollarde longe before he was lorde of

the maner he dyd dewell at the plase there called the newe plase
and beynge a grett bulder Annes Furse came wythe her plowe
to helpe home som tymber and in truthe did showe hym the
wrytynge of Bromeham and Kynstere in her son John Furses
presenes, when he hadde throffeleye redde hyt he did demonde
of them what rente they payed they awnsered x^s for the one and
Sargente
Pollerdes on
cunsell xvij^s for the other then Mr Pollard sayed the more foweles you,
for you are not bownd by this to paye anye rente for that yt is but
a rent secke your relese dothe discharge hit; not longe after Mr
Pollarde bofte the maner then John Furse my granfather did go
to plowe wythe there one calfe for the fyrste denayede the rente
and that by Mr Pollardes on cunsell beynge then a lerned man
and a sargente at lawe so ever setheres the dethe of Ser Lewes
The statute
our helpe Polard the rente for Bromeham and Kynstere was never payde;
by the Statute of Westemester the thyrde[45] all this rente sute and
serves ys clerely voyde becose yt is but a rente secke reserved
The polle dede
a second helpe onlye by a polle dede for no man sethenes the makynge of that
statute but the prynse onlye can create a newe tenure, therefore
no dowte the londes in truthe muste nedes be holden as the reste
A trewe
defynysion of the maner ys holden proporsyonately in rente sute & serves. I
have harde the maner ys holden of the lorde of Northemolton this
The excepson
of the relese of
no forse you see whatsoever the menynge of the partes in the begynnynge
was bothe the reservasion in the dede and excepson in the relese
ys all voyed by lawe, but here note that ons sethenes the dethe
A distrese
taken for the
rente of Ser Lewes Ser Hewe Pollarde did dystrayne Bromeham for
the rent the distresse was a blacke mare whiche a longe tyme
remayned in the pownde but in the yende wythe owte payemente
the dystrese was turned owte of the pownd and sethenes never
Prescrypsion
also a barre dystrayned but mony tymes thretened and charged upon all the
reves but never payde these lxx yeres so theye are now clerely
barred of all there rente sute and serves bothe by statute ther
An other tytell
to Bromeham relese and perscryppsyon for John Furse of Sombryge, John
Furse of Torryton nor yt Robatt Furse never payded them
anye. Note that after the dethe of Willyam Furse John Furse
his son and here did by Mr Pollardes intysemente enter upon
Bromeham & made tytell by forse of the laste will of John Furse
his grandfather but the tytell not good for that Willyam Furse

---

45. Statute of Westminster the third: 1289, 'Quia Emptores', or 'Quia Emptores
terrarum', 18 Edward I, st. 1, c. 1. This abolished subinfeudation and protected
the rights of chief lords.

was my granfather John Furses tenant & was content to holde
the londe of hym by dede so after a lytell trobell the lawe sessed.
This londes called Bromeham ys devyded into dyveres closes as
here after folloyethe, yt is nowe in the tenure of John Furse &
is worthe by the yere abowve all charges xxxiij^s iiij^d. There was
som stryfe for a lytell ylonde betewexte Mr Curteneye and Furse
but in the xvj of El' [1573/4] a fynall yende was made in the
presenes of dyveres; the note remaynes amonge our wrytynges.
Note the fyftyedole for one hole payement for Bromeham ys x^d.

Kepe sure your wrytynges

The order for the ilonde

The particuler names of all the tenements callede Bromeham,
viz:
The BRODAPARKE xvj akeres, the utter gratton xij akeres, the
three corner close vj akeres, the Inner more xvj akeres, the utter
more lx akeres, the knappe x akeres, the lytell haye ij akeres,
the Ayshe parke one aker, the lytell parke iij akeres, the furse
parke xij akeres, the Esteparke xvj akeres, the more meddowe
iij akeres, the longe medes ij akeres, the iij hames or marche too
akeres, The weste wode vij akeres, the Estewode xv akeres, the
Towne plase and gardens one aker.
        Sm^a to. Clxxxiij akers.

fo. 12

Westekynstere in Kynges Nymett

fo. 13

WESTEKYNSTERE[46] ys also a tenemente, yt dothe lye wytheyn
the paryshe of Nymett Regis; yt was parsell of the maner and
copyeholte lond as Bromeham was and yt is holden as Bromeham
ys and that all by one tytell. There was reserved xvij^s rente yerely
a releve and sute to the lordes curte of Kynges nemet but yt was
never payde sethenes the dethe of Ser Lewes Pollorde but yt is
clerely discharged by lawe by the same menes that Bromeham
ys. The laste copye holder was one Draper. This londes nowe
ys in the tenure of one Water Tossell and yt is worte by the yere
abowve all charges xxx^s.
        Yt payeth for a hole fyftydole vij^d.

Bromeham and Kynestere all one tenure

and bothe of them discharged by our menes

46. Weste Kynstere in Kings Nympton is Kingstree (SS714196). In the tithe award it
    is 137 acres; Furse gives it as 126.

The pertycular names of all the closes of the Tenemente called Westekynstere viz:

THE NORTHE downe xxx^{ti} akeres, Loveleye xvj akeres, the layes x akeres, the more lx akeres, the pese wythe owte garlonde yate by pyllondes londe halfe one aker, the meddowe x akeres.

Sm^a to. Cxxvj akeres.

[ADLER FAMILY AND THEIR PROPERTIES]

This is the juste lyne and dyssente of John Addeler als Atheler and of his proyenytors of whom we are dissended

fo. 15

THERE was sometymes one Henrye de la Wodehyll was sesede of londes in Herpeforde of the grante of John de la Pytte, and Henry hade issue John. This John as I suppose dewelled at Harpeforde and by that menes he and his sequele were fyrste called John de Harpeforde. This John in the laste yere of Kynge Edwarde the fyrste [1306/7] fyrste bofte the fee sympell of Henbere. He marryed one Rose att More the dofter of one Elles at Mowre, he bofte this londes called Henbere of one Crysten Coppen and yn the seconde yere of Edward the fyrste [1273/4] he purchased one tenemente in Kerton towne of the foresede Elles at Mowre he also in the vij of Edward the Seconde [1313/14] purchasede one other tenemente in Kerton towne of one Gorsenne in fee sympell. THYS JOHN and Rose hadde issue John Herpeforde and Roger Herpeforde. John Herpeforde the younger he hadde issue Thomas. THIS Thomas marryed one Jullyan of what kyndered I do not understonde; he was sesede of serten londes called Mowre in Certon of the grante of John att Mowre the sonne of the foresed Elles in the xj^th yere of Edwarde the thyrde [1337/8] and Thomas and Julyan had issue John.

THIS JOHN Herpeforde was sesede of londes in Pytte Holcombe and Chydyngebroke; he marryed wth John at Mowres dofter and here as I do suppose but I am serten he had issue ELLEZABETHE.[47] This Ellyzabeth was marryed to one Rafe Dabernon of Munkeleye

The originall of the lyne of the Harpefordes

Elles at More

Ellezab^t Dabernon

---

47. Elizabeth Dabernon's conveyance to William Sprye or Spree is DRO Z1/10/42, and that to John Ruffe or Roff, 1453, Z1/10/45.

and they hadde no issue, but Ellezabethe survyved and beynge a wyddowe she made dyveres convayens of her londes in Mowre Pytte Hollacombe Chydyngebrok Henbere Harpeforde and the londes in Certon towne to her cosen John Addeler. I rede that John Herpeforde in the fortye yere of Edward the thyrde [1366/7] convayed all his londes to one Richarde Frynche of Exon'[48] and the same Rycharde Frenche reassured all the same

Rafe Dabernon

londes to the foresed Ellezabethe in the ij yere of Henrye the IIIIth [1400/1]. Rafe Dabernon and Ellezabethe hys wyfe in the

Roger Adeler

xij yere of Henrye the VI [1433/4] paste all there londes to one John Dabernon; that yere Rafe dyede. I do suppose that one Roger Addeler of Munekeleye fyrste maryed the foresede Rafes syster and here or else the foresede John Dabernones dofter and

Ric' Adeler

here. He hadde issue one Richarde Addeler whiche marryed one John Harpefordes dofter the son of the foresed Roger for this is serten that Richard Adler was ryght here to Rafe Dabernon and

John Adler cosen and here to Ellz Dabernon

Richard hadde issue John Addeler whych did wryte hymselfe also cosen and here of Ellyzabethe Dabernon, whiche can not be, but he muste lyneallye dyssend from the foresed Roger Harpefordes heres. Rafe Dabernon was sesed of a garden in Grett Torryton whiche came to the Adleres by dyssente and agayne the foresed Ellezabethe in the xiij of Henrye the VI [1434/5] convayed all

John Adler did marye Annes Hoper

her londes to one Sprye, and so did Richard Adler convaye all his londes to the same Spree and otheres and the same Spree and too feffees reassurede all the premysses to the foresede Richard Addeler for the terme of his lyfe, the remender in fee tayle to John Addeler and to Annes hys wyfe the dofter and here of Roberte Hoper of Erygge.

Grette trobell and of longe tyme

BUT HERE marke after the dyssesse of Ellezabethe Dabernon then began gret trobell vexasyon trobell [*sic*] and dyvers sutes in lawe for Ellezabethes Dabernones londes betewexte Roger Herpefordes heres & John Addeler and so contynewed dyvers yeres for Roger Herpeford the seconde son of John Herpeford and Rose his wyfe hade issue John and Thomas; this John hadde issue John whiche John was marryed and theye had issue John and Alse. This laste John dyed wythe owte issue and his syster Alse was marryed to one John Ruffe of Certon and they hadd issue John which dyd dewell at Exon and this John Ruffe of

48. John Harpford's conveyance to Richard Frenssh, 22 March 1366, is DRO Z1/10/22.

Exon immediately after the dyssesse of Ellezabethe Dabernon *fo. 16*
did in truthe enter ynto all her londes as nexte cosen and here of
the same Ellezabethe, and when he myghte not prevayle then in
the xxvj of Henry the VI [1447/8] he alynated the londes to one
Bobyche. He contynewed the sonne styll yn trobell but in the xij
yere of Edward the IIIIth [1472/3] he then solde all his interres to
one Willyam Lobbe; he contynewed the same in lawe too yeres   All yended by
then the mater was compermytted to serten wardes men so by   a warde
awarde the mater was ended in the xiiij yere of Edward the IIII[th]
[1474/5] and by the same awarde John Adler payed to Lobbe xiij[li]
vj[s] viij[d], and then he by good assuranes con[v]ayed all the londes
to John Adler and his heres for ever.[49] So yt sholde seme that
John Adler came to this londes more by dede then by dyssente
butt ever sethenes the londes have bynne quyett.

ROBERTE HOPER was sesede of londes yn Erygge wytheyn the   Roberte Hoper
perysshe of Nemett Regis; he was marryed to one Rose the dofter   and Rose his
and here of Thomas Garlonde of Chymleye and by Rose he   wyfe
hadde a good tenemente in Chymleye by good convayans to hym
and his heres for ever, and he hadde the use & possessyon of the
londes durynge of her lyfe but sethenes none of his heres never   Garlonde loste
inyoyede hyt. This Rose was a wyddo when Hoper marryed her
and she hadde a sonne and by that menes I suppose we loste
Garlonde. This Roberte and Rose had issue Annes. Roberte dyd
dewell at Eggerudege and there he and his wyfe dyed.

JOHN ADDELER afte the dyssesse the foresede Rafe Dabernon &   John Adler &
Ellezabethe his wyfe and Roberte Hoper and Rose his wyfe was   Annes his wyfe
as ys aforesede at laste sesed of all there londes. He dewelled at   hade issue
Erygge and ther kepte a good howse and was in the yende of good
welthe, but trulye I have harde John Furse payde hym myche
monye to marrye Annes his dofter, but in consederasyon thereof
he presentelye gave hym Henbere Scorehylle & a tenemente yn
Certon towne.[50] This John Adler and Annes his wyfe hadde   viz. Annes &
issue but too dofteres that is to saye Annes and Johan. This   Johan

---

49. The sale to John Bobeche, 20 July 1472, is DRO Z1/10/52, and that to John
    Lobbe, 20 July 1472, Z1/10/53. William Lobbe's transfer to John Adeler 1 May
    1475 is Z1/10/54 and concerns an arbitration on the title to land in Crediton,
    More, Holcombe, Pytte, Chedyngbroke, Herford and Hembere, which all once
    belonged to Richard Harford.
50. For Crediton and Crediton Hamlets see Major T. W. Venn's *Crediton*, and O. J.
    Reichel, 'The manor and hundred of Crediton', *TDA* 54, pp. 146–181.

Kyngewill
maryed Johan

Johan he did marrye to one John Kyngewyll of Kerton & in consyderasyon thereof he dyd assure to Kyngewyll & to his heres all his londes in Hollacombe and one tenemente in Kerton towne in Prystenlane and ij^s of stocke rente. John Kyngewill and Johan his wyfe hadde issue Bennett Kyngewyll. This Bennett and John Furse of Sumbrydege after made a full partysyon of all Adleres londes. John Addeler and Annes his wyfe both of them dyed at Kyngesnymton and be ther buryed, and more I can not saye of John Addeler and Annes his wife and of all the reste abowve wryten but God sende them all a yoyefull daye in ther ressurrexsyon.

They hadde
issue Bennett

They made dyvers leses I never sawe but too of them; that was John Adler in the xxxvth of Henry the VI [1456/7] made a lese of Mowre to one Lyndon for liij^s iiij^d rente and Pytt to one Hunte. He did homage for Mowre Pytte Chydyngebroke and Erygge. Note here that the foresede Robert Hopers name was Eggerudege alias Hoper.

Hoper als
Eggerudege

fo. 17

What londes
Robarte Furse
did lye to
mortgage

NOTE that Roberte Furse of Denepryer at the vj daye of Maye yn an° dni 1580 did lye to morgage to John Dunsecombe of London for one hundred powndes to be repayed the xxvij daye of November then nexte insuyng all his londes on More Chydyngebroke and Certon.

The juste
discharge

ITEM the C^{li} was truly repayed at the tyme and plase appoynted to John Dunsecombe yn the presens of Phyllyppe Bassett Humfrye Preddes and John Hoayell and for the same I have a suffyciant acquyttans under Dunescomes honde and sele and the mortgage dede redelevered. Note this dede was knowleged but never inrollede & c. Kepe sure that acquyttans.

fo. 18

What Addeleres londes was in quantyte and where yt did lye and howe hathe the same.

Mowre

MOWRE[51] was devyded Kyngewill hadde the howses and all the londes by the sowthe syde of the waye and Furse hadde all the reste whiche was by existmasyon lxxxx akeres of good londes, yt lyeth wythe yn the p[a]ryshe of Certon and maner of Uton, yt was holden by knyghte serves, yt was sette at justemente to

---

51. Mowre, in the manor of Uton (SX812991): Moor Farmhouse is grade II listed, but as mid-nineteenth century.

dyveres persones and by that menes the rente was incresede from xxvj^s viij^d to xj^{li} xvj^s viij^d for one parte.

CHYDYNGEBROKE[52] lyethe also in Certon, yt was a tenemente and ix akeres of good londes. Yt was holden by knyghtes serves the rent was xij^s the londes all good pasture.

HARPEFORDE[53] lyethe also in Certon, yt was a tenement and xlv akeres the moste parte but mene londes the rent home xj^s.

SCOREHYLL[54] lyethe also in Certon paryshe, yt was nere xxx akeres but very sympell londes, but latelye inclosede and a powre howse ther bulded yt was holden in socage tenure, yt was holden of Mr Prestewod as of his maner of Venyetedeborne. Yt was worthe abowve all charges iij^s iiij^d by the yere.

CERTON IN THE towne[55] was one howse and one garden or meddowe the hole nere halfe on aker of londes. Yt lyethe in the westetowne and ys holden of the bysshope of Exon' by socage; yt was in grett decaye the olde rente but x^s by the yere but nowe xxvj^s viij^d abowve all charges.

HENBERE[56] ys a tenemente and nere xl akeres, the moste parte but mene londes. Yt lyeth wythe yn the parysshe of Sente Marye Tedborne and yt is holden of Mr Hewe Ackelonde in socage tenure and was worthe by the yere abowve all charges xiij^s iiij^d.

NOTE THAT ROBARTE Furse of Denepryer solde v perseles of the foresede londs called Mowre to Willyam Kyngewill of Certon when he dyd fyrste purchase Erygge, viz one meddowe called

Margin notes:

Chydyngebroke

Harpeforde

Scorehyll

Certon

Henbere

Robarte Furse to bye other londes solde

52. Chedenbrok, now Chiddenbrook (SS818005), is in Newton St Cyres according to Devon RO 64/12/9/1,3, but a grant 1399/1400 defines it as in Crediton on the west side of the chapel of St Lawrence (Z1/10/27, 28, 29). *PNDevon* merely puts it in Crediton Hamlets (II, p. 407). On the tithe map there seems to be no building.
53. Harpeford is now Harford (*PNDevon* II, p. 405, SX812962). Great Harford is a farmhouse listed as grade II, probably sixteenth century, and Little Harford as grade II*, late fifteenth to early sixteenth century.
54. Scorehill, or Scoreland, supposed to be the poorhouse, has not been found referred to as such in other sources. In 1626 it was conveyed, as a messuage and a farthing of land, in the tenure of Luce Hawkyns, widow, from John Tucfelde of Crediton, gentleman, to Walter Deyman, cooper (DRO Z1/10/264).
55. Crediton, house and garden in the West Town, held of the bishop, is too vague to be traced.
56. Henbere is now Hembeer (*PNDevon* II, p. 452), in Tedburn St Mary. In the tithe award it occurs as Lower Hembeer, owned by Richard Hippisley Tuckfield, and as Lower Hembeer. The OS map 1809/10 shows Higher and Lower Hembeer in SX8095, both now deserted.

all the foresed
vj parseles of
londes

the brode mede, on close called the Bromeparke, on other percell callede the Starehyll downe, too other closes called the Slades, the hole londes by existymasyon xxiiij^{ti} akeres of londes and of the yerelye rente of iiij^{li} xiij^s iiij^d over and abowve all charges.

THE RESTE of all the fore sede londes called Mowre Chydyngebroke Harpeforde Scorehyll Certon Townehowse and Henbere, the same Roberte solde the same to Richarde Predes of Feber for iijC^{li} when he did fyrste purchase the maner of Skyrrydon, and Mr Predes hathe bande of vjC^{li} for the inyoynge there of and Kyngewyll hadde a bonde of ijC^{li} for the inyoynge of his porsyon. AND at the same tyme Mr Predes resevd all the wrytynges of Roberte Furse consernynge the same londes.[57]

THE LONDES YN Torryton ys but one lytell garden nere halfe one aker, yt lyeth in Newestrete wythe yn the Burrowe of Torryton.[58] Yt is socage tenure & holden of the lorde of the Burrowe of Torrryton by the payemente of vj^d for all maner of rente sute and serves and yt is nowe in the tenure of one Henry Vynaye and yt is worthe by the yere abowve all charges ij^s ij^d.

fo. 19

Yerndege in Kynges Nymett

YERERNDEGE ys a tenemente and yt ys devyded yn to dyveres perseles: yt lyethe wytheyn the perrysshe of Kynges Nemett. Yt is holden of the maner of Kynges Nymett by knightes serves, the heye rente ys xvj^s yerelye and sute to the curte. Note that all the maner of Kynges Nymett ys awnsyente demene. We paye for a hole fyftyedole for Yererndege x^d. Yt is nowe in the tenure of John Furse the sonne of Water Furse, yt is worthe by the yere above all charges xxvij^s vj^d.

Note the releve for all Erygge ys xvj^s payed after that rate.

fo .20

The pertyculer names of all the closes of the foresed Tenemente called Erydege

THE NORTHE down xvj akeres, the Whyteleaye xiiij akeres, the Sondeparke vj akeres, the Weste Sondeparke ij akeres, the otesangger xvj akeres, the Beareparke iij akeres, the grene iij

---

57. Writings to Predes, that is, Prideaux. Now DRO Z1/10. Did Furse keep copies or an abstract, to write so precisely in 1593?

58. New Street in Torrington is extant, but an individual building unlikely to be traced, especially considering town fires.

akeres, the Rode mede on aker, Shortelonde mede one aker, the longe mede iiij akeres, the Weste Shortelonde iij akeres, the este Shortelonde iij akeres, the balle one aker, the ockeparke iij akeres, the too gardenes one aker, the Towneplase one aker, the brodaparke xxiiij akeres, the knappe xxx akeres, the mowre xl akeres.

   Sm^a to. Clxxj akeres.

JOHN FURSE [died 1549/50] the sune and here of the foresede John Furse and Annes his wyfe after hys father and mothers dyssesse by dyssente was also sesede of all the foresede messuages londes and tenements yn Furse Westewaye Bromeham Westekynstere Henbere Scorehyll one howse in Certon and the garden in Torryton. He was also as coo-here juntely sesede wyth hys Cosen Bennet Kyngewyll of the foresed londes in Mowre Herpeforde Chydyngebroke and Pytte. He fyrste bofte the fee sympell of one tenemente in Comemarten[59] yn the xxviij yere of Kynge Henry the VIII [1536/7] of one Willm Breckenocke. This John Furse bofte the tynnemyll at Lydeforde, he also was sesede of the thyrde parte of an other tynne myll in Ockehamton called Cordedon Smythe, he hadde a grette delyte to be a tynner, I am sure he was honer of too hundred tynne workes in Devon and Cornewall whiche yn his tyme theye were very profytabell unto hym.

fo. 21

What londes he had

The purchase of Commarten

The tynne mylles

His tynne workes

THYS JOHN Furse was a mane that dyd farre excyde all his proyenytores yn wysedom lernynge credytt welthe strenth manhode and personage for his personage he was the goodelyste man that ever I did see for he was grette and clene growen stronge myghtye and welle favorede, he always delyted to be desente and tryme yn hys apparell and well horsede, he ferede no man for he often tymes was surelye tryede, he was a grete wraxseler and geven myche to plesure, he was at the yennes of the curte and there sweren an atturneye but he dyd not myche use that, but he dyd procure dyvers good and in thos dayes profytabell offyses for he was too severall tyme undershryfe of Devon and onse chefe colector of the fyftyedole, he was xvj yeres Stuarde

His abyllyte and credet

His practyse & offyses

---

59. A tenement in Combe Martin is impossible to trace.

of the Stannerye[60] and monye yeres Stuarde of the Dewchye of
Lankekester,[61] he was hedde Stuarde of all the abbetts curtes of
Tavystoke and Bockelond and of dyveres fees, and chefe Stuarde
to dyvers others by menes whereof his fees were large and his
gaynes grette. Yn his yuthe he was one Mr Reneyes clarke and
for his manhode and good quallytes Mr Shylston hadde hym
in serves and after hym he served a worthye knyghte one Ser
Thomas Dennes, he was wythe hym yn Scottelonde and laste
of all he was yn serves wythe the Ryght Honerabell Henrye
Curteneye Erell of Devon and Marcus of Exon' and yn grete
favor and credytte wythe hym.

His fyrste
marrage

Holstrom &
Wallonde

The dethe of
Marye one of
the cooheres of
Foxsecombe

THIS JOHN Furse fyrste marryed one Marye Foxsecombe als
Truncharde one of the dofteres and cooheres of John Foxscombe
of Grette Torryton and by that menes yn the yende he hadde
for his porsyon serten londs called Wallonde and on tenemente
calede Holstrom. What John Foxsecombe was and what londes
he hadde yt shall appere here after.[62] When this John and Marye
were fyrste marryed they hadde but lytell theye did dewell at
Grette Wyke in Torryton and god did so prosper thym that
before she dyed they hadde CCCC bollockes and grette store of
monye and other quycke stuffe and were as well furnyshede of
all thynges in ther howse as any one man of ther degree was yn
all ther cunterye. This John and Marye hadd issue John Furse
Jerome Furse Edwarde Furse Crystean Johan Pasco Tomsen and
Margarette and serten otheres whyche dyed infants. What is
becom of ther issue hit shall here after appere.[63]

THIS MARYE Furse to all our grette loste and henderanse in here
beste tyme when she was some fortye yeres dyede and ys buryed
nere to the dore that dothe goo yn to Jhus yele in Grett Torryton

---

60. Steward of the Stannary: the stewards' courts began in the thirteenth century
and were abolished in 1836, and were courts of common law administered as
at Westminster, except where expressly varied by stannary custom. They dealt
with debt, trespasses to streamworks and ore and actions for nuisances such
as flooding or silting-up. The Vice-Warden's court acted as a court of appeal
(Pennington, *Stannary Law*, p. 29).

61. Steward of the Duchy of Lancaster: see Revd J. A. S. Castlehow, 'The Duchy of
Lancaster in the County of Devon', *TDA* 80, pp. 193–209. The authority was
of feudal lordships, chief rents and the profits of holding courts. The Duchy
courts were held at five centres, honours or seignories: Broadhembury, Spreyton,
Witheridge, Goodleigh and Holdsworthy.

62. See below, p. 52.

63. See below, pp. 49, 52.

Churche for ther adyunynge lyethe dyveres of her proyenytores. This Marye was a very tryme comlye woman a paynefull wyfe and carefull for her busynes, gentell and fryndelye and belovyd of all men and grettleye estemed for her vertus lyfe and good and honeste quallytes.

Thys John Furse after the dyssesse of Marye he marryed one Anne Remonde a wyddowe, a gentyllwoman boren. She did dewell at a berton in Swymbebrygge called Mearche[64] this was an unhappe marrage for she leved wythe hym but too yeres yt was, he fyve hundred pounds the worse and ever after durynge hys lyfe and his executores after hym longe yn trobell, and yt the woman a verye good woman but thys hyt happened; she hadde monye chelderen and a myghtye kyndered. This John at his fyrste comyngde dyde in truthe delever unto hyr grett somes of monye in golde and she hadde myche monye of her one remanynge in her hondes dewe to her one chylderen and dyvers spessyaltyes where yn dyveres of her fryndes did stonde bownde for the payement of severall somes of monye, yt happened that he beynge yn the Sowthe hames in kepynge of the curtes and all his chylderen verye younge, she sodonelye fell sycke and when she was dedde all the monye golde and dyvers spessyaltyes were gon, so when he came home he never reseved one grote, but what so ever her dett was he sureleye payed hyt.

His seconde marrage

fo. 22

Then after the dyssesse of this Anne he marryed one Margerett Cutteleyefe of Norcote in Estedowne a vere tryme wyfe and a dyscryte woman. This John and Margerett a longe tyme dyd dewell at Marche where they kepte a bowntefull howse. No man yn the cunterye of his abyllytye did the lyke but spessyally at Crysemas for then he hade his lorde of mysserule his mynstereles and some viij tall fellowes in his leverye and there made grette waste whiche myght have bynne better spente for by thes menes he dyd lacke no companye for the assestans of his howsekepynge. He helde dyveres justements and dyvers tenementes. He was alwayes orderlye served att hys tabell, he alwayes kepte som too or three clerkes and for the moste parte he did usuallye ryde wythe too men and sometyme wythe iij, but after the execusyon of my Lorde Marcus he was never jocante nor merye in harte.[65]

His thyrde marrage

His ydell charges

---

64. March, in Swimbridge, was never in Furse's hands. Marsh is a listed building.
65. Henry Courtenay, Marquess of Exeter, was executed 9 December 1538.

The Lords of Kyngenymton havynge a hatred unto hym for the denyall of the rente for Bromeham and Westekynstere dyd myghtelye hate hym for by the intysemente of Ser Hewe Pollard and on Hanford, Ser Hewes mane there was a noftye pryste[66] that falselye did accuse this John Furse of heyght treson but he most honestelye dyd acquytte hymselfe to be a good subyecte to ther grette shame and reprove, good be therefore praysed; Ser Hewe for the recompense of this wycked interpryse made the pryste presentelye person of Ockeforde this wycked pryste was after Bysshoppe of Exon' and longe after John Furse was dedde he by chanse dyd lye at Marche where he did confesse to on Crysten Remonde John Furses dofter that he hadde falselye accused her father.

Falselye accusede (margin)

Marke well this (margin)

THYS John was also gretelye spoyled in the comosyon[67] in Kynge Edward the VI tyme for he was then geven bodye and goods leke a rebell and yt durynge all the time of that Rebellyon he was contynuallye in his bedde sycke and not abell to travell. That trobell coste hym sevenscore powndes but his wyfe Margerett after his dyssesse by verdytt in the Castell of Exon' tryed her husebond a good subyecte and by that menes she was relesed of som charge whiche otherwyse she hadde payede. After this John wente from Marche he did a longe tyme dewell at Mowretowne[68] in Grette Torryton all the dayes of hys lyfe.

The commosion a grett charge (margin)

THIS John Furse and his cosen Bennet Kyngewill yn the xxxiij yere of Kynge Henrye the VIII [1541/2] made pertysyon of all the londes in Mowre Pytte Herpeford and Chydyngebroke, this was donne by the order and awarde of Remonde Norleye gentylman and Thomas Harres of Certon: so John Furse hadde for his parte Harpeforde Chydyngebroke and all the londes of Mowre that lyethe on the northe syde of the waye that ledethe from Certon to Gonston Crosse to hym and hys heres for ever and Kyngewyll hadde for his parte all the howses of Mowre and all the londes that lyethe on the sowthe syde of the waye and all that tenemente called Pytte to hym and his heres for ever,

This John Furse made partision with Kyngewill (margin)

of all except Erygge of Adleres londes (margin)

---

66. The naughty priest of Oakford who became bishop seems to be William Alleye, d. 1570.
67. The Commotion is the local name for the Prayer Book Rebellion, 1549. See Rose-Troup, *The Western Rebellion.*
68. Moretowne is Moortown in Great Torrington, and is Grade II listed as early seventeenth century (SS516201).

but for that Philyppe Furse hadde before that tyme bofte the fee sympell of Kyngewylles parte of Eggerudege there fore that was never parted.[69] Soo ever sethenes this partysyon every man hathe bynne contented wythe his porsyon and for the reste of all Adderes londes yt was particulerly convayed by dede som to Furse and som to Kyngewyll as ys aforesede. Thys John Furse when he dyd dewell at Moretowne hadde ther a Chapell[70] and hade a pryste mentayned yn his howse a longe tyme he also hadde one old nobell, and for that the same was better then his wyghte, for he wolde waye a ryle, he did delever the same olde nobell to hys sonne John and his will and comondement was that the same olde nobell sholde remayne from here to here for ever.[71] Thys John Furse did also reseve of his father a cowe accordynge to his grandfathers will and yerely upon Sente Rosemondes daye[72] he did at his one howse releve the powre wythe mete drynke and monye the valye of a calfe accordynge to his grandfathers and fathers wille and plesure. This John in truthe in my one herynge andyvers otheres did charge his son John Furse as hys father charged hym wythe the foresed cowe and calfe and that he sholde do the leke to his heres. This John Furse made his last will and testemente by the whiche he did geve all his Tynneworkes in Devon and Cornewall to Edwarde Furse his sones sonne and to his heres for ever and to Roberte Furse his sones sonne and here all his sylver plate to remayne from here to here and dyvers other good impelmentes worthe myche in valye. Dyvers other legasyes he gave to dyvers persones, and made Margerett his wyfe sole executryxse. He dyed the xiiij daye of Februarye yn the yere of o^r lorde god 1549 [1550] and ys buryed yn the Chansell of Grette Torryton faste by the quiere havynge a blewe stone upon his grave. He levede lxviij yeres; this you see for all his welthe wysedome and strenthe he indured monye

Marginal notes:
His chapelen

Of the olde nobell

Of the cowe reseved

What charge he gave to his son

His laste wille

To Roberte Furse his plate & c.

His dethe

fo. 23

---

69. The allotment of land from John Furse to Bennet Kingwill 30 April 1541 is DRO Z1/10/67.
70. Moortown chapel's dedication does not appear in any of the published bishops' registers, the most likely being that of Bishop Lacy (Dunstan, *Register of Edmund Lacy*).
71. The value of the coins, ryal and noble, could vary according to time and place. See Glossary.
72. Although a Rosamund does appear in *The Golden Legend*, a book of saints' lives, she is far from saintly and no day of celebration is ascribed to her (Ryan, vol II, pp. 368–9). The reference is more likely to be to Rosamund Clifford, mistress of Henry II, who was venerated before the Reformation, and celebrated on 6 July.

sharpe stormes and yt in the yende dyede yn credytt. He in his lyfe tyme procured dyvers leses viz the wyghtes of Holseworthye to his sone John and lekewyse lytell Weke and Moretowne to his wyfe, to Crysten his dofter and to John Furse the sonne of John Furse. This Margeret contynewed wyddowe monye yeres and dyd alwayes kepe a verye good howse. This John Furse in his lyfe tyme made dyvers leses, that ys to saye yn the xv yere of Henry the VIII [1523/4] he made a lese of Holstrom to one Weke for xxvj^s viij^d rente and in the xxxv [1543/4] of the same Henry he made a lese of Bromeham to William Furse his brother & others for xxxiij^s iiij^d rente, and in the xxxij yere of the same Henrye [1540/1] he made a lese of Westekynstere to Water Hoper for vj^s viij^d rente and in ann^o 19 H 8 [1527/8] he made a lese of Furse to one Hockewaye for vij^s vj^d rente, and in ann^o xj of the same Henrye [1519/20] he made a lese of Westewaye to Wode for xiij^s iiij^d rente, and in the xxvj [1534/5] of the same Henry he granted the same londes in Westewaye to one Xpofer Wode. This John did also procure a lese for 99 yeres of Stabeldone more of Phillyppe Hoper the whiche chatell lese he assyned by his laste wyll to Margerett his wyfe, the reste of his terme to his cosen Roberte Furse, and more I cannot saye of John Furse and Marye his wyfe but god sende unto them a joyefull daye in ther Resurrecsyon and lyfe ever lastynge.

fo. 24

THERE WAS on of our proyenytores that did geve a sylver gurdell full of sylver barres well worthe xiij^{li} vj^s viij^d that hyt sholde remayne from here to here and for wante of heres the same sholde remayne to the holy Rowde of Certon. Howe gave hit or howe longe hyt contyned I do not understonde, but I am sure that John Furse hadde the same. There was also a pere of bedes of sylver and vj sylver spownes that sholde remayne from here to here, but yn the same John Furses dayes the Rode of Certon was burned and therefore the foresede Margerett in shorte tyme after her hussebond John Furses dyssesse solde the foresede gyrdell bedes and sexse sylver spownes, whiche in truthe sholde have remayned from here to here. BUTT her husebonde did charge her to mentayne one John Patye a naturall innosente whiche of longe tyme hadde bynne in his howse and she fayethefullye dyd promyse to fulfylle his requeste, but she solde not the pore mane, but convayed hym from Torryton to Denepryer to Roberte Furse

Marginal notes:

His leses

What leses he made

Stabeldon More

All is loste

Except John Patye

and the same Roberte for that John Furse his granfater favored hym and for charytye kepte the powre fowle at his one charges durynge his lyfe.

THE PLATE that sholde remayne from here to here by John Furses wyll was three saltes of sylver persell gylte one goblett of sylver wythe a cover persell gylte too pownsede or flatte peses of sylver and one dosen and halfe of verye fere sylver spownes; of all this plate there was but onlye one salte of sylver that came to the possessyon of Robarte and that by chanse by forse of his father John Furses wyll for Robert Remonde by crafte and forse compelled the foresed Margerett by menes of award to delever hym not only all the foresed plate, but all other thynges what so ever geven to the same Robarte by his granfathers will excepte Stabeldonmore whiche durynge the foresed vij yeres the wrytynges there of was spoyled so for that Robarte was but a chylde at his granfathers dyenge daye and not of hym selfe abell to resyste the wronges he loste but all yt was never worthe hym but lytell for what so ever came ynto Remondes hondes all was loste.

What plate was geven to Robert

Remondes false practes

What ys becom of John Furses issue

fo. 25

WHAT John Furse his son and here was yt shall appere in an other plase.[73] Jerom Furse Edwarde Furse and Tomsen Furse all three dyed unmarryed but all were of fulle yage. This Jerome was a goodlye tall man and of grett strynthe, he was buryed at Sombryge. Edward beynge at scowle at Tavystoke by sherpyng of a sparre wythe his knyfe a litell hurted his knee the syne beynge ther hit coste hym his lyfe. Tomsen dyede w[th] syckenes.

Jerom Edward & Tomsen dyed w[t]oute issue

MARGERETT Furse his dofter was marryed to one John Erell of Aysheperton and John and Margerett had issue one dofter called Necoll Yerell. This John Erell was a good freeholder, he hadde nere xx[li] land of yerelye rente; he and his wyfe dyed ther chyld but younge, then John Furse her granfather was her garden he marryed her to one Willyam Norleye the son and here of Remonde Norleye of Idugegeleye, a man of proper levynge. This Willyam was marryed to Necoll and hadd issue too dofters; this Willm was a lerned man of grett credett and a fyne and

Margerett Erells issue

73. See below, pp. 52–3.

personabell a man as I have sene and he made a grette accownte of his wyfe and yt she but a lytell woman and rudelye brofte upe for before she came to xvj yeres she was kepte close for in Kynge Edwardes the VI dayes, there one Erell that came from the curte that hadde lettores to have marryed her, & by that menes she was marryed younge: a very gentell curtes wenche. This Willyam moste unfortunatelye and to the ruen of all his posteryte he beynge a moste excellente cunseler commynge in syrcute wythe the jugges at Salseburye fell sycke and there dyed. His wyfe before anye of her fryndes did understonde the

Norles harde delynge

same by the requeste of her fatherynlawe presently convayed all her londes to Willm Norles chylderen & for wante of shuche issue to the olde Norles heres, and so paste hit by fyne and to recompense this good torne the olde Norlye presently moste falselye conayed his one londes from Willm Norles heres. This Necoll hadde mony good tynneworke plate and other good thynges from her father & fryndes and all Norle hadde and all she loste, and after theye hadd there purpose small fryndeshyppe she hadd at anye of the Norles but wythe yn shorte spase she havynge no fryndeshyppe she by happe marryed one Escotte a very honeste man: he dewelled in Cornewall and had by her

The spoyle of all at laste goodes & londes

dyvers sones. Willyame Norles dofteres proper wemen and bothe marryed the one to Trevet the other to one Drewe and wytheyn shorte tyme all Ereles londes consumed.

Crysten

CRYSTEN Furse maryed the foresed Roberte Remonde and the were of grett welthe & never hadde issue. Crysten survyved and made one Hewe Hanford, which marryed Jenefa Chechester her cosen, hole executor.

Pasco

PASCO Furse was marryed to one John Marten of Holsewortheye. He was a man of grette welthe and had good levynges theye had issue onlye John wh[ch] nowe dewellethe at Holseworthye. Pasco dyed then her hussebonde marryed an other woman.

Johan

JOHAN Furse was marryed to one John Toychen w[ch] hadde a plowe londe and by her dayes he was of pretty welthe. He dewelled att Sente Gylses; they hadde issue Henrye and others. Johan dyed then he marryed agayne. He always after leved in grete myserye and a longe tyme for dett he was in pryson.

One burgage in Comemarten

COMEMARTEN ys a howse and a garden in Comemarten Towne, yt is holden in fre socage of the lorde of the burrowe. The heye Rente is xij^d a yere and sute to the curte. Note here that one Ellen Brekenocke was honer of this londe & hadde issue Willyam. Shee in her tyme made a lese whiche ys yt indurynge to one Bennett and to his wyfe to then to ther executores and assynes. This lese will ende the xij daye of Desember in an° d^i 1602. Note farder that nere xxx yeres paste one Willyam Hancocke bofte Bennets interres and he became tenante to John Furse & to Roberte Furse his son, and of Robarte Furse Hancocke resevede of hym xij^d for a releve. The rente reserved upon the lese ys but xviij^d the whiche we muste allowe all the hole ys our fyne, for sute be not ther entered that is xij^d for rente and v^d for our sute. There ys now dewellynge in the same howse on John Toker; yf the howse were in honde yt wilbe worthe xxvj^s viij^d a yere. Inquere what estate Toker hathe for Willyam Hancocke is dede and his son pretendethe to have the fee sympell by what tytell I do not understonde.

WALOND AND HOLSTROME[74] was Foxsecomes londes as afore sayede. Wallonde was a proper thynge, yt lyethe in Cockeberye and yt was holden by knyghteser[v]es, yt was worthe abowe all charges xlvj^s viij^d. This londes called Wallonde when they bofte the maner of Skyrrydon Roberte Furse solde hit to John Curter for a C^{li} and delevered hym all the wrytynges consernynge the same and he ys bownd in CC^{li} that Curter and his heres shall inyoye the same. HOLSTROM YS NOT YT SOLDE, yt is a tenemente yt ys devyded into dyveres severall closes as here after yt shall appere. Yt lyethe wythe yn the perryshe of Lewetruncharde, yt is holden of Antonye Quicke esquyre, lorde of the maner of Lewe, in free socage for the yerelye rente of one penye for all maner of rentes sutes servyses relefes and demondes. Yt is nowe in the

---

74. Walond, in Cookbury, and Holstrom, in Lewtrenchard. Walland agistment appears in the tithe award, 117 acres with no apparent building. Holstrom is now Holdstrong, and appears on the tithe award and is at SX487857. Lewtrenchard court rolls 30 June and 14 October 1593 refer to Sir Samuel Tucker and Robert Furse as tenants of 'Bemamen', a place or personal name not identified, amerced 3d. for default. Benjamin does not appear to be a local name. In October 1610 the heirs of Robert Furse were amerced, but the mystery name is not repeated (British Library Add. Ch. 9403, 9415).

tenure of Edwarde Furse; yt is worthe by the yere abowve all charges xxvij^s iij^d.

fo. 28   The pertycular names of all the tenements call Holstrom

[*blank*]

THE FORESED tynnemyll the one lyethe nere Lydeforde, yt was fyrste made by the foresed John Furse, yt is holden of the Quene in free socage for the rente of [*blank*]^d and sute to Lydford, yt is nowe in the tenure of Water Borrowe for vj^s viij^d rent.

[*gap*]

John Furse hadde the thyrde parte of one other myll called Cornedon Smythe but this fyftye yeres we hadde nether rente nor profytte.

fo. 29   ## The lyene or petygrewe of Foxsecombe

JOHN FOXSECOMBE otherwyse Truncharde by dewellynge at Foxsecombe[75] was callede Foxsecombe for here note I was credybell informed by my cosen John Chychester that there was one Willyam Truncharde lorde of Lewe Truncharde that hadde

Foxsecomes armes

dyveres sonnes and his armes were iij blewe barres in a whytt fylde, and to his youngeste son he did grante for his mentenans the foresed londes callede Foxsecombe Holstrom & serten other londes to hym and his heres for ever. Chechester sayethe that the here of the Trunchardes do nowe dewell in Dorsettshere and do geve the same armes this presente daye, and by this menes Chychester did geve the same armes and yf he maye geve them even soo wyll I and our cosen Toker. The armes remayne in dyvers wyndowes in the churche of Grettorryton. The foresed John Foxsecombe in the xxx yere of Kynge Edwarde the fyrste

Foxsecom Holstrom

[1301/2] had londes in Foxsecombe and Holstrom. He hade issue John; this John the younger was marryede to one Margerye the dofter and here of one Axseworthye and by that menes wee hadde the londes called Axseworthye and theye hadde issue Willyam.

John de la Walle

This Wyllyam marryed one Johan the dofter and here of John de La Walle and by that menes he fyrste hadde the foresede londes in Wallond Weke Ketehyll and a howse in Grete Torryton, and

---

75. Foxcombe in Lewtrenchard (SX483873); a John Foxcombe is recorded in 1330 (*PNDevon* I, pp. 187–8), and the place was farmed in 1939 (Kelly's Directory).

Willm and Johan had issue Willyam. This Willyam marryed one Alse and Willyam and Alse hadde issue John; this John marryed one Annes and John and Annes hadde issue John; this John the younger marryede one Johan and theye did dewell att Wyke and theye hadde issue Marye Luse and Ellezabethe. This laste John was a man of grett accownte he myche delyted huntynge and was a myghty stronge man he mayntanyed a good howse and was of good welthe and bothe he and his wyfe are buryed in Grettorryton churche. He made his dofter Marye his executor. Marye marryed John Furse as is aforesede, Luse marryed Steven Tuker and had issue onlye Nicolas: this Nycolas had issue but he and his issue solde all ther londes. Ellezabethe marryed one Hewe Chechester and by hym she hadde issue John and dyveres dofteres, then Hewe dyede and after his dyssesse she marryed one Edmond Pennefownde and by hym she hadde but one dofter whiche marryed one Mr Nycolas Pynes sonne and here of Estedowne. This Edmonde Pennefownde & Ellez^bt his wyfe all her systeres beynge ded abowte the xxx yere of Kynge Henry the VIII [1538/9] compelled the cooheres to devyde the londes, but where hit was by a wryte or order of Ser Richarde Pollarde Sargente Harres and Mr Humfrye Colles I am not serten, for that the wrytynges never came to my hondes, but true hyt ys that yt was devyded and so ever sethenes the same hathe so contynewed quyett. Furse hadde for his parte the foresede londes called Holstrom and Wallonde, Chechester hadde Weke and Axseworthye, Tuker hade Foxsecombe and Ketehyll, but here note Foxsecombe hade more londes in Skeyte Overmyll and Lydforde. I do not understonde that ever anye of these perseles were ever devyded but I am sure that Chychester hathe solde the same and all the reste of Foxsecomes londes, the londes called Foxsecombe lyethe wythe yn the parryse of Lewetrunchard, Axseworthye wythe yn the parryshe of Thrustelton, Ketehyll withyn the parryshe of Brodewode, Skette & Overmyll[76] in Lydforde parryshe. This partisyon was more for plesure than profytt but John Furse the younger and his heres be a good C^li the worse for that partysyon.

Farde understonde also this petygrew: Rafe de la Walle hadde issue Gylberte, this Gylberte had issue John, this John hadde issue Henrye Willyam and John, Henrye and Willyam were

Margin notes:
Foxsecomes cooheres
Marye Luse
Ellezabt

Pennefownde
Pyne

A wryte of partision

Furses parte
Chychesters parte
Tokeres parte

Rafe de la Wall

---

76. Skette in Lydford is not traced, but Skit was at some time the name of the upper part of the East Ockment river, and the vale known as Skit Bottom (Hemery, *High Dartmoor*, p. 871).

bothe of them made prystes and as I have redde parsones of Torryton. They did grante all ther londes to John their brother. This John marryed one Annes Bere by whom we sholde have hadde a howse in Torryton, and they hadde issue Henrye and Johan. Henrye dyed wythe owte issue then Johan was marryed to Willyam Foxsecombe as yt is above wryten. Note the Foxscombes hadde grette and costelye sutes in lawe with one Holstrom for the londes of Holstrom and after longe sute they did recover the same and ever sethenes quyett.

fo. 30
What lond John hadde

JOHN FURSE [*c.* 1506–72] the son and here of the foresede John Furse and Marye Marye [*sic*] his wyfe, after his father and motheres dyssesse by juste tytell was also then lawfullye sesede off all the foresede londes callede Furse, Westewaye, Henbere, Scorehyll, one howse in Certon towne, Harpeforde, Mowre, Chydyngebroke, the garden in Torryton, Bromeham, Westekynstere, Comemarten, Holstrom, Wallonde and the moyte of Erygge and of one hole tynnemyll and of the thyrde parte of

He marryed fyrste Johan Moreshed

one other tynnemyll called Cordon Smythe. This John marryed one Johan Moresehede the dofter and here of John Moreshede of Moreshede wythe yn the parryshe of Denepryer. This John

His fyrste dewellyng
Then to Come

fyrste did dewell at Weke in Grette Torryton where he prospered well but not longe after he was removed to his grett loste and then he did dewell at a plase called Come in Torryton; he hade not all but som parte and that he helde at justemente but yn the

And at laste in the towne

yende he was by polyse and fasehode ther lekewyse dysplased; then he was forsede to dewell in the towne and there contynewed all his lyfe. John Furse in the ryght of his wyfe hadde londes in dyvers plases what hyt ys yt shall appere here after. Thys John

His issue

and Johan were marryed iij yeres before theye hadde anye issue they hadde issue Roberte Furse John Furse Edwarde Furse Steven Furse Johan Furse and Margerye Furse. What become of them yt

Johan buryed

shall also appere here after. This Johan in the yere of our Lord God 1549 [1550] dyed in her fathers lyfe tyme she is buryed in the Chansell nexte before her father John Furse, she was dede juste iij wykes before hym. Her dethe was gretelye lamented of all men. She was a comelye woman welbelovyd plesante a wyse paynefull and carefull woman for her howseholde a grett decaye and loste to all her chelderen. She was marryed some xvij yeres

His seconde marrage

and dyed when she was xxxviij yeres of yage. Then not longe

after her dyssesse the foresed John did marrye wythe one Richard
Powles dofter called also Johan, a very younge thynge; her frynds
did myche mysuse hym the daye of marrage and his companye in
plase and dyner provyded he was feane to goo hom unmarryed
for that tyme the cose was theye never payde hym but xx marke
with her and theye wolde not be contente with vi^{li} xiii^s iiij^d junture
but wolde have all his londes in Certon but yn the yende theye
were marryed and trulye she usede hym well and all his chylderen
for theye were marryed more then xx yeres and hadde never any
chylde.

THIS JOHN was of good welthe and welbelovyde of all men. His
gretes delyte was in good howsekepyng verye gentell gevynge
credyt to all men whiche monye tymes did torne to his one grett
henderans. Yn his uthe he was verye stronge lustye and well tryed
for wraxselyn, lepynge, casten of the barre and also wythe his
suorde and buckeler, his exercyse was kepyng of curtes he wolde
wryte well he was myche trobeled wythe syckenes as the pyles
and yn his later dayes wythe the colycke splene and stronge gurye.
He cosede in hys lyfe tyme a cowe to be delyvered to his son and
here to the use of the powre and comonded hym to do the lyke to
hys heres, he also delevered the foresede olde nobell accordyg to
his fatheres requeste. He by his laste wyll gave all hys tynneworks
to his son Steven Furse and hys heres for ever. He made dyveres
other legasyes viz. to Steven by will & other wyse to my knolege
C markes besydes dyveres impellmentes and quycke stuffe to
Edward, dyveres bullockes plowe stuffe & howseholde stuffe to
Roberte all hys apparell harnes a sylver salte serten quyckestuffe
& to all the reste of his chylden som thing. He made his wyfe
executor. He leved 66 yeres he died the xxiiij daye of Auguste in
the yere of our lorde god 1572; his wyfe was CC^{li} the better for
hym and by his dethe she durynge her widdood hadde by custom
monye thynge & vj^{li} xiij^s iiij^d for her junture.

THYS JOHN Furse did paye v^{li} to one Richarde Davye of Tottenes
for one annueltye of iiij^s to hym & his heres to be payde owte of
serten close of londes called Hachemore parke in Grett Torryton;
he never hadde the rente payed nor no convayenes for the same
so he was grettelye deseved. This John Furse in his olde yage
was myghtelye oppressed and that wrongefullye by dyverse busy
persones in lawe. He toke monye grett and dongerous jurnes

His welthe and
most delyte

His most
exersyse

The cowe &
olde nobell

His laste wylle

fo. 31

Hachemore
Parke

Myche
oppressed by
lawe

in kepynge of his curtes he alonge tyme leved a solytarye lyfe
and did refuse companye for that he was myche subyecte to the
stowle; he was of goodlye stature but not leke his father. He
wolde goo verye nete and trym yn his apparell and som tymes for
his recreasyon he wolde playe at tabeles, fynallye he was not to

His liberalite
to the powre

be blamed for anye yevell, he delyted myche the churche, he was
a fryndelye man and lyberall to the powre he did comonly upon
all solen daye feaste the powre and in ther companye he wolde be

His buryall

most meryeste, he lyethe buryed in his one fatheres grave in the
chansell in Grett Torryton. His wyfe after his dessesse marryed
one John Seller, he before the makynge of this bowcke was too

Hys wyves
good happe
in her second
marrage

tymes mere of Torryton. This Seller and his wyfe at all tymes
fryndye used all her fyrste husbondes chylderen and fryndes. So
all the goodes and levynge bestowed on them was welbestowyed.
And more I can not saye of John Furse and Johan his fyrste
wyfe but god sende them a joyefull daye in ther resurrecsyon and
lyfe everlastynge. He hathe now upon hym a blewestone where
yn hys father and hys one name and the tyme of ther severall
buryalles ys trulye wryten.

This John Furse yn hys lyfe tyme made monye leses, that ys to

What leses he
made

saye he sett his parte of Mowre to dyveres persones so the hole
rente of Mowre was xj^{li} xvj^s viij^d. He made a lese of Kynstere to
John Tossell for vij^{li} rente, he made a lese off his parte of Erygge
to John Furse his cosen for x^s rente, he granted Henbere to John
Westyngeton for xvij^s vij^d rente, he granted Furse to Willyam
Hockewaye for xv^s rente, he granted Herpeforde to Nycolas
Ballaman for xij^s rente, he granted Westewaye to Crystopher
Wode for xiij^s iiij^d rente, he granted Chydyngebroke to Mathewe
Gollocke for xij^s rente, he granted the towne howse in Certon
to Alse Brodemede for xxvj^s viij^d rente, he granted Holstrom
to Thomas Gregorye for xxvj^s viij^d rente, he made a lese of
Bromeham to John Furse his son for xxxiij^s iiij^d rent.

fo. 32

What is becom of the foresede John Furses chylderen

What Robert Furse his sonne ys yt shall appere in an other plase.

John Furse

John Furse was marryed to one Cateren Lake, he dewelled at
Bromeham. He was a verye good husebonde, he was cunstabell
of the parysshe, he was of good welthe and had issue dyveres

sones and dofters videliset John, George & Hugh & Cateren & Cristen.

EDWARD Furse marryed on Margerye Cowcke alias Best, he dewelled at Holstrom, he proved not the beste husebonde, he leved but bare and did myche decaye his tenemente. He hade issue John Furse and too dofters, vid[t] Johan & Blanc[h]e.

Edward Furse

JOHAN FURSE was fyrste marryed to one John Sowthewode of Newneham in Chymley paryshe to one that had a verye good berten, but he was a badde fellowe and consumed all. That marrage was costelye to my father, yt coste hym C marke more then his promyse and all wayes in trobell durynge hys lyfe and I thynke yt was the shortenynge of his lyfe. This John Sowthewode and Johan had issue Roger and Hewe, then he dyed, then she marryed one Richard Norramore of Sowthe Tawton whiche hade pretye londes, but he beynge so often surtye for his brother in the ende consumed all hys goodes and she dyed very pore, but Richard and Johan had issue Roger.

Johan Furse

Too tymes badely marryed

MARGERYE Furse from a chylde was with her awnte Remonde and by her menes moste unhappylye marryed to one John Chychester a younger sone of Ames Chychester of Arlyngeton. This Chychester hade juste no goodes nor levynge but that Remonde provyded for hym, he was geven all to the spoyell and lose lyfe, he made small accownte of his wyfe or of anye of her fryndes he dyed a begger, whiche yf he had survyved Crysten Remonde, the berten of Merche was hys for the terme of his lyfe, he was a proper wyse man. This John and Margery hadde issue iiij dofters viz Jenefa Crysten and Mary and dyveres others that dyed infantes. This Jenyfe had serten londes convayed to her from Roberte Remond and yn the yed hadde all Remondes goodes, she was marryed to one Hewe Hanforde of Deniton.

Here unlucke marrage

STEVEN FURSE was trened upe in lernynge, he was pryntes to a marchante and had his frenche and castell tonge perfytt, for he was nere too yeres in Rone & so myche in Luysheborne. He was skylefull in his trade but made monye bade vyages to his grett loste and not for wante of skyle or care but by yell fortune. He hadde grett fryndeshyppe of Mr Seller & his wyfe and of Crysten Remonde. He was nere xlv yere olde when this was wryten he was not then marryede.

Steven Furse

[MORESHEAD FAMILY AND THEIR PROPERTIES]

fo. 33   **A Trewe Dyscorse of the heres of Moreshedde**

Semston:
Adam le Bonde

Moreshedde
bofte and
Rowdon by
Walken le
Bonde

Then Marten
he bofte
Nuston

Rafe le Bonde

Made us free
of sute &c.

ADOM le Bonde was sesede of londes yn Sempeston[77] and he hade issue Walken le Bonde. This Walken lebonde he fyrste bofte the fee sympell of Moreshede and Rowdon of one Willyam le Hurborneforde not longe before the dates of dedes by too severall dedes Walken le Bonde had issue Marten le Bonde, Marten after his father was sesede of all the foresede londes in Sempeston Mowreshede and Rowdon.[78] This Marten fyrste bofte the fee sympell of londes in Nuston[79] of the grant of one Ser John Shybleston knyght. This Marten did homage to Richard prier of Plymton for the londes in Moreshede. This Marten le Bonde hade issue Rafe le Bonde, this Rafe after his father was sesede lekewyse of all the foresede londes in Sempeston Moreshede Rowdon & Nuston. Thes Rafe made us free from all sute and serves by dede for all our londes in Sempeston and Rowdon to the lordes of Northehurborneford by the payemente onlye of viij^d yerely at Micaellmas for all maner of rentes sutes and servyses of the grante of on Bennett then lorde of the maner of Northehurborneforde in the xj yere of Kynge Edward the

77. Sempeston in Dean Prior (SX712692), manor of Northharborneford, is now Zempson (*PNDevon* I, p. 299). The farmhouse is Grade II listed, but as being seventeenth century or earlier, remodelled and extended in the eighteenth and nineteenth centuries. Furse describes his land there (p. 86) as a mere close, with the old walls of a tenement burnt down.
78. Rowdon occurs in the tithe award as part of the 'Moor's Head Estate', as two arable fields, 620 Middle Rowdon, and 621 Borrough Rowdon. They are very near and a little to the north of the homestead of Moreshead, SX713634.
79. Nuston, now Nurston, in Dean Prior (*PNDevon* I, p. 299, SX719640).

seconde [1317/8] and yn the xiij yere of the same Kynge Edward [1319/20] he did procure a relese of londes in Nuston of one Roger Moyeles. This Rafe had issue as I suppose one Willyam whiche was called Willyam de Moreshed for as I have sayed before the custom and use was of olde tymes to call men after the names of ther mansyon howses but spessially thos that then were freholders for I have redde that wytheyn the paryshe of Denepryer there was Steven of Smallacombe, Sempeston of Sempston, Tordene of Tordene, Nuston of Nuston and so of dyvers others. Agayne I do rede that before and longe after Willyam the name of the Bondes did in dyvers plases dewell in Denepryer but howe so ever yt was ever sethenes the laste yere of Kynge Edward the seconde [1326/7] theye and all ther sequele have bynne knowen by the name of Moreshed and the howse of Moreshed was ther contynuall dewellynge as longe as anye of the Moreshedes remayned. Yf this be not trewe then no dowte Rafe hadde no issue but then this Willyam maye be his syster or dofter son yf he had anye dofter for after this Willyam the Bondes loste all the foresede premysses. THYS WYLLYAM de Moresehede marryed one Amye of Nuston, this Amye was also sesede of londes in Nuston as hytt dothe appere by dyvers wrytynges, but here note that I have redde in an olde bocke of survaye of the pryor of Plymtones concernyngge the maner of Denepryer that Willyam Moresehede solde his wyves londes to one Henry Stape, and this Henrye Stape had issue one dofter whiche marryed one Sterte and ever sethenes Sterte and his heres have inyoyed the same. This Willyam and Amye hadde issue Rafe Moreshede, this Rafe did homage in the iiij yere of Edward the thyrde [1330/1] to John Pryer of Plymton for londes in Moreshede and Nuston. This Rafe hadde issue Symon Moresehed this was maryed and hadde issue Symon Moresehed. This younger Symon was marryed to one Ellezabethe the dofter and here of Richard off Sympeston and by that menes he was sesed of other londes in Semston as hit apperethe by dyvers grantes from one Bryscome and otheres in the ix yere of Henry the VI [1430/1] and from one Knyghte and otheres in the viij yere of Ric the second [1384/5]. This Symon was also sesed of londes yn Overdene by what tytell I am unserten. He was also sesed of londes called Bulston in Sowthebrynte but by what tytell where by purchase or dissente I do not underston, but I did lerne by an

Willm de Moreshed

Amye de Nuston

Stertes tytell

Rafe Moresed
Symon de Moresehed

Symone de Moreshede
Ric de Sympston
had londes in Semston

Penyton

olde bocke of survaye of the maner of Sowthebrynte that Symon Moresehed was sesede of londes in Bulstone and that the Abbett of Buckefaste and Moresed ded excambe Bulstone for Penyton. This Symon made a lese of all Richar of Sympestones londes to the lorde of Hurborneford for serten yeres and by an other dede he did acknolege the resevynge of xviij yeres rente, so in xviij yeres ther was no rente payd and theye beynge myghtye men when Moresed demonded rente they wolde paye none and the rente but vj^d a yere the valye so small and Moresed not abell to resyste them, so by sufferans we have loste the londes and by no other menes to my knowlege. Symon in the viij yere of Henry the VI [1429/30] made a lese of Peneton to one John at Wode and in the iij yere of the same Henry [1424/5] he did his homage to Nicolas pryor of Plymton. This Symon and Ellezabethe hadde issue Richarde Moresede Thomas Moresede and iij dofteres. THYS RYCHARDE Moresehede after his fathers dyssesse was also sesede of all the foresed londes in Moreshed Sempeston Rowdon Nuston Overdene and Penyton. He also marryed one Elyzabethe the dofter and here of one Wether and by that menes he was also sesede of one other tenemente yn Moresehedde this Richard in the x yere of Henry the VI did homage [1431/2] to Nicol pryor of Plymton. This Richard was not the beste husebond for hym selfe nor yt for his sequele but a man geven holye to the spoyell for he leved powrelye and consumede his levynge chyldyslye for he was prowde in mynde and unfaythefull of his promyse as hit shall appere by his doynges. In his later dayes he was blynde, he leved untyll he was lxx yeres, he dyede at Moresehed and ys buryed at Denepryer. This Richarde and Ellezabethe hadde issue John Moreshede Willyam Moreshed and serten dofters. This Willyam was an unresonabell wylfull fellowe for by happe ther was a balyefe that upon som occasyon did take a dosen of clothe for a dystres, this Willyam at Rowdon yate mette the balyefe and ther presentely did murder hym; the optanynge of a pardon coste myche monye so by thes menes Richard was in grette dette and upon accyones of dett he yn the yende was uttelawyed. To salve this sore Richard did conclud that his sonne John sholde marrye one Margerye Downynge one Downyng dofter of Estewyke in Sowthetawton perryshe, and that she sholde have for her junture Wetheres londes and that John Moresehed sholde then presentelye have a perfyt assurans to hym and his heres of all Richard Moresedes londes, and yn consederasyon here of John

The loste of Semston

fo. 34

Ric Moreshed marryed Wethers here

So more londes in Moreshead

His issue

John Moreshedes marrage

sholde paye all Richarde Moresedes dettes and fynde hym and
his wyfe suffyciante mete drynke and loggynge and to paye hym
yerelye to his mentenans iij^{li} vj^s viij^d, so yn dede this marrage was
solempysed and the assurans of the londes by good convayenes
under the honde and sele of the same Richarde. John payed all
his fathers dettes and performed his promyse in all thynges and
yn truthe was in actuall possessyon of all Richarde Moresedes
londes and there of made dyveres leses and dyede there of sesede
and upon his dethe his son was in warde in the lyfe tyme of
Richarde. This John and Margerye hade issue John Moresehed
John Willyam and Thomas and John and som iij dofters. This
John the son of Richard dyede, his father fenynge hym selfe not
well, the powre wyddowe thynken no gyle folloed the dedde
corse to his grave then whyles the companye was to the burynge
this Richard and his wycked sonne Willyam bruke all the cofers
and toke awaye all the wrytynges and then presentely concluded
wythe the pryor for the warde of the londes but not for the bodye
of the here. He kepte the wyddo owte of the possessyon and was
a menes of grette trobell and expenses to her before she by order
of lawe myghte recover junter or dower. The powre wyddowe
and her chylderen beynge powre and yn grett dystresse god
provyded for them all for in the yende all the chylderen came
to grett welthe and credyt but spessially the sonnes for by good
happe this Margerye hadde a wyddo to her syster dewellynge yn
Trowleye a verye ryche woman she was one Wonstons wyfe and
had no chyde, she hade the iij younges sones they all had londes
and grett welthe and were men of grete credet and so ther issue
dothe remayne to this daye.

This Richarde by the helpe of his lawles sone became more like
a madde man then a man of reson agaynste all ryghte and good
consyenes entered yn to all his sonne John Moreshedes londes; to
some he made leses to otheres he did lye londes in morgage and
to som he paste the fee sympell. He sette the Wylleparke to one
Wylseforde, Semston to Trynke, Nuston to Crobere, Peneton
to Smythe and Leye, he after grantede our londes yn Overdene
to the churche of Denepryer to have the too formest setes in
the Churche. At that tyme one dewellynge at Tordene taken the
mater ingrefe presentelye procured the same to be forfyted for
that yt was fownd morte mayne and by this menes he bofte the
londes so here Moresed and the church bothe lese the londes

To Dunnynges dofter

Ther issue

The falsehodes of Ric'

Yt god provided for them

Ric' false & ungodly practes

fo. 35

then he leaye Peneton to morgag when he hadde nothynge yn the

Moresede the Leyeparke solde

londes and by that menes we loste the one halfe he also alynatede one close of londes parsel of Rowdon and a tokenmyll called the leeyparke and all Wetheres londes yn Moresede to Willyam Moreshed his son and to hys heres for ever, but some did reporte that he did sele that wrytynge after he was dede. He solde also the Comeparke but by good happe he dyed before the wrytynge was seled and yf ther were ever anye alynasyon made of the londes at Hambrygge I do thynke yt was his doynge. He dyvers

John the son & here of John marryed

tymes kepte curte at Moresehede and bownde all his tenantes there to do ther sute to his curte but when John Morsede the sonne and here of John and Margerye came to his full yage the pryor marryed hym to one Ellenor his buttelers dofter a verye proper woman and a wyse. Theye were marryed in Richarde Moresedes lyfetyme so when he sholde kepe howse he was powre younge and wythe owte fryndes the howses hagges and alle thynges owte of order and in grett decaye. He was not abell to goo to lawe nor yt to dele wth his unruly unkell, but by menes

The order duringe Ric' lyfe

of good nyghtebores and fryndes an order was taken for the olde man durynge his lyfe so John hadde all the londes excepte the londes that Willyam hadde and so hit contynewed durynge Richardes lyfe whiche was xx^ti yeres to longe that he leved yf hit hadde plesed god but god for geve hym. This Richard dyed in

Downynge did geve this

Kynge Edward the IIII tyme. Note that Downnynge of Estewyke did geve sexse sylver spownes wth ockekernes one brasen panne and one lytell andyron to the Moresedes to remayne from here to here, thoffe the valye not grett yt the man ys to be remembered for his good wyll, surelye I reserved all thos thynges but the thynges yt selfe ys so woren that hitt ys clene spente but I hope

John issue

to leve the same in valye. The foresede John and Ellenor hadde issue John Roberte and fyve other chelderen he did leve well and was a good hussebonde yndede he bulded the barne he hagged and planted and was at grett charges. This John did homage to Roberte pryor of Plymton yn the xvij of Ed' the IIIIth [1477/8] and in the same yere he granted dyvers leses whiche I do omytt. This John in his beste tyme in the plage dyed and v of chyldenen.[80]

---

80. Plague was prevalent in Exeter in 1503–4, 1537, 1546–7, 1557–8, 1563–5, 1570, 1586–7 and 1590–1 (Slack, *Impact of Plague*; Shrewsbury, *History of Bubonic Plague*). Dean Prior parish register records, 28 July 1570, 'Here began ye plague', and 6 December 1590, 'ye plague end here'. This does not imply 20 years continuous plague, indeed Slack thinks the 1590 outbreak may have begun with the burial of Richard Budmere of Exeter, found dead in the way (Slack, p. 86).

His wyfe was after iiij tymes well marryed excepte her laste hussebond. She was a myghtye woman of welthe but her laste husebond beynge a lustye servynge man sone consumed hyt so in the yende she was powre and fayne to tryste to a dofter that she hadde, but presently after the foresede John Moresedes dethe his son John was a warde to the pryour but beynge nere of full yage he also dyed, this his brother Roberte was in warde and he also dyed unmarryed. Then all ther landes by a juste tytell dissended to John Moresede ther unkell beynge the seconde sonne of the foresede John Moresed and Margerye his wyfe.

Too of there chylderen in warde

THYS John Moresede farre exyded all his proyenytors yn welthe wysedom and credytt but when his father was dede then he was forsed to tryste to hymselfe for he never made reconyng to be honer of Moresehede but bound hymselfe pryntes to a carpynter which occupasyon he usede all his tyme and he kepte dyvers men and pryntyses to hys grette gayne; his exercyse was moste upon mylles and frames for belles. This John was taken for a sodyer and yn the fylde wonderfullye wonded stripped and lefte for dede he reperynge for soker happened amonge the sodyers of his enymy yt he fownde mersye for one of the s[a]me sodyers for charytye beynge mere strongeres gave hym his sodyers cote and monye in his purse and under the color of this cote and the helpe of good peopell he came agayne ynto his cunterye but after he came home he was complayned that he then dowted here to remayne but then he wente to Blacke Awton where he dewelled a longe tyme then by happe he marryed on Necoll Churchett and when they were marryed theye were forsede to make ther weddynge apparell ther bedde clothynge but wytheyn a lytell tyme by menes he hade men and pryntes all this was reformed and he optayned a good bargayn called Cottaberye and after one other bargayne called Tolsone.[81] He was in grete credyt amonge the marchantes of Dartemowthe and gave som venter wythe them. Yt happed that the churche of Blackeawton was robbed

John Moresede of Blackeawton
His welthe & credytt
His exercyse

fo. 36
A worke of grette mersy

his marreg

81. Cotterbury and Tolsone, in Blackawton. Cotterbury, now Lower Cotterbury (SX816509), is recorded from the fourteenth century. John Moreshead, Furse's grandfather, died in 1525 and so probably acquired it in the late fifteenth century. 'Tolsone' is Oldstone (SX818517). Polwhele describes these as two of the four gentlemen's seats in the parish. Cotterbury remained in the Pinhay family to the later eighteenth century. It is the subject of an archaeological survey by Stewart Brown (Brown 2007). Oldstone, the mansion of the Cholwich family, burnt down in 1893 and is now a neglected ruin (Pevsner, p. 186). It is, nevertheless, Grade II listed.

Falselye
trobeled

and nor dore nor wyndo broke, John Moresede when he came to the churche sayed to the perysheners howe maye our churche be robbed wythe owte the consente of our Clerke for here ys no dore wyndo nor locke broken; this Clerke had myghtye fellowes to his kyndered and as Naab[82] was accused so was Moresede and comytted to the gale but god gave hym favor of his keper that he was never in pryson but over nyghte but he wente to worke ever daye and hadde hys wages iiij[d] for everye day, thus he contynuede a prysoner too yeres and by no menes myght com to his awnsere. Then he made a supplycacion to Kynge Henrye the VII and by that menes a comyssyon was dyrected to the Errell of Devon so when he came to his awnser there was no mater obyected agaynste hym and by that menes he was delyvored; I fownd and have the same supplycacion amonge the Erelles wrytynge when I sarched the evydens for Skyrrydon.[83]

One
tenement in
Dartemowth

More he did
bye

A good lode

His charge in
buldynge

THYS JOHN Moresede fyrste bofte the fee sympell in the xvj yere of Kynge Henry the VII [1500/1] of one tenemente in Dartemowthe[84] of one Thom' Powre and yn the xix of the same Henrye [1503/4] he bofte serten olde walles of one Hamydes and others and made there of too tenementes. Then after the dethe of the foresede Robarte Moresehede his brothers son he did remove from Blackeawton and dewelled at Moresehede, he trulye reported to on of his frynds that his plowe and one lode that he dide brynge yn to Moresehede was then worte CC[li], he brofte dyveres other lodes ther besydes bestes cattell corne and shepe and when he came to the londes yt was in grett decaye by menes of the wardeshypp, and the londes som in one manes hondes and som yn an other, and weyenge also his grett charge in the lawe I do thynge he sholde as good chepe have bofte so myche londes in them dayes as he possessede, for he bulded the bakehowse and kychen newe and the stabell. He also newe bulded the halle shyppen and all the howses excepte the barne, he was at grett charges in plantynge and makynge of the hagges and gardenes. He was a longe tyme in sute wythe Margery Certon and Lewes

---

82. 'As Naab was accused'. The only sense to make of this is Naboth, in I Kings 21, already cited by Furse in his introductory exhortations, falsely accused of blasphemy and stoned to death by the trickery of Jezebel, wife of Ahab, who coveted Naboth's vineyard.

83. Note that Furse had access to the Earl of Devon's documents, presumably at Powderham, when he was writing up evidence for Skyrrydon.

84. Tenement in Dartmouth; cannot be traced.

Burye for Penyton the mater came to a nisyepryus & the jurye sweren and fullye agreed to fynde with Moreshede but polyse was wrofte to delaye the gevynge of the verdett, the same Moreshede was softe from howse and brof[t]e before the Erell of Devon and the lorde Broke and by them compelled to compermyt the mater to the too Judeges, and by ther award Moreshede loste halfe the londes of Penyton as hyt dothe manyfestelye appere by serten convaynes made from Certon & Berye to Rowe and others and from them to Moresed. BUT HERE mark this, Berre longe after was for treson and rebellyon condemned & executed[85] and as wente to his execusyon he callede to one Mr Willyam Gybbes whiche hadde the gyfte of all Beryes londes he did desyre hym to restore to Moresedes heres the foresed londes in Penyton for we have donne them grett wronge and I thynke God in the revange thereof hathe layed this plage justely upon me, but Gybbes helde faste the londes from Moresehede, he solde the londes to Ser Wyllyam Peter. This John Morehede was longe yn lawe wythe his cosen Nycoll[86] Moreshede for the leye parke & the londes in Moresede and hyt came to commyssyon but never sertyfyed; the mater was compermytted & the partes bownde by oblygasyon to abyde the awarde, but before anye awarde made one of the wardesmen dyed, so all the charge loste, and he beynge olde and werye of the lawe and abell to travell did lett hit remayne. Durynge the sute our potte water was torned a waye so Moreshed was forsed when he did brewe to youke his oxen and in vesell to brynge his water from Hambrygge for in the mede he myghte not come, then to revange this John Moreshede did stoppe ther water curse to ther tokenmyll in the leyeparke and was yn the x yere of Henr' the VIII [1518/9] that where as our potte water curse was over the leey parke this John by arte of tynners recovered a newe curse and brofte hit to Meddes yate wher hyt dothe nowe ronne and so into Rowdon & from thens home. Then Nycolas Moresed wyfe one Jenett she wolde com for water but this John wolde breke her pottes so after longe stryfe an order was ag[r]eed that John and his heres sholde frelye have water in ther mede

In lawe for Penyton

The rewarde of wronge

fo. 37

In lawe for Moresede

Owr potte water and mylle streme

A newe curse

The order taken for the water

---

85. John Bury was attainted and executed for treason in the 1549 rebellion, and the inquisition on him shows that he had land in Peneton, and refers to John and Margery Kyrton, and Sir William Peter's lordship. Either Furse has confused him with Lewis, or he was Lewis's heir and Furse has failed to make the distinction (WSL IPM transcripts).

86. Robert Furse uses Nycoll as an abbreviation for Nicholas, but Necoll for the female version of the name.

and theye frelye to take water in our curte, but here note theye did alwayes com to the redynge of our lettes and by thys menes ther myll was decayed.

THYS John and Necoll hadde issue John Moreshed and Margerye. This John leved untyll he was lxxx yeres he was geven myche to prayer fastynge and gevynge of almeses he was myche blynded by the freeres ~~of Sente Nycolas at Exon~~ at Exeter he no dowte gave them grette gyftes non of his fryndes did knowe what but when he was then dedde in dede the freers themselves dyd reporte that he was the beste and moste lyberall gever that cam ther in moye yeres. He was a man ernes in his talke a very wyse sadde and grave man as ever was of his kyndered, a man of no grett stature but verye stronge and well growen. His dofter hadde alle his bargaynes and that full stuffed in his lyfe tyme, she marryed one John Pynnhaye and hadde som xij chylderen men and wemen he gave to every of them xxˢ by his wyll and to som more. His wyfe beynge a very grose woman he did ordayne by his will that she sholde have her mentenanse at Moresehed and a horse and the profyt of serten shepe and som rente all at hys sonnes charges he gave by word the howse in Dartemowthe that he bofte of Powre to Willyam Pynhay after his son John Moreseds dyssesse. He made his sonne John his fulle and sole executor he dyed the xviij daye of Apryll in xvj yere of Henr' the VIII [1525] and lyethe buryed by the fore sege havynge a blewe stone upon hym. This you se he paste grett dongeres and sustayned grett wronge and trobell and begane powre and in the yende came to grette welthe and credett and indede was a good husebond for all his sequele and for all his lostes he never demynyshed hys levynge but incressed the same god be therefore prased and after hym hys wyfe contented herselfe with the porsyon appoynted unto her she leved a wyddo nere xx yeres but that she had wente all to her dofter when she was dede, she was also buryed in Dene churche agaynste the fonte & at my charges she hathe a blewe stone upon her grave and more I can not saye of this John Moreshed and Necoll his wyfe but god geve them a joyefull daye in the resurreccyon and lyfe ever lastynge.

fo. 38

THEN AFTER the dyssesse of the foresede John Moresehed all the foresede messuages londes and tenementes in Moresehed Sempston Rowdon Nuston Peneton and the iij tenementes in Dertemowthe by juste tytell came to the foresede John Moreshede the son and His marrag here of John Moresed and Necol hys wyfe. This John did marrye on Necoll Sperke the dofter of one John Sperke of Blackeawton His issue and John and Necoll hadde issue John Moreshed. This John in hys yuthe was lustye and geven to all plesure as to hunte dyse cards and all other pastyme but spessyallye to shottynge and tennes, he was so myche geven to lybertye that his father made myche the lesse accownte of hym and hadde bynne myche to his henderans yf his wyfe hadde not bynne for her paynefullnes grett labur and wyse behavor did monye tyme pasyfye the olde manes anger, but here remember the comon saynge that the catte dothe not growne before he hathe the mowse, so surelye the olde man was deseved in his son for after his fathers dyssesse he became a verye wyse man sober sadde and grave myche more extemed then his father or anye of his proyenyters, he was xx yeres cunstabell of the hundred of Stanbur'[87] he was retorned yn monye juryes he allwayes mentayned a good howse a good Followe this plowe good geldynges good tyllage good rerynge and was a good hussebonde indede he wolde never be withowte iij copell of good hownds he wolde surelye kepe companye with the beste sorte. He myche mended the howses the hagges and orchardes and made his londes better som wythe marell and som wythe the see sonde. The gentyllemen grettely estemed hym, he served his prynse in the warres he was a verye fortunate man to bye and sell cattell or other bestes, he did use to fede cattell ande for the same he helde alwaye justemente grownd, he aggemented mych his welthe and impellementes of hys howse, he myche inlarged his howse orchardes and meddowes by clensynge of them of allers & shuche leke. He fyrste bofte the fee sympell of one tenemente in Nuston of one Thomas Bastarde yn the xix yer of Henrye His purchas the VIII [1527/8]. He was a man of good strente of som greter stature then his father well growen well lymed well faced but yn his yage he wente monye yeres very lame. This John to our grett quyettenes made an excambe wythe one Sterte for londes yn Nuston, viz Sterte hadde one persell of our londes called the Foreberye and on meddowe called Puntersedowne mede and lybertye to yoke and unyoke ther oxen agaynste John Moreshes hagge and Moresede was to have for hys porsyon a corner of Stertes londes lyenge in weste parte of Moresede Close to make The excamb by Sterte & Moreshed Moresedes Close square and all the meddowe lyenge agaynste

87. See p. 75, note 93.

Moresedes Close and a water curse from Stertes londe to Watelete the same [*blot*]ede and a fowte pathe to go over Stertes lytell close adyunynge to Rocheford at all tymes but when the same lytell close ys in tyllage. This ever sethenes this order on bothe partes hathe bynne quyettelye performed. This was don in the presenes of Willm Hele John Hele Hewe Hele & Richard Pernyll in the xxviij yere of Kynge Henr' the VIII [1536/7] and before the wrytynge was made Sterte was dede. John Morsh^d did homage to John pryer of Plymton in the xvj yere of Henry

His leses

the VIII [1524/5]; he made dyveres leses of his londes Penyton to Florens Alman the reve thereof to Roberte Pynhaye, he granted Nuston that he bofte to Ellezat Tolchard, and one tenemente in Dartemowthe to John Gagllaway, an other to Willm Robarte for 90 yeres, and the thyrd tenemente he did delever to Phillyppe Pynnhaye brother of Willyam Pynhaye and all the wrytyngs.

His testament
His dethe

This John leved untyll he was lxviij yeres he gave legasyes to all his dofteres chyldren and to dyvers otheres and he beynge the laste of that name dyed the xxvij daye of Marche in the yere of our lord god 1557 and ys buryed dyrecketely agaynste his father havynge a fere blew stone upon hym. This John in the commosyon by procuremente his goods was geven wrongefullye but yt hit coste hym xxvj^{li} xiij^s iij^d. This you see John did increse his londes and by the marrynge of his dofter myche the credet of his howse & sequele.

fo. 39

He made his wyfe Necoll and his cosen Roberte Furse his hole executores. This Necolle leved a wyddowe som xiij yeres after her husbondes decesse and the fyrste iiij yeres she and her cosen Roberte Furse. Then when Roberte was marryed she gave over all thynges unto hym som small thynges she dyd excepte and Roberte was to fynde her and to mentayn her a horse and paye unto her iiij^{li} rente yerely durynge her lyfe whiche in all thynges was faythefullye performed.

What Necoll
Moreshed was

THIS NECOLL was a good prosperus fortunate and a most happye graundemother for Robert Furse for by her menes he was in favor wythe hys granfather and yn her yothe she was a grett laborer and surelye her father was clerelye bente agaynste her hussebond, som by menes of his one destretes and som by the intysemente of Pynnehaye whiche was a cravynge companye and a costely for Moresed & his heres. The marrage of Margerye to Pynnehaye stowde faather mother and brother fyrste and laste CC^{li} for he hadde too bargaynes full stuffed he was to pay serten rente he never payd penye, what he hadde in secrett no man knowethe but all that the olde Necoll hadde the surelye hadde; the hadde one howse frely in Dartemowth and Peneton for a powre som but the foresede Necoll by her wysedom curtysye and gentyll and fryndelye behavor pasyfyed the olde man, and yn the yende he usede his son well for her sake for so he wolde often tell her that the good that he dyd to his son was for her sake, and AGAYNE immedyatelye after my mother John Moresedes dofter was dedde the Pynnehayes in grette favor and for that his dofters chylderen were all but younge and he hymselfe lame and olde determyned and I suppose partely granted to ylde upe all his stocke to one Phill Pynnehay and to make unto hym a lese of Moreshed and to be at his fyndynge, but when Necoll hard of this she was the cose that this practyse toke non effecte, and for thos coses in secret she was never belovyd of the Pynhayes agayne. Longe after the dethe of John Moresehed her father her good happe was to fynde lxxx angeles xxvij olde ryeles and vij olde nobeles and serten other olde golde but all she delevered to her husebond so by her menes in the yende Moresede goodes and londes came almoste holye to Robarte Furse. This Necoll hade dyveres brother of verye good welthe: Fynsen Sperke deweled at Blackeawton and he hadd many sones and dofters rychely marryed, Tasye Sperke a very ryche man, he hadde too sonnes Willm & John bothe of grett welthe the one dewelled in Blacke Awton the other viz John in Brente. Ther was Richard Sperke he dewellede at Curneworthye, one other brother that dewelled at Harteleye and one other brother wch was father to Steven Sperke and Thomas Sperke of Fuege. This Necoll was a good and godlye mynded woman she hadde grete delyte to the churche and to faste and praye everye Frydaye in the yere she of devosyon did faste and lekewyse she dyd yerely faste the fortye daye in Lente. After she was lxxxx yeres olde she was a verye good alme woman and lyberall to the powre she was curtes and fryndely to all peopell and beloved of all men and yn her yuthe she was a very bewtyfull woman desente in her apparrell and a perfytt good hussewyfe she levyd untyll she was nere C yeres of yage and yeven at her laste tyme a lustye woman for she did go

She was always happy to do us good

Her good qualytes

commonlye to the churche. She made Roberte Furse her executor
and gave dyveres legasyes but to every of Robertes dofters she
gave one olde ryell she dyed the xiiij daye of June in the yere of
our lorde god 1573 and she is buryed in Dene churche in her
father John Moresedes grave havynge a blew stone upon her and
more I can not saye of my granfather John Moresed and Necoll
his wyfe but god sende them a yoyefull daye in ther resurrecsyon
and lyfe everlastynge in the kyngedom of heven Amen & c.

fo. 40   **The perfytt petegrewe of Willyam Moresehed**

Rychard Moresehed as yt is aforesed hade issue John and
Willyam. Willyam Moreshed hadde issue Nycolas Moreshed,
Nycolas hadde issue Robarte and Johan. Robart hade issue
Crysten. Robarte dyed and one Willyam Synge his fatherynlawe
hadde the warde of Crysten but yn the xxx yere of Kynge Henr'
the VIII [1538/9] Crysten dyed wythe owte issue, then the londes

Annes Andros   did dyssende to the foresed Johan Moresede. This Johan marryed
petigrew   one Roger Harres, Roger and Johan made a lese of the londes to
Johan Berde and others. Roger and Johan had issue Willyam and
Phyllyppe. Willyam was marryed and had issue Annes, Willyam
dyed in the lyfetyme of his parenes, then the foresede Johan dyed
and then Annes a warde to John Gyles, Gyles solde her to on
Andero this Andero did marrye her to his son Thomas Andero
and Thomas and Annes hade issue Willyam and dyvers others
this Thomas and Annes solde ther londs to Roberte Furse as
hereafter yt dothe appere.

   John Moresede my granfather called Roberte Moreshed
to the Chancerye and ther was longe in sute but before anye
judegemente Roberte dyed and so the sute sessede and for that he
was not abell to travell he never procured no farder sute.

[*Fos. 41 and 42 are blank.*]

[FURSE AND HIS INHERITANCE]

ROBARTE FURSE the sonne and here of John Furse and Johan
hys wyfe and cosen and here of the foresed John Moreshede,
after the dyssesse of the sayede John Furse and John Moresede
he by a juste tytell and a lyneall dyssente was also sesede of
all the foresede messuages londes and tenementes yn Furse, What londes
Westewaye, Bromeham, Westekynstere, the one moyetye of by dissente
Erygge, the garden yn Torryton, one tenement in Commarten,
Wallond, Holstrom, the too tynnemylles, the howse yn Certon,
Chydyngebroke, Mowre, Harpeforde, Henbere, Scorehyll,
Moresehede, Nuston, Sempston, Rowdon, Penyton, and of too
tenementes in Dartemowthe. This Roberte dewelled at Dene
Pryer in his mansyon howse of Moresehede he dyd marrye His marrage
on Wyllemott Rowelonde one of the dofters and cooheres of incressed his
Edmond Rolonde of Nymettrasye by which menes he was also londes
sesede of dyvers parselles of londes. What Rolonde was his issue
and where the londe lyethe yt shall hereafter at large appere. This
Roberte fyrste bofte the tenemente yn Dartemowthe of Philyppe
Pynnehaye that John Moresed did geve to Willyam Pynnehaye. What londes
He also bofte one other persell of londes in Sowthe Brynte called he purchased
Thenecombe, of one Richarde Wanell of Moreton. He also dyd
bye the fee sympell of one close of londes in Dertyngton, of one
Andro Foxse of Denepryer. He also bofte the fee sympell of
one other tenemente in Uggebur' called Cuttewyll of one Phi'
Whyte. He also fyrste bofte the other moyete of the berten of
Egerudege[88] of Willm Kyngewyll of Certon, he also bofte the

---

88. The purchase of a moiety of the barton of Egerudge in 1574 is confirmed
   by a final concord in The National Archives, Easter term of that year (TNA
   CP25/2/109/1333).

fee sympell of the londes in Moresed and the leye parke that
was Thomas Androes londes lyenge in Denepryer of Thomas
Andro and Annes hys wyfe. This Roberte also fyrste did bye
the fe sympell of the maner of Skyrrydon Hokeneye Lytell
Kynedone Stancombe Churchebere and Fostardes Parkes of
Philyppe Bassette Esquyre.[89] He also bofte one lytell garden and
parsell of londes in Nymett burrowe of one George Davye. He
also bofte to hym and his heres one annuyte of iij^{li} of Henrye
Harte of Holle. Roberte Furse also payed vj^{li} xiij^s iiij^d to Edward
Lakyngeton gentylleman to make parfyt his estate and interres
in serten londes called Ocke in the parysshe of Bysshopes nymett.
What all thys purchase londes ys and where hyt dothe lye yt

An increse of
his levynge by
polisye

shall hereafte at large appere. Thys Roberte for the increse of
his levynge fyrste bulded one grestemyll and too tokenmylles
upon his londes called Rowdon and iij severall dewellynge
howses, he lekewyse bulded one other dewellynge howse at
Nuston. Thys Roberte did myche inlarge his orchardes, he made

A good
practyse to
inlarge his
comodites

the hopeyard the moste parte of waste grownde, he made the
arbegar[d]ynge nusserye the plase for benes. He planted monye
ockes aysshes elmes and other trees and planted monye newe

His buldyngs

hagges. He made of his kychchen a parler he made the backe
curte of waste grownde and his mylke howse lykewyse, he fyrste
bulded the wenehowse in voyed grownde and wythe yn to yeres

Some parte
burned

the same by menes of the bakehowse was all burned and all
moste all the bakehowse, then he newe bulded the wenehowse
and made hit longger by the towellehowse, he also newe made the
bake howse and inlargege the same for he made the oven mantell

Gretely
alterede

& drye in the este parte in voyed grownde where before the same
did stonde in the weste parte of the howse. All the barnes rofe
fell downe and a grete parte of the walles, Robert newe made the
same barne and made hyt from thache to shyndell and to avoyed
the inconvenyenes of pulles he then in voyed grownd made the
crosebarne and a polle dore. He also bulded the syder howse
newe and the chamber, he yn voyed grownd fyrste made the
shyppen and wthyn x yeres all the rofe by neclygense of workemen
fell downe so onse more he did make hit perfytt. He made the

fo. 44

hall larger by all moste the iij parte and incresed one mor lyght
to the same by one wyndowe, and of the olde shyppen he made
a kychen and a paste howse, he made all the chambers over the
same he made the porch and enterye and syled the hall and glaste

---

89. See below, pp. 93–126.

Drawing of Moorshead, home of Robert Furse, in the early twentieth century (*Western Morning News*, 1 May 1937, p. 13).

all the wyndoes. He made the lytell larder and the lytell howse by the parler and altered the wayes in to the buttery, he made close the grett curte and sette there the too yates.

This Roberte was myche oppressed by lawe but he defended hym selfe and kepte surelye his one; ther was no thynge that came to his hand but that som one or other made tytell to hit but all in vayne he systayned grette loste by loste of his quycke stufe he loste CCxl shepe in one yere, iij or iiij of his plowe oxen in a yere but iiij or v horsses in a yere, he was myghtelye dyseved by his credytors. Thys Roberte hadde issue Roberte Furse John Furse Johan Furse Annes Furse Marye Furse Ellezb^t Furse Willemott Furse Grase Furse Jane Furse Susanne Furse and Anne Furse: whatt ys becom of Robertes issue yt shall hereafter appere.[90]

Still in lawe

Grett lostes

His issue

THYS ROBARTE FURSE at his grette charges did grettelye increse all the impellementes of his howse and furnyshed the same yn mycke better valye then he reseved the same bothe yn sylver plate yn pewture brasse yeron fetherbeddes bowlsteres pyllowes coverlettes shettes stondynge beddestedes bordes chestes a presse treen vessell and generallye in all other necessaryes whiche were to longe and yn vayne here to resyte for as the howses were inlarged and the old impellementes som stolen som loste and som woren and growen owte of use and fasshyon of forse he was compelled to supplye everye wante and to furnyshe the same in farre better order and at gretter charges then ever anye of his predyssessores did use.

The charge of his howsehold stoffe

90. See below, pp. 76–7.

The charges of
his dofters

THIS ROBERTE WAS also at grette charges and payed grette somes off monye to the marrage of his dofteres whyche here after hit shall more at large appere.

The marrage
of his son

THIS ROBERTE FURSE also in his lyfe tyme viz at Mic in an° dni 1593 havynge a grette care for the preferremente of John Furse his sonne and here of his sequele and dowttynge grettelye his sunes tender yeres then beynge but ix yeres of yage and iij monthes and for fere that he sholde incomber hymselfe wythe an unequall mache or a mache to his utter decaye, he then fullye concluded wythe Edmonde Furse of Ochamton in the cowntye of Devon gentylleman and wythe the Wyllemott his wyfe late the wyfe of John Alforde[91] dyssessede theye havynge then the warde and beynge then the lawfull gardeneres of John Alfordes too dofters and cooheres Ussula and Susanna that the foresede John Furse the sonne and here of Roberte shal by gods permyssion marrye and take to wyfe the foresede Susanne Alford the seconde dofter and coohere of John Alforde yf the same John Furse and Susanne shall thereunto agree when theye shall accomplyshe the yage of xv yeres. Susan ys nere sexse monthe yelder then John Furse by whiche marrage yf hit shall plese god hyt shall take plase no dowte John Furse shall grettelye incresse his londs for John Alforde her father dyed sesede of the thyrde parte of the maner of Rowcom and of [blank] burgage and serten other closes and meddowes in Murton hamstede, of too tenementes in Samforde Curteneye of the maner of Chechecotte of the moytye of Puttehanger, of serten londs in Sowthecote and of [blank] burgages in Ockyngeton & of the iiij parte of the howse in Ockyngeton whereyn John Alforde did dewell and of [blank] meddowes and certen other londs there. What John Alforde was and where his londs dothe lye & the valye thereof shall more at large hereafter appere.[92]

fo. 45
Tynneworkes

John Alforde was lekewyse sesede of dyveres tynneworkes he was of grett welthe and dyed unteasted and what was porsyoned to Susan I am not serten.

91. John Alford's widow Wilmot married secondly Edmund Furse of Okehampton, gentleman. This Edmund does not appear elsewhere in Furse's narrative, nor in Vivian's Furse pedigree, so his relationship is unknown. In fact, John Furse did not marry Susan Alford, but Welthian Snelling of Plympton St Mary, who may have been a better match. This may have come about because his mother Wilmot, two years after Furse's death, married Arthur Hart of Plympton. Susan married Peter Ebbsworth or Ebbsworthy, *c.*1605, and her sister Ursula married John Calmady of Saltash (Vivian, *Visitations of Devon* pp. 318, 129).

92. See below, p. 138.

Note that Roberte Furse when he bofte the moyete of Erygge he then alynated serten quylletes of londes parsel of Mowre to Willyam Kyngewyll and when he bofte the maner of Skyrrydone then he solde to Mr Predes off Feber all the reste of his londes in Mowre Certon towne Chydyngebroke Herpeforde Henbere Scorehylle for CCC^{li} and Walonde to John Curter for Cx^{li} and lekewyse when he bofte Thomas Androes londes in Moresehed and the leye parkes he then solde Cuttewyll for l^{li} to Thomas Byckeforde. This Robert Furse was gretely charged with the prynses serves, he was xvj yeres cunstabell of Stanbury hundred and for xxx yeres he was a comon juror but in the yende he suede for a wryte of prevylege, agayne he was commonly one of the grande jurye and dyvers tyme fore man of the grande jurye, he was lekewyse gretelye charged in subsydeye farre excidynge anye of his predisessors, he was x^{li} in londs he was not forgote in the charge of armor his charge was a corselett furnyshed, a muskett furnyshed too callyvers furnyshed iij alman ryvets furnyshed a bowe and a shefe of arrowes furnyshed, all this armor[93] he bofte; his charge yerely to the powre of Dene pryer xvj^s and iiij^s to the mentenans of the churche & monye other extraordynarye charges he payde on yere xv^{li} for mersements for hymselfe and his father. When he was cunstabell he hadde the conduccyon of a C sodyers from Exon' to Barnestabell by that menes he loste iiij^{li} and all his travell. John Gyles rector of the shefe of Denepryer sette the shefe of Denepryer to Robarte Furse for v yeres for xv^{li} a yere by worde and for that he hadde hyt not by dede Gyles moste falselye made a lese to one other and by that menes yt coste Roberte Furse xx^{li} and myche trobell and sorrowe.

What londes Roberte Furse did sell

Robertes charges for the serves of the prynse

Deseved by Gyles

[*Fos. 46–48 are blank. Fo. 49 contains sentences written in a separate hand indicated here by italics, and words written in a further hand indicated by bold italics.*]

---

93. Constable of Stanborough Hundred. The constable was responsible for keeping the peace, maintenance of watches, and mustering armed men (Cam, *Hundred and Hundred Rolls*, pp. 18, 86). A common jury was a jury consisting of ordinary jurors, as opposed to a special jury, of persons of a certain status. A grand jury was an inquisition of 12 to 23 freeholders of a county returned by the sheriff to sessions of the peace, and commissions of oyer and terminer and general gaols delivery. Furse's obligations to provide arms are confirmed in Howard and Stoate, *The Devon Muster Rolls for 1569*.

fo. 49   ## What ys becombe of Roberte Furses issue

ROBERTE Furse the sonne and here of Roberte and Wyllemett his wyfe dyed presentely when he was boren, whatt John Furse his brother ys yt shall here after in ordere appere.

JOHAN Furse was married to one John Cake the sonne and here of John Cake of Marytavye gentylleman. Robart did geve yn marrage to the same Johan his dofter C^{li} in monye & all his londes yn Moresede Sempeston Rowdon & one close at Rowdon hedde in spessyall tayell, but yf Robert had issue male at his dyenge daye then in lewe of the londes one other C^{li}. John and Johan hadde issue Roger Cake Grase Cake Marye Cake & serten wothers wch dyed infants.

This Jone Furse had issue ~~Roger Grase Mary John~~ *John William Jone & 7 more she had whether the ware christned or no I know not she died the 23th daye of June beinynge of the age of 42th in anno Domini 1603.*

ANNES Furse was marryed to one John Wolcomb of Plymton. Roberte gave in marrage wth the same Annes Cxx^{li} and the thyrd parte of the maner of Skyrrydon yf John Furse her brother dye wthowte issue of his bodye and Roberte the father wytheowte here male. John and Annes hadde issue Marye Wolcombe Jane Wolcom Wylmote Wolcom & Willyam; Willyam ys dedde. Note that John Wolcome hadde dyveres good perseles of inherytans and good chattal leses.
Willian Wolcombe & Agnis Wolcome was borne after there granfathers desese.

MARYE FURSE was marryed to one John Redeclefe the son and here of Wyllyam Redeclefe of Marytavye one that purchasede all his londes. This Marye hadde in marrage Cx^{li} in monye and one other thyrde parte of the maner of Skyrrydon yf John Furse her brother did dye wythe owte heres of his bodye and Roberte the father wythe owte here males. John and Mary hadde issue Wyllemott Redeclefe, *Siblye; then she was a wyddowe & maryed John Reddeclife, the other brothers sunne & had issu Jhone & Marye & William.*

ELLYZABETHE FURSE: She was marryed to on Rafe Wodeleye lord of the maner of Bockelonde in the mowre. He hadde in marrage wythe Ellezabethe Cxxxj^{li} xiij^s iiij^d in monye and the laste or other parte of the maner of Skyrrydon yf the foresed John Furse dyed wythe owte issu of his bodye and Roberte the father wythe owte here males.

This Elizabeth Furse had isue Rafe Elizabeth Innes and Annis & the she died.

WYLLEMETT Furse was marryed to one John Byrdall of Sente Thomas parryshe, he by arte a brasyer, he had serten londes but dyveres good leses. She hadde lxxx^{li} in monye and the reversyon of one tenement for the terme of her lyfe in lewe of xxx^{li} and all Furses parte of all Rolond londes yf John Furse her brother do dye wythe owte issue. *She hath issue Mellerye wch dyed & a sonne what his name was I know not he lived a most 2 yeares & then dyed she hath livinge Elizabeth Birdall Margret Burdall & Welmot Burdall & the she died.* *fo. 50*

GRASE FURSE *maryed one John Hackesworthye but hee lived wth hir but a quarter of a yeare beefor hee* ~~made a waye wth 33^{li} of his Mr Arthur Hyles what is becomeof him I know not~~ *parted fro' her.*

JANE FURSE *maryed one John Horwill. She had issue Alse and Sarra & then hir husband dyed & the maryed one Charels Sactfeld. John Furse her brother payde her a C^{li} & Jane & Charels had issu Welthian.*

SUSANNE Furse *maryed one Thomas Parnell. John Furse her brother payde her C^{li} she hath issue John Parnell, Ane Parnell.*

ANNE FURSE

John Furse maried on Welthian Snellinge he had issue Elizabeth and one that was borne to sune a woman childe and Robert and Francis and John and Fardonando and then died.[94]

[Moreshede]

MORESHEDE *als* Moreheved ys a tenemente, yt lyethe wythe yn the perryshe of Denepryer, yt is holden nowe of John Gyles lorde of the maner of Denepryer by knyghtes serves and xij^d rente and *fo. 51*

---

94. For further details of Furse's children see Appendix III.

sute to the curte. Yt is also yn my one occupasyon and ys devyded into several persell as here after shall appere. By forse of this tenement we have comon of pasture and common of turbarye in all Buckefaste more gratis we do inyoye that comones by menes we are tenantes to the maner of Denepryer.

We paye for everye hole fyftyedole for all our londes in Moresehed Sempeston Rowdon and loyer Nuston but onlye viij^d and yerely for sherro rente j^d at Micaellmas for all the foresed quylletes of londes and no more. I payed for a releve for all my londes wythe yn the maner of Denepryer to John Gyles but onlye ix^s iiij^d ob. Note that I do immagen that he will demand vij^s ob. for the londes that I did bye of Thomas Andero whiche ys more then we ofte to paye for more none of the Moresheds payed when bothe the tementes in Moresehed were in one manes possessyon for prove loke to the olde letteres of homage.

Note also that the hole vyllage of Moreshede did usuallye take there potte water yn our curte at Moreshed for the whiche Parnyll and Gylbertes tenantes payed yerely one penye everyche of them at Micaellmas and came yerely to clense our lete but Androes tenant payed no rente becose wee hadde water in ther meddow, but a bowte the xvj yere of Ellez^at [1573/4] Parnyll and Ascott then Ser John Gylbertes tenante did not paye ther rente; we did alter the water curse soo we lese ij^d rente & theye ther water but better loste then fownde. Note farder there was a common fowte pathe throffe our curt & over the wheteparke and becose yt was but by sufferans yt was no lawfull waye therefore abowte the xxx yere of Ellez [1587/8] Roberte Furse did denaye the pathe and ever sethenes quyet.

Note that Moresede hadde the too foremost seges in Dene church but when the churche was newe made yt was gretelye altered and John Gyles patron and one of the iiij men[95] in an° d' 1581 havynge a myre malles to Roberte Furse toke upon hym to plase and dysplase Furse and all his tenantes but Furse resysted his order for the whyche by spessyall presepte was called befor Mr Sparrowe and Mr Townseyend then to justes of the pease and Mr Townesyend then chancelor to our bysshoppe of Exon' after longe debatynge of the cawse yn the yend by the consente of the

Marginal notes:
- Buckefaste More
- Fyftydole
- For the releve
- Pottewater
- A pathe stopped
- It was but a waye for our one yease
- Seges in the churche

---

95. The 'Four Men' had a particular status in Dean Prior. A book of parish accounts 1587–1599, chiefly churchwardens but also the four men, constables and collectors of the poor rate is deposited in Devon RO but unfit for production.

ordenarye patron incombente fower men churchewardens and the consente of all the hole perrysshe all the setes were ordered by Mr Townesyend and so ever sethes hathe contynewed so by Furses resystans where before we hadde but only too setes not too seges now we have iij hole seges to our one pryvate use, that is the fore sege yn the norte yele and the loniest shorte sege w^{th}owte the yele dore and the longe sege adyunynge to the same.

Note that by paynge of the foresede penye for Sheryfe rente at Micaell we be free from goynge to the hundres curte for makynge of sharches from conductynge of prysoners to the gayle makynge of buttes reparyng of stocke pyllorye cuckenstole and from all other charges what so ever consernynge the tythenge of Denepryer. We must wache at the becon but not to make the becon and to warde wth the tythen. Note Gyles did threten to compell Roberte Furse and all his ten' to grynde all ther corne to his milles but Furse made awnser he was none of his copyholderes he helde by dede and more then his dede forsed hym he was not bownde to do. Agayne note the free ten' do not presente with the cust' ten' but are exempte.

Oxilion rente

Marke well this

Grynd no corne ther

The pertyculer names of all the closes of the tenemente called Moresehed

fo. 52

THE WHETTEPARKE x akeres, the Sowthedowne xiiij akeres, the Grette Slade xj akeres, the lytell Slade one aker and halfe, Hedeman perke vj akeres, Greder parke vj akeres, the mede too akeres & halfe, the Oteparke iij akeres, the Okeheye or undertowne one quarter of one aker, the Benehaye the gardenes hoppehaye curtelage nursaryes in all iiij akeres.

Sm^a to. lxviij akeres one q^r

THYS be the bondes of Buckefastemore[96] from HURBORNE WYLL dissendyng towardes the sowthe to Fenforde, from Fenforde goynge upwardes towards the weste unto Blackeover from Blackeover dissendynge to wardes the weste to Smallabroke fowte. From Smallabrokefowte assendyng by the Ryver of Aven

Buckefaste more bondes

---

96. The bounds of Buckfast Moor may be compared with those in Buckfast Abbey documents (British Library Add MS 37,640) cited by Rose-Troup in *TDA* 61, p. 258, and in *The Register of John de Grandisson, Bishop of Exeter*, vol. III, ed. F. C. Hingeston-Randolph, p. 1608.

to wardes the northe to the Utter Welbrokefote and from thens
styll assendynge by the Ryver of Aven northe wardes to the hedde
of the same Utterwelbroke, from thens beryng som what to the
este unto Powpaborowe, from Powpaborrowe berynge sowthe
lyneally by the Rowe Rewe to Duckestone, and from Duckestone
dyrectelye to the foresed Hurborne wyll.

ij^s rente

Note for all these comones was payed by the pryer of Plymton
to the abbott of Buckefaste for common of pasture for all his
tenantes of Denepryer free and customarye but only ij^s by the
yere. This too shyllynge was monye yeres payed by John Gyles
Willyam and by John Gyles untyll the v yere of Quene Ellez.
[1562/3] but sethenes he never payed penye.

Note this

Note there hathe bynne dyveres questyones and quares for this
commons betewexte Ser Willyam Peter lorde of Brynte More and
Ser Thomas Dennes lorde of Buckefaste more and Sowtheholl
mowre but yn the yende hyt was quyettelye yended. Note Ser
Thomas did in dede dysmember Brynte more from Brynte maner
so Ser Willyam hadde Brynte more from Ser Thomas and not
from the prynse.

Where the
daystes went

Agayne note that wythe yn a verye small tyme before the abbe
londes came to the Kynge bothe Brynte more Buckefastemore
Sowtheholle more all the cattell and strayers wente to
Dommabrygge pownd.

The waye
undertown

Note there ys a lytell waye betewexte our mede and Mr Gylbertes
londe, this waye was seldon usede before Willyam Ascott did
sette a yate there and som tymes he carryed his haye that waye
for by my granfatheres tyme yt was not so usede but Mureshed
did alwayes burye his carren there when pygge or bollocke did
dye in the fellon. I have harde the olde inhabytans of Moreshed
saye that yn olde tymes in that lytell waye was a well where all
the hole vyllage hadde ther potte water but for wante of use
and mentenans the water hathe nowe som other curse. Before
I dyd bye Androes londes there was som dowte howse londes
that waye was for Ascott clemed hit to be his lordes londes but
that myght nott be, for marke the olde meddowes hagge and the
yate is clene benethe the curse of the olde hagge and therefore
no dowte ledde owte of our londes, for in Kynge Henr' the VIIth
tyme all the lyell Slade leaye open and som parte of the meddowe

so no dowte we were the last inclosier: lett them use ther waye but loste not the londes.

Note John Moresede did lye his tymber under towne and ther wrofte the same and none but he and yt was Roberte Furse that fyrste planted the same wythe ockes and aysshes in the yere of our lorde god 1588 and sethenes he hathe dyveres tymes pared the ockes and polled the aysshes and fylled serten apses ther growynge and all to his one use.

For under towne

ROWDONE ys nowe dyveres tenementes and dyvyded ynto dyveres severall closes. Yt lyethe in Dene pryer wythe yn the maner off Northehurborneforde, yt is soocage tenure we holde hit and serten other londes called Sempeston of Richard Voyele Esquyr as a free tenante of his maner of Northehurborneforde by fealty and payemente of viij^d yerelly at Micaelmas for all sute and serves. Howe yt is devyded yt shall here after appere but in the xth yere of Henrye the VIII [1518/19] yt was then but v closes and one token myll and at that tyme there were too seeverall weres upon Meddeles the one for the token myll the other for our potte water for the whyche the heres of Moresehed payed to the lorde of Brynte vj^d yerelye at Micaelmas, but as I have sayed before upon the stryfe betewexte John Morese and Nycolas Moreshede bothe weres and water curses loste ther use, then was John forsede to make an newe were in Meddeles and a newe water curse for his potte water and for the same contynually payed to the lorde of Brynte the foresede yerelye rente of vj^d and ever sethenes the water curse quyett, and beware do not alter that curse but contynewe stylle the same. At the lawe curte holden at Sowthe Brynte the xxiij^{ti} daye of September in the xvth yere of the rayne of Quene Ellezabethe [1573] John Peter knyght then lorde of the same maner in open curte dide grante to Roberte Furse and his heres for ever lybertye to have too severall weres the one in Medeles the other yn the Comeparke for the same Furse muste paye yerely viij^d that ys vj^d for the were in Meddeles and ij^d for the were yn the Comeparke and for not paymente to dystrayne Furses londes at Thenecombe. Then Furse beynge sure of his weres he wythyn a shorte tyme beganne to bulde the gryste myll and too Tokenmylles, BUT THE buldynge of thes mylles was to Furses grett coste and the onlye menes of his grette trobell

fo. 53

The olde weres

The newe weres

Grete sutes in lawe for the milles

and expenses yn the lawe, for then presentelye one Mr Richard
Voyell Esquyre then lorde of Northehurborneforde a myghtye
man havynge dyveres justes and almoste all the gentyllemen
to his cosenes procured one Franses Dodde and Ellezabethe
his wyfe then Mr Voyeles tenantes for Hurborneforde mylles
to brynge an assyse of annoyanes agaynste Roberte Furse and
Willemot his wyfe. The under shryfe and the jurye came and
made there vewe, this sute contynewed too yeres and more they
had a decem tales octo tales sexto tales quarto tales and att
everye assyses cosede Furse to retayne cownsell and to have som
viij men for wyttenes, and all was but showe to make Furse to
submytt the cose to som awarde, but Furse knowynge his cose to
be good defended his tytell, so yn the yende after grett expenses
on bothe partes and for that ther cawse was not good, Mr Voyell
sente Furse word that yf he wold be quyett and geve over his
sutes so wolde he do the leke, and this not ended by tryall but
by bothe the partes consente, and ever sethenes yt hathe bynne
quyett. Mr Voyes accyon not good for dyveres cawses, the fyrste
cose for that his grystemyll was but xij yeres yelder then Furses
mylle, for before that tyme yt was a gyggemyll a myll belongen

fo. 54

to a toker and for that thos gyggemylles was the spoyle of myche
clothe the same by a statute made in Kynge Edwarde the Sexte[97]
tyme clene taken awaye, the second cawse for that the water
curse was altered som xviij ynches or more by newe buldynge
of the mylles so by that menes he loste his prescrypsyon, agayne
Furse hadde a were and a water curse for lxx yeres for the rente
of vj^d and by that menes he myght well justyfye his water curse
by perscrypsyon whiche were and lette Furse dothe contynewe,
and beware do not alter that were nor letes for that was the only
poynte that served my purpose, agayne we cane prove we hadde
a token myll in the leye parke in Richard the secondes tyme &

An other
practes

so contynewed untyll x^o Henr' the VIII [1518/19]. But when
all this wolde not serve there false and malysyus pretens to
overthrowe Furses mylles, then another myscheffe was invented:

by Cholwill

there was one John Chollewyll otherwyse Wyllyames a myghtye
and the onlye man to rule almost all the tynneres that no man
durste to resyste hym he was brother by marrage to Mr Voyell[98]

---

97. The Statute against gig mills is 5&6 Edward VI c. 6:30.
98. Richard Fowell's sister Margaret or Margery was married to John Williams alias
Cholwill, possibly as his second wife (Westcote, *View of Devonshire*, pp. 521–2;
Vivian, *Visitations of Devon*, p. 369).

and chefe stuarde of all the stannerye; this Chollewyll did cose one Willyam Gale of Sowthebrynte to pyche[99] the tynneworke called Meddeles the worke lyeth or bothe the sydes of the ryver of Hurborne and by that menes he mente to convaye the water from Furses myll, for in dede the worke was fyrste sesed of the water and he gave warnynge to one Wyllyng[s] wyfe whiche had no other ryght but by her dower, the whiche warnynge I do suppose the custom of the stannerye will not allowe. Furse presentelye to prevent this cosede one John Langeford lekewyse to pyche the foresede tynneworke called Medeles and gave the warnynge to one Water Adam an olde honer yn dede, and he the same Langeford dyd leke wyse geve the same warnynge to Roberte Furse, so the same tynneworke was three severall tyme pyched and iij severall tymes entered, and all yn one yere. The nexte yere Chollewyll cosede his man one Thomas Tonye to newe poyeche agayne the same tynneworke and Tonye dyd lekewyse geve warnynge to Wyllynges wyfe. The cawse of this newe pyche was for that the custom of the Stannerye was that howe so ever will pyche a tynneworke the pycher muste make a newe hedde and a newe tayell wythe yn the bondes of the same worke. Wyllyam Gale that fyrste pychede the worke yn truthe made newe hedde and tayell, but not in the tynneworke called Meddeles, but he made the hede in Meddeles and the tayell in another worke adyunynge and by that menes his pyche not good, and for that cose Thomas Tonye whiche was also an honer wythe Gale in the fyrste pyche did newe pyche agayne the same tynneworke. Upon this newe pyche made by Thomas Tonye Roberte Furse in his one person came ynto the tynne curte at Aysperton and there proved the tynneworke called Meddeles laufully renewed accordynge to the forme of the statute and by

Marginal notes:
- Gales pyche
- Langfords pyche
- Tonyes pyche
- The only menes to avoyde ther tytell

99. 'The procedure for bounding land in Cornwall and Devon was simple and was known technically as pitching a pair of bounds. Thomas Beare, writing in the second half of the sixteenth century, described it as follows. "The manner of bounding is more commonly to make four corner bounds, two at the head of the work and two more at the tail, in cutting up three turfs in every corner, and so consequently their side bounds and head bounds with three turfs on every place, one directly against the other . . ."' A later writer described this as in the form of a molehill. 'Beare was writing of bounding streamworks, and "the head of the work" was the higher part of the alluvial bed towards which the work progressed. The lower end of the bounds would have water brought to it through a channel called a tye or leat, so that the ore could be washed and the waste matter or tailings washed away downhill.' (Pennington, *Stannary Law*, p. 77, citing Thomas Beare, 'The bailiff of Blackmore', in Thomas Pearce, *The Laws and Customs of the Stannaries of Cornwall and Devon*, 1725).

that menes Tonyes pyche voyed. Sethenes the foresed Langeford paste all his ryght to Roberte Furse and becose Furse wolde not be pestered wythe the serves of the tynners he did convayed the same to Grase Furse hys dofter so by thes menes Furse ys nowe lawfull honer of all the foresede tynneworke called Meddeles and beware that the same worke be lawfullye renewed yerelye and then dowte no man for the tytell.

Note also that yn the xxvij yere of Kynge Henrye the VIII [1535/6] a statute was made for the preservasyon of serten havenes,[100] this statute ys good for us. Rede the statute at large for Hurborne water hath curse to Dartemowthe haven that was an other menes that yf the worke hadde bynne loste yn dede I wolde surely have tryed the worke men in the Escheker.

Yt another practes to overthrowe our myll. Gyles, Furses enyme, thretened hym to compell hym and all his tenantes by forse to grende all ther corne to his custommarye myll and that he wolde plucke downe Furses mill. Roberte Furse made hym awnser that he was not his custommemarye tenante nor no copyeholder but the londes that he helde of hym was by dede and becose his dede did not charge hym wyth shuche serves he wolde and all his tenantes be free and not grynde to his mylle, and as for pluckenge down of his myll Furse made hym awnser that his myll did stonde not yn his maner nor upon his soyell but wythe yn the maner of Northehurborneforde and that upon Furses one soyell. Then upon this awnser he procured his homage to presente vj persones at his lawe curte at Denepryer that then dyd inhabytt & were resydente upon the foresede londes called Rowdon to be sweren sensores to his curte and there to pay ther sensores rente that lekewyse Furse refusede becose yt was wythe owte his lybertye and for the discharge there of made the stuarde and homage p[re]vye of his polle dede & dyveres offyses and other wrytynges whyche upon the syght there of the mater was ended. Thus you see Furse hathe bynne hardelye be sett for his myll. But here note that the customarye myll of Dene was nere adyunynge to Nuston and hadde ther powle in our londe and where the myll was ys now made a dewellynge howse. The myll at Denetowne was fyrste bulded when that myll was lett downe.

100. 27 Henry VIII c. 23, An Acte for the preservation of Havens and Portes in the Counties of Devon and Cornwall.

THE lordes of Northehurborneforde do demonde of us sute to there curte fealtye and knyghtes serves for our londes of Rowdon and Sempston but we do none nor will not. Our awnsyent rente was a pere of gloves but by forse of a dede made in xj° Ed the Second [1317/18] this rente was altered so nowe we paye for rente sute and serves but viij^d yerely. Note that one Symon Moresehede did homage to one John Voyell for londes in Rowdon in an° vij Henr' VI [1428/9], but never non of our awnsettores sethens nor before for in truthe by our polle dede yt is socage tenure.

For our sute and serves to Mr Voyell

AGAYNE NOTE Mr Voyell can not amerse us for by lawe he hathe ther nowe no maner, a maner can not be wythe owte free tenantes and he hathe but one free tenant, then yf he can not justyfye to kepe a curte then we nede not to do sute nor yt fealtye yf we hadde no other helpe.

Marke this also

The pertyculer names of all the closes and severall devysion of the tenement called Rowdone

fo. 56

THE LAYE PARKE nowe devyded ynto iij severall closes xij akeres. This was but one close and a tokenmyll upon the same but when the water was taken a waye as ys a foresede then one Robert Berde tenant pulled down the howse and sette the same at Moresede, and ther yt nowe remayenethe. This leyeparkes be nowe in lese with serten londes in Moresed all for one pertyculer rente granted to one John Berde and otheres for the terme of their lyves.

THE GRYSTEMYLL ys persell of Rowdon, yt remaynethe yn my one hondes, yt is but the myll and mill howse, yt was fyrste bulded yn the xvj yere of Quene Ellezb^t [1573/4].

THE WYLLEPARKE ys one close of londes viij akeres, the newe mede sontymes persell of the sam close ij akeres, too other closes of londes called Meddeles xij akeres, all in my one occupasyon and parcell of Rowdon.

STABBES howse ys persell of Rowdon and ys bulded upon one close of londe called Meddeles, yt is a howse and a garden and nowe yn the tenure of Roberte Stabbe and Catteren hys wyfe for terme of ther lyves for the yerelye rente of vj^s viij^d, and yt was fyrste bulded the xxx yere of Quene Ellezabeth [1587/8].

fo. 57   THE COMEPARKE ys persell of Rowdon yt ys nowe made a tenemente and ys devyded ynto iij severall closes & one appell garden and upon this ys also one tokenmyll. There ys also annyxsed unto thys tenemente one lytell persell of the foresede Willeparke where of som parte ys made an arbegarden, the hole londes by existymasyon ys viij akeres. Yt is all nowe in the tenure of Mathewe Torner and otheres for the yerely rente of xl^s ij^d. Note this Torner fyrste bulded the mylle in the xv yere of Quene Ellezabethe [1572/3] and sethenes all the reste of the howses he devyded all the severall closes and was at grett charges in makynge clene the Comeparke of stones.

MEDDELES ys but a persell of Medeles and ys nowe also a tenement devyded ynto iij severall perseles of londes or closes and one arbegarden. The hadde the one halfe of the mylle howse whiche ys nowe ther dewellyng howse. Mathewe Lenarde fyrste bulded the token mylle yn the xxiij^{ti} yere of Quene Ellezab^t [1580/1], all this ys nowe yn the tenure of this same Matthew Lenard and otheres for the yerelye rente of xl^s. Mathewe at his one charges devyded the londes.

[From here on some sums of money and acreages are left blank. Furse must have intended to complete them later but had no opportunity. The rest of this page is blank.]

fo. 58   SEMPESTON lyethe in Denepryer, yt is holden of the lorde of Northehurborneforde as ys aforesede, yt is but one close of londes of ix akeres and one other percell of londes adyununge one aker, all in my one occupasion. Note ther were monye olde walles ther therefore no dowte a tenement but in settynge an ocke there verye depe I fownde aysshes crockeshurdes & olde iron so I judege that yt was no dowte burned.

fo. 59   MORESHEDE ys allso one other tenemente, yt lyethe yn Denepryer, yt ys ho[ld]en of John Gyles by knyghtes serves by the yerely rente of viij^d and sute to the curte, yt is nowe in the tenure of John Berde & otheres for the yerelye rente of xlj^s. We paye for fyftyedole for one hole fiftyedole [ ]^d and for shryfe rente [ ]^d for the whyche the londes ys free from all tythenge charges as Moresede ys.

This londes Roberte Furse fyrste bofte of the foresed Thomas Anderowe and of Annes his wyfe yn the xxvij yere of Quene Ellezabethe [1584/5] for Cxx^{li}.

After thys londes was bofte one Water Hele made a tytell to the hole londes for that Roberte Moresehedde did morgage all his londes to one Nycolas Hele by dede of bargayn and sale, and the condysyon broken, yt was for the deleverye of serten tynne but non of the Heles never was sesed nor hadde anye use or profytt there of, but Robarte Moresed dyed sesed so did Crysten his dofter and John Hanes and Roger Hanes. Thomas Anderowe and Annes were sesede, and so sesede theye solde hit to Furse by fyne. Agayne the londes when Moreshede shold passe this assurans was intayeled so no dowte of Mr Heles tytell. The fyne & tayell dedes wilbe a barre &c.

Heles tytell to Moresehed

The pertyculer names of all the several closes of the londes called Moreshede:

fo. 60

SHORTACOME downe [ ] akeres, lytell Shortacombe v akeres, the lytell grove one aker, too closes called Rowedon, too appell gardenes, one arbegarden, one meddowe one aker.

NUSTON ys a tenemente, yt lyethe also in Denepryer, yt is holden of John Gyles lorde of the maner of Denepryer by knyghte serves. The heye rente ys one pere of gloves or one penye for the same at Ester, but tyme owte of mynde in lewe of the gloves we have and do paye iij^d and sute to the curte. Yt remaynes in my one occupasyon. By this tenemente we have comones in all Buckefast more as one of the free tenantes of Denepryer.

fo. 61

The pertyculer names of all the severall closes and devysyones of the londes called Nuston:

fo. 62

NUSTON CLOSE vij akeres the lytell parke one aker and halfe and one meddowe one aker and halfe one other close lyenge at Rowdon hedde xij akeres.

NUSTON the tenemente was taken owte of Nuston Close yt is a thynge newlye erected by one John Edwardes yn the xxiiij of Quene Ellezbethe [1581/2] he payethe for the same vj^d of yerelye rente.

NUSTON ys also a lytell meddowe persell of the foresed Nuston this meddo ys nowe in the tenure of John Typpett & otheres for the yerelye rente of iij^s iiij^d.

fo. 63 NUSTON MESSUAGE ys a tenemen yt lyethe also in Denepryer yt is holden of John Gyles of his maner of Denepryer by knygh[t]es serves & vj^d for heye rente and sute to the curte. Note farder we paye yerelye for this londes xv^d yerely to John Hele at Micaell; yt is nowe yn the tenure of Edwarde Prowse for the yerely rente off xxvj^s viij^d. This tenemente hathe also comones yn all Buckefaste more by the same tytell that we cleme for Moresehed and Nuston, we paye for fyftyedole [ ] and for shryfe rente [ ] and by this menes we be free from all tythen charges as Moreshed & all the reste of our londes ys.

Note this Note this londes and serten other londes in Denepryer was
petygrewe somtyme one Dunselese londes whiche hadde issue one dofter called Alse this Alse marryed one Somer. Somer and Alse hadde issue iij dofteres the one married one Bastarde the other one
Devysion Hewett the thyrde one Scryche so the three cooheres by an agremente fyrste devyded this londes that is to saye Bastarde hade the howse & the londes nowe in the tenure of Edward
and alinasion Prowse and that Bastardes son solde all his parte to John
- Moreshedde, Scryche hadde for his parte vj closes viz one called the Bromeparke one other called the Threcorner parke too other closes called the Grenewylles and the too other closes called the Byckewylles, Scryches sonne solde his parte to Mr Gyles. Hewett hadde for his parte one close called Rowdon one other close called Wasawaye and too other closes called Someresparkes and the foresede socke rente of xv^d owte of Bastardes londes thys Hewets sones sonne sollde his parte to the foresede John Hele.

fo. 64 The perticuler devysyon of all the foresede tenement called Nuston:

ROCHEFORDE one aker and threquarters, the meddowe one aker, Forchen parke ij akeres and halfe, the Fursehyll iij akeres and halfe one aker, and halfe the garden and all the reste iij akeres.
  Sum^a to. [ ]

DARTEMOWTHE[101] ys a howse and garden w^thyn the burrowe   *fo. 65*
and lybertyes of Dartemowthe but the londes lyethe wythe   The tenure
yn the perryshe of Sente Pederyeckes yt is holden of Thomas
Sowthecote Esquyre lorde of the burrowe in free socage for the
yerelye rente of xij^d and sute to the curte yt is in the tenure of
Water Gonne for the yerelye rente of xiiij^s iiij^d and the tenante ys
bownde to dysharge for all maner of offyses what so ever dewe
for all our londes in Dartemowth durynge his terme.

This londes was one Powres londes he solde hyt to Moreshede   Powres londes
Moreshede by worde gave hyt to one Willyam Pynnehaye he
dyed wythe owte any leverye possessyon or atturnemente and
wythe owte issue then John Morsehede the younger did delever
the howse and wrytynges to one Phillyppe Pynnehaye Willyams
brother whiche Phillyppe for that the homage myght not fynde   Pynhayes tytell
hym tenante becose he code not showe any convayenes to prowe
anye grante from Moresehed but he showed the conayenes from
Powre to Moresehed and for that he was not Moreshedes here
the jurye fownde Moresedes here styll to be lawful honer of
the londes Phillyppe Pynnehaye then solde the same to Roberte   Solde
Furse for viij^li in the iij yere of Quene Ellezabethe [1560/1] but
for that Phyllyppe Pynnehaye nevere hadde anye grante from
the Moreshedes after he hadde payde the viij^li and reseved from
Pynnehaye agayne all his wrytynges Roberte Furse did then
presentelye enter yn to all the same howse and garden as cosen
and here of John Moresehede and inyoyed the same quyettelye
and made dyveres leses there of and Furse was fownd tenante
to the lorde and dyde fealtye for the same londes and therefore
becose Pynnehayes wyfe sholde cleme no dower Furse refused to
have anye convayenes from Pynnehaye but trusted holye to his
one wrytynges.

DARTEMOWTHE one other howse adyunynge to the foresede   *fo. 66*
howse & holden of the foresede Thomas Sowthecote by socage
tenure & the yerely rente of ix^d and sute to the curte yt is nowe
yn the tenure of Willyam Robart for the yerelye rente of vj^s ix^d.

DARTEMOWTHE an other howse adyunynge to the same and a
garden and holden of Thomas Sowthecote by socage tenure by
the yerelye rente of ix^d yt is nowe in the tenure of John Gallawayes
executores for the yerelye rente of vj^s ix^d. Note the too laste resyted

---

101. The property in Dartmouth cannot be traced.

tenementes were olde walles John Moresed bofte the same and made too severall tenementes and too severall gardenes.

fo. 67   THENECOMBE Denecombe als Tunecombe[102] ys serten londes yn Sowthebrynte yt is holden of the lorde of the maner Ser John Peter knyght in free socage and iiij^s v^d for the heye rente yt is in my one occupasyon and wee muste do sute to the curte we paye for fyftye dole iiij^d and to the churche one halfe boyshell of otes.

Spessiall   This londes was one Fryees londes of Bockelonde Brewer he hade
note for   issue Nicolas Frye this Nicolas solde this londes to one Richard
Thenecombe   Wanell of Moretonhamstede; Richard Wanell in the seconde yere of Quene Ellezabethe [1559/60] for xxvj^{li} xiij^s iiij^d solde the same londes to Roberte Furse and to his heres. Roberte dowtynge his assurans in decimo of Quene Ellezab^t [1567/8] hadde a relese wythe warrantyse from the foresede Nycolas Frye to Furse & his heres for ever. Furse did by fethemente convayed this londes to dyveres feffes and theye reassured the same to Furse and his heres but Furse in the xx yere of Quene Ellezabethe [1577/8] did by grante paste all the foresede londes in Thenecome to one Phi' Whyte & his heres and leverye & atturnement paste and then presentelye Phillyppe Whyte reassured the same to Furse & his heres and did passe the same by fyne and dyvers other londes; this fyne and relese from Frye and the severall discontynewans will barre Frye and all other.

Comones in   Note in ryghte of this londes we have comones yn all Brynte more
Brynte more   and thes be the trewe bondes of Brynte more[103] that ys to saye from the plase where the too Glases do mete goynge upwardes to the northe to the hedde of Glase from thens styll assendynge to the northe by the Rowe Rewe to the myds of the threeburrowes from thens to the Utterwhytaburrowe alwayes northewardes & from Whytaburrowe towardes the yeaste to Bockelonde forde from thens dessendynge downeward by the weste syde of Aven to Smallabroke fote from Smallabrokefote from Aven more to the

102. Thenecombe, in South Brent, is Thynacombe Barn (*PNDevon* I, p. 292), and variously as Thinnicombe in the tithe award, which shows a barn, but not apparently a house.
103. The bounds of Brent Moor are cited from the Buckfast Abbey cartulary in Grandisson's *Register*: see above, note 96, p. 79. A lengthier inquisition on the boundaries of Dartmoor and Brent Moor of 1557 is quoted by Stuart A. Moore, *Rights of Common upon the Forest of Dartmoor*, p. 50.

yeaste to Blackeover from Blackeover goynge downe to wardes the yeaste to Fenforde.

The pertyculer closes of Thenecombe: *fo. 68*

THE TOO Flowdeparkes xiiij akeres, the lytell parke ij akeres, the grett Hele nowe devyded in to fower perseles xxvj akeres.
    Sm^a to. xlij akeres.

PENYTON[104] ys also a tenemente yt lyethe wytheyn the maner of Aysheabbett but we do our sute to Brynte curte and yt ys holden of Ser John Peter knyghte lorde of the maner of Sowthe Brynte in free socage, the heye rente ys iij^s xj^d yerelye; note the maner of Brente and Ayshe Abbett ys nowe but one maner for theye kepe but one curte and that yn Brynte Churchehowse but theye have yerelye too tythenmen & they and ther homage do make severall presentementes. There ys adyunynge to Penyton one lytell more callede Brodamore, that more ys a comones for Bulstone and Penyton and we have also in the ryghte of this tenement commones and common of turbarye in all Brynte more. What Brynte more ys yt is wryten in the laste tenement called Thenecome, we paye for one hole fyftydole xij^d and yerelye to the churche one pecke of whete.

Marginal notes: fo. 69 / The tenure / Commones in Brynte more / and Brodamore

The pertyculer names of the closes of the londes called Penyton: *fo. 70*

THE BRODEPARKE nowe devydede yn to fower closes the lytell meddowe one aker and halfe the longe mede ij akeres and halfe the Sowthe parke v akeres the gardenes curtelage & waste q^r ac.
    Sm^a to. xix akeres quarter besydes the comones in Brodamore & Brynte more.

There was more londes belongen to Penyton but we did loste hit by a warde so we have but the one halfe note when the warde was made then there were but olde walles the howse was newe bulded by one one Alman yn John Moreshedes tyme.

Marginal note: Londes loste

The lorde of Brynte will demonde a herrett for Penyton and an other for Thenecombe but paye hym none for non of our predissessores did ever paye anye herrett theye saye that the custom of the maner ys to paye for everye farthynge of londes

Marginal note: Beware what you paye

104. Penyton in Ash Abbott manor. This is Pennaton in South Brent parish (SX686594), which belonged to the abbey of Buckfastleigh, and where there is a village called Ash or Aish (*PNDevon*, I, pp. 291–2); Broad Moor is at SX683597.

for a releve xij^s vj^d. Surelye upon the dethe of my granfather John Moresehedde I payed for Penyton vj^s iij^d and no other herrett.

Folo this

By the olde dedes this relefe ys expressed so is a herrett sute to the mylle x^d but paye no more but as our awnsetores have payde.

[SKYRRYDON MANOR,
BOUGHT BY FURSE]

Skyrrydon Maner[105] wythe all his memberes Roberte Furse yn
the xxij yere of Quene Ellezabethe [1579/80] for the some of
nyne hundred powndes dyd by the same of one Phillyppe Basset
of Collom John Esquyre for the some of the same ixC[li] this maner
ys holden of our soverante ladye Quene Ellezabethe in capyte and
so be all the memberes by the fortye parte of a knyghtes fee. This
maner and his memberes ys devyded yn to severall tenementes
and hyt dothe lye in severall parrysshes the names qualytes and
the valye there of sall more at large here after appere.[106] The
maner hyt selfe ys a free hamelett and ys a lette of hyt selfe
yt hathe the goodes of all felones owtelawreyes felons de see
fugatyves strayeres wayeffe and all other thynges and lybertyes
belongen to a lette and vewe of frankepleges. This maner yt selfe
ys vendevyle that ys free yn all the foreste of Dartemore for all
ther bestes and cattall and maye frelye make cole and cutte fenne
and carrye the same to ther one use yn consederasion there of
the tenantes of the manner do yerely paye vij[d] for vyndevill rente
and too tenantes appere at the Castell of Lydforde at everye lawe
curte ther holden.

The tenantes of this maner hathe also common of pasture
and common of turbarye in all Buckefastemore for the whyche
the lorde of the maner dothe paye yerelye iiij[s] at Micaell to Ser
Thomas Dennes Knyghte lorde of Buckefaste more.

The purchas
of Skyrrydon
maner

The tenure

The previleges

Vendevile

Buckefaste
more

---

105. Skyrrydon manor meant a great deal to Furse and he relates at length the legal
difficulties he had in securing its purchase from the feckless young Philip Bassett.
For amplification and corroboration of his account see Appendix I.
106. See below, pp. 102–26.

How this
maner
hath bynne
possessed

Boyvyle

Curteneye

The Kynge to
Ser Gawyn
Carewe

The Erell of
Devon

Bassett and
Cholmeleye

A false
practyse

Bassetts dethe

THYS maner wythe his memberes yn Kynge Richarde the secondes tyme Kynge Henrye the fowerthes tyme and yn Kynge Henrye the fythes tyme was one Boyvyles londes but yn Kynge Henrye the sexte tyme the Curteneyes were honeres of the maner and so contynewed styll untyll the xxx yere of the rayne of Kynge Henrye the VIII [1538/9] then one Henrye Curteneye errell of Devon and lorde Marcus of Exon' was executed for treson and so hit came to the possessyon of Kynge Henrye the VIII thene yn the xxxiij yere [1541/2] Kynge Henry the VIII by his lettores patens did grante this maner and dyveres other thynges to one Gawyn Carewe and to Marye his wyfe for the terme of ther lyves for a small rente reserved, the fee sympell of thys maner wythe all his memberes remayned in Kynge Henrye & yn Kynge Edward the sexte. Quene Marye yn the fyrste yere of her rayne [1553/4] by her lettores patens did geve the maner of Skyrrydon and dyvers other londes to one Edward Curteneye Errell of Devon and to the here males of his body; this Edward Curteneye was the onlye sonne and here of Henrye late Marcus of Exon' but the clargye then dystrustynge his relygyon and for that the Quene then unmarryed dyd grettelye favor hym he was sente yn to Italye and there yended his lyfe wythe owte here males of his bodye. Then after his dethe Kynge Phyllyppe and Quene Marye yn the iiij and v[th] yere of ther rayne [1557/8] by ther lettores patens did sell the foresed maner wythe all his ryghtes & memberes to one James Bassett and to Ranolfe Clomeleye, this Ranolfe Clolmeleye was in truthe but putte yn by Bassett in truste onlye to defrewe the prynse of the wardeshyppe of Bassettes chylderen for Chomleye never payed one penye for the londes nor never by Bassettes dayes nor after did converte one penye to his one use by forse of thes lettores patenes but as Bassett made Cholmeleye junte patonye in tryste so yn tryste althoffe he hadde wyfe and chylderen brotheres and cosenes yt he made the same Cholmeleye his hole executor.

AND YN truthe hyt happened that James Bassett yn a verye shorte tyme dyed then one Ser Peter Carewe knyghte hadde the wardeshyppe of Phillypp Bassett the sonne and here of James Bassett and there was grette trobell and sute in lawe for the wardeshype of Phyllyppe Bassette but after longe and costelye sutes in lawe the mater was determyned yn the Curte of Wardes.

AND FOR that Cholmeleye survyved the hole londes was invested yn hym and the younge Bassett by that menes no warde. THEN WHEN all thynges were thys yended and all yn pease Cholmeleye beynge bothe worshyppefull trustye wyse and juste and mente to dele faythefullye wythe Bassettes heres accordynge to the truste reposede yn hym he cawsed all the chefeste of the younge Bassettes fryndes namelye Mr Roper his granfather Thomas Roper and Edward Roper his unkeles and dyveres other the infantes fryndes at a tyme and plase sertayne there to mete and then and there made them fully acquaynted yn what estate Mr Bassett dyede and what charges Cholmeleye hadde bynne yn the defens of the wardeshyppe of the younge Bassett and payenge of the grett legasyes geven by James. When all this was reveled yt dyde appere that James Bassett was at leste iij or iiij thowsante powndes in dett.

fo. 72

The sute for Bassetts here Chylmeles trew delynge

THEN by all ther agrementes yt was thofte better that serten londes to be solde to acquytte the dettes then the here sholde remayne charged wythe userye. Then Mr Cholmeleye in consederasyon that he myghte by ther fulle consente and agremente have to hym and his heres the maner' of Henton and Mudevynne he wolde dyscharge the hole of all Mr James Bassettes detes and legasyes and assure all the reste of the londes to Phillyppe Bassett and his heres. This of all partes there was verye well leked and by all ther condyssente fullye agreed and acceptede. THEN presentely dyd Cholmeleye by fethemente and fyne paste to the foresed Thomas Roper and to Edwarde Roper the maner' of Collerudege, Colrudege parke, Byrchehayes, Cullom John, Ponseforde, Paddebroke, Skyrrydon, Sowtheallyngeton to them and to ther heres for ever and reserved the use to a pere of indentures, but here note for that Colmeleye for that hadde justelye and trulye nowe payed monye for the foresed too maneres Henton and Mudeven and by no menes myghte have anye perfytt assurans from Phillyppe Bassett beynge verye younge and to avoyede the trobell and exclamasyon that Bassettes heres myght make and beynge survyvor as ys aforesed and suffycyante tytell yn hymselfe and to avoyed the exclamasyones of all other and for that he myght quyettely have and inyoye the same the uses in the foresede indentures were this expressed that ys to saye fyrste the fefes to stonde sesed of all the foresed londes expressed in the

Mudven & Henton solde

Cholmele grante to the Roperes

The use referred to the indents

foresed fethemente to the use of Marye Bassett wyddowe mother to the infantes ~~and~~ for the terme of her lyfe the remender after her to Phillyppe her son and to the heres of his body and for defawte of shuche issue to Chareles Bassett and to the heres of hys bodye and for lacke of shuche issue to the ryght heres of James Bassett for ever for and untyll shuche tyme as the foresede Marye Phill' Chareles or one of them ther heres or assynes shall yn ther one ryghte enter yn to the foresede maner' of Henton and Mudeven that then and from thens forthe the foresed feoffes shall stonde and be sesede of all the foresede maneres expressed

But marke this provyso

yn the foresed fethemente to the onlye use of the foresed Cholmeleye his heres and assynes for ever, wythe this proviso expressed yn the same indenture, that ys to saye provyde alwayes that hyt is fullye concluded betewexte the foresede partes that yf hyt shall happen anye shuche enterye to be made yn dede and a re enterye to be made upon the same, that then the foresede Cholmeleye and hys heres shall detayne and kepe the foresed maners and londes granted unto the foresed feoffes no longer but untyll the same Cholmeleye and his heres shalbe fully satysfyed and contented for all shuche hurtes loste and dammages as the same Cholmeleye his heres or assynes shall sustayne by forse of the same enterye.

fo. 73

Mary is dedde

Phi' in possession

Marye Bassett by forse of these assurans was sesede and so dyed sesede then Phyllyppe Bassett after her did enter and was lekewyse sesede of all the foresede londes contayned yn the foresede fethemente he hadde issue too dofters. Phyllype Bassett dyd passe the foresede maner of Skyrrydon to Roberte Furse as ys aforesede by dede of bargayne and sale inrolled in the Chanserye, he also did acknolege a fyne and made hyt also to Furse by fethement and relese wythe warrantyse agaynste all men and dyd also acknowelege yn the Chanserye a recognysans

of all thos maneres

of xviiiC^{li} for the performans of the same and Phyllyppe Bassett was at the same tyme then in actuall possessyon of the maner of Grett Torryton the maner' of Collerudge, Colrudege parke, Byrchehayes, Colom John, Ponseforde, Padebroke and of a manor called Swaneborne yn Bockenhamshere and of serten londes yn Kente nere to Sandewych and for that the possessyon of the maner of Skyrrydon was then yn Ser Gawyn Carewe and the londes intayled to Chareles Bassett and Furse myght not have hyt by recovarye becose Ser Gawyne was not hys frynde Roberte Furse to strenthen and make sure his tytell procured a farder convayenes of the maner of Skyrrydon wythe all his memberes by dede relese and fyne from Chareles Bassette. This maner and serten other maneres was to paye to the prynse xxxix^s vj^d so after James Bassett hade Skyrrydon and Sowthealyngton there was porsyoned unto the same Bassette in the eschecor xxiij^s and that Ser Gawen payed to Bassett but when Phillyppe solde Skyrrydon to Furse he then porsyoned Skyrrydon to xij^s a yere so wythe myche adoo yn the yend Ser Gawyn atturned tenante to Furse and payed hym full iiij yeres the foresed yerelye rente of xij^s at Micaelmas. The maner of Skyrrydon and all his memberes when Furse bofte hyt was all copyeholte londes. Ser Gawyn Carewe dyede the xxv daye of Marche yn the xxvj yere of Quene Ellezabethe [1584] but his wyfe ladye Marye was dede longe befor. So the hole rente of the maner sethenes Ser Gawyn dyssesse wythe the pasture of the wode was xvj^{li} xiiij^s one pownde of waxse.

Chareles Bassett to Furse

Ser Gawyns rente xxij^s to Bassett

To Furse but xij^s per an'

Carroes dethe

CHARELES BASSETT yn shorte tyme fledde the reame for relygyon and becom a freer or a moncke and ys dede beyonde the seayes wythe owte issue. PHYLLYPPE he wytheyn a verye shorte tyme solde all his londes and then beynge moste wyckedlye bente he practysed moste falselye and unconsyonabelly to defrowde all thos that hadde delte wythe hym. Fyrste he did thynke wythe monye to have corruptede Mr Cholmeles here howse name was Ser Hewe Cholmele of Cholmeleye in Chesse Shere a man bothe honeste and worshyppefull and he was cosen and here to Rafe Cholmeleye viz his brotheres sone for Ranolfe hadd no issue he was Recorder of London I mene Ranolfe Cholmeleye a longe tyme. This Phillyppe Bassett yn truthe repayred to Ser Hewes howse and moste lamentabellye revayeled unto hym that he was utterlye decayed and that he beynge young was by cunnynge defrowded and compelled for tryfelles to sell his londes and prayed Ser Hewe to be good unto hym and to recompense his curtesye he wolde geve to the same Ser Hewe one thowsante markes yf he wolde accomplyshe his requeste for by lerned cownsell he was putte yn mynde that by Ser Hewes helpe he myght frustrate all the assuranses that he hadd paste for anye parte of his londes that was contayned in the foresede fethemente, for

Chareles is fledde

Phi' solde but all

His develyshe practyses

to do grett wronge

A starke lye

that Phyllypp Basset hadde in all the same premisses but a state upon condysyon whiche condysion broken the hole interese was then forfyted and all the hole ryghte agayne in Ser Hewe and his heres so his menynge was to enter upon Ser Hewes maners of Henton and Mudaven havynge by no colore anye juste ryghte or tytell to the same and by that menes the condysion broken and there upon Ser Hewe to enter upon all Bassetes londes and after shuche eneterye to convaye the same londes in truste to some of Bassettes fryndes.

BUT WHEN the good knyght hadde fullye harde all Bassettes wycked requeste he made hym awnser that he wolde never consente nor yelde to do so vyle and unresonabell thynge. Ser Hewe sayede yt maye be that there be som men that have wyfe and charge that have solde ther one londes to bye your londes and so by this menes yf this sholde take plase theye be by connynge utterlye undon. Farder then Ser Hewe Cholmeleye sayed Mr Bassette yf you have bynne a badde hussebonde the fawte ys yours for my unkell delte justely trulye plenely and fayethefullye wythe you and wythe your fryndes; your father was a man of grett worshyppe and my unkell was of some credyt and the worell knowethe that my unkell was but putt yn by your father in tryste yt never coste hym penye. Mr Bassett yf you will make to me a relese of my londes I will make a relese to you accordynge to trewe menynge and that gratis, I will not have my unkeles name nor yt my one to com yn questyon upon shuche a connynge parte for all your londes or love of a thowsante marke. So Bassett for that tyme departed yn the menetyme ther fell som

stryfe betewexte Ackelonde Donsecome and Russewyll for the maners of Colom John, Ponseforde and Paddebroke all three clemed the same from Bassett and the one of them to begyle the other made an newe supplye to Ser Hewe Cholmeleye. Ther ys

an other knyght in Chesse shere caled Ser John Savege a myghtye man and Ser Hewes nere nyghte burre and grette frynde; this knyght hadde a sonne called John beynge his son and here lyenge in London he was cosened by Bassett so he payed for hym som sexse hundrede powndes and never restored one penye

the foresed Ackelond and his consortes promysed the younge gentylleman that yf by menes of his father he myghte procure Ser Hewe to satysfye ther requeste they wolde of ther one monye geve hym fyftye powndes and Bassette promysed to restore hym agayne the foresed vjC^{li} and in truthe Bassett was bownde in too thowsante pownd to Donsecome to enter in to Mudeven & Henton att all tymes when he sholde be requyred and there upon after Ser Hewes enterye they wolde have all ther convayenes newe from Ser Hewe. The younge Savage thynken thos men wolde have performed ther promyses by all menes porsibell but chefely by his father yndede procured Ser Hewe for the releve of the younge Savage to ylde to ther requeste; then came Bassett downe ynto Devon hopynge to have hadde som gentell rewardes amonge the reste of thos that bofte his londes and when he myght make no more then he rode by Donsecomes requeste and made his enterye upon Mudeven and presentelye Mr John Savage procurede from Ser Hewe a suffycient letter of atturneye to enter yn to all Bassetts londes to the use of Ser Hewe. Bassett made his enterye in September in an° xxix of Ellezabethe [1587] & Savage entered in January in the xxx yere of Ellyzabethe & xvj daye of the same monthe [1588] in to Skyrrydon maner and after and before in to all the reste of Bassettes londes.

When thys was donne then the chefeste procurer of this vyle & unresonabell practes was fyrste begyled Donsecom by name for yn Marche then folloynge Ackelonde Bassett and Russewyll prevylye rode to Ser Hewes howse and ther in there presenes Mr Bassett seled iij severall releses of all his interres in Muddeven & Henton to Ser Hewe all iij of one effecte and Ser Hewe seled the leke releses to Bassett for all his londes and then and there presentelye for one thowsante markes payed to Ser Hewe and to Bassett Ser Hewe made new convayenes of the maner of Colom John to Ackelonde and serten other londes to Russewyll. And the foresed thre releses do this remayne the one wth Ser Hewe the other wythe Ackelonde the thyrde wythe Russewyll: at the doynge of all this there was then presente one Rychard Ewenes boren at Collerudege and then sarvant to Mr Ackelonde whiche dide informe me all the hole mater but when Donsecome harde what was donne then he procured Bassett and they rode to Ser Hewe and ther Donsecome payed one or too hundred powndes and he hadde also newe convayenes for serten londes from Ser Hewe. All this tyme Mr Rudegewaye and I stode styll but when this was donne we hadde thretenynge letteres from Ser Hewe

Bassetts entere

Cholmeles enterye

fo. 75

The desever dissevede

Releses seled

A thowsant markes payd

Londes convayed

My awtor

Dunsecombes jurneye

Letores sent by Cholmele

or at leste yn hys name but in truthe we never made awnser to that letter and sethenes we never harde more from Ser Hewe but the curtes younge gentylleman Mr John Savayge for all his travell and fryndeshyppe never hadde one penye to his charges of Bassett nor of anye of the reste.

Agayne I do note and thynke hit to be trewe that yf Chomles reenterye were good yn dede as I thynke hit not good for that he entered where as he hadde no tytell nor ryght and agayne yt muste be shuche an enterye to putte owte moleste or trobell the honer or tenantes by the menynge of the indenture and there by must sustayne some loste ther was no shuche enterye made by Bassett for he never toke dystresse nor occupyed anye parte of the londes but beynge upon som parte of the londes sayed here I do enter that the selynge of the foresede relese by Bassett and that Ser Hewe accepted the same and the foresede severall somes of monye he muste nedes holde hym selfe fully satysfyede for by the foresede provyso in the indentures Cholmele ys to have the londes but untyll he be satysfyed and yf he have reseved vij or viijC^{li} for a penye damege and a relese of the otheres tytell for the maneres of Henton and Mudeven I hope he muste nedes be satysfyed. Agayne note that Bassettes enterye was made of a myre wronge onlye to defrowe his one actes and dedes a mater agaynste all reson and equyte and there fore no dowte the statute made in the xxvij yere of Quen Ellezabethe [1584/5]^{107} wolde have bynne for us agayne hit were an unresonabell mater that Cholmeleye for no thynge sholde have hadde all thos londes that other men trulye payed for yf the mater sholde have bynne putt in execusyon no dowte the Chanserye wolde have releved us but by the newe covaynes Ackelond Russewyll & Dunsecombe do thynke we shall never take anye advantage of ther londes by menes of our reconysanses but by thes menes will frustrate the same but I do not thynke hyt.

Ther was grett speche delevered by on Trystram Gorge Esquyere and a justes of the pease whiche marryed one Coles dofter and here^{108} that the maner off Skyrrydon was his wyves inherytans and that the Curtenes hadde no tytell nor ryght to the same I hope we nede not to dowte ther tytell for the Curtenes have

---

107. 27 Elizabeth c. 4 An Act against covenous and fraudulent Conveyaunces.
108. Trystram Gorge was of Budockshead, now a ruin, Budshead, at St Budeaux near Plymouth, and married Elizabeth Cole.

hadde the maner in Henrye the VI tyme and ever sethenes untyll the attendor of the Marcus and sethenes the prynse Ser Gawyn and I have hadde hit quyettely and for that dyveres fynes have paste Mr Gorge & his heres are clerelye barred.

Agayne I have bynne thretened that yt sholde be persell of the erreldom of Devon but dowte not that for this maner was one Boyvyles londes and from hym yt came to Ser Hewe Corteneye of Hackecom and yn the yende to the Erell of Devon. I have sene in wrytynge under sele that one Bonyfante bayelefe of the Castell of Exon' reseved of Boyvyle then lorde of Skyrrydon iij^s for a heye rente so hit sholde seme that the maner was then holden of the lorde of the Castell of Exon', the dede berethe date in Edward the III tyme. I have harde that Boyvyle lord of Skyrrydon was attaynted in the stryfe betewex Henrye the VI and Edward the IIII.

The ereles tytell

Exon

Ther ys Recordes in the Eschecor in the pype offes that one Water Debenies ofte to paye three arroes to the kynge when he commethe to hunte in the forrest of Dartemore for serton londes in Skyrrydon for the whyche we goo yerely iij^s to mersementes and I was forsed to paye the same to one Willyam Foxsewill when he was undershryfe and never before nor sethenes.

Marke this

Agayne yt dothe appere by all our olde accowntes that there was yerely payed to the pryer of Plymton ij^s for the heye rente of Skyrrydon but sethenes the attendor of the marcus never now payed.

The priers tytell

But howe or of whom so ever the maner or memberes were holden yt is serten that nowe the prynse hathe created a newe tenure so that nowe we muste holde the same of the prynse yn capytye and that by the fortye parte of a knyghtes fee. Item ther was a condysyon yn the dede of bargayne and sale that yf Roberte Furse did not paye to Phillyppe Bassett the viC^li the xxv day of November in an° 1580 then the sale or grante of no forse. Item accordynge to the same condysyon or covenante the viC^li was trulye payed to Basset yn the presenes of Humfrye Predeaxse John Machen John Hoyell Willyam Foxsewill George Pollarde John Fetherstone Fardenando Fryckelton and Water Foxse for the prove there of I have a suffyciante relese or acquyttans from

The tenure in dede

This condic' performed

Phillyppe Bassett under hys honde and sele yn the presenes of all the foresede persones berynge date the xxv daye of November an° xxiij Ellezab[t] [1580] kepe sure that acquyttans what so ever happen.

Note my charge for Chareles Bassetes assurans coste me x[li].

The mony payde

Farder note that at Mr Bassettes requeste yn truthe for hym I was bownde by recognysans in the Chancerye in CC marke to one Willm Stonynge for the payemente of C[li] the xxvj daye of November in an° xxiij of Ellezb[t] [1580]. Item this C[li] was also then trulye payed to Willyam Stonnynge accordynge to the condysyon of the recognysans in the presens of John Yoaye and Water Foxse for the whiche I have also a quyttans from Stonynge but kepe sure that acquyttans becose the recognysans ys not yt canseled.

[*There is no fo. 77.*]

fo. 78

The perticular devysyon of all the severall parsels or closes of the berten:

The berten off Skyrrydon[109] yt lyethe yn Denepryer John Hele the yelder and John Hele his son do nowe cleme to holde the same by copye of curte roll for the terme of ther lyves for the yerelye rente of iij[li] vj[s] viij[d] and sute to our curte and to Lydforde curte and yn all other respectes charged as a customarye tenante theye paye ther beste beste for a herret and xij[d] for fyftydole and [ ] for vendevyle rente.

The mansyon howse the curtelage and towne plase ij akeres The Furse parke xv akeres the Sondeparke x akeres the Wester Parke viij akeres the Brodaparke xij akeres The Brodemede vij akeres The Clevaparke viij akeres the Bromeparke vij akeres Brendon parke vij akeres the Bromeball iiij akeres the Bere one aker and halfe The Willeparke vj akeres the Barne parke x akeres the medes fyeve akeres the gardenes halfe one aker Skyrrydon downe Cl akeres Hollagrepe xl akeres.
Sm[a] to. CClxxxviij akeres.

Note that this Hollagrepe ys nowe usede for persell of the berten but yn truthe yt was persell of the lordes waste and was fyrste

---

109. Skyrrydon. Skirraton Estate (Yarde-Buller) was recorded as a house and curtilage in the tithe award. It survives as a farm but the house is not old.

inclosede by one Wyllyam Hele yn Quene Maryes tyme but now by an agremente Hele ys to have hyt.

Yn the xvj of Kynge Richard the seconde [1392/3] Boyevyle then lord of the maner dyd dewell at Skyrrydon and there the tenantes were bownde to do ther dewe dayes yt dothe appere that yn Kynge Henry the VII tyme one Croppen helde hyt by dede but in xij of Henry the VII [1496/7] was the fyrste coppye and ever sethenes helde by copye.

For the dewe dayes

THERE ys also serten other londes adynynge to the barten parsell of the maner som parte knowen by stones and the reste by bankes but no parte ther of as yt inclosede, yt ys nere C akeres but here note the free tenante of Rede Clefe dothe cleme some xl akeres but yf theye wyll have hyt lett them showe for hyt.

fo. 79

Note that Hewe Hele the free tenantes tenante for Redeclefe dyd cutte the fearnes in som persell of the wastes that they cleme for the soyle of Redeclefe by my lycens. Agayne note that fyftye yeres paste one James Maddycke then bayelyefe and depute to Ser Thomas Dennes then lorde of Buckefastemore was resysted by the tenantes of Skyrrydon for drenynge of this waste and ther well betten. Agayne Willm Hedde was accusede in Skyrrydon curte for dyggen of stones yn this waste or open grownde yn the xxv yere of Quene Ellezab* [1582/3] and for the same made fyne.

Marke this

And note this

This waste hathe bynne dyveres tymes vewed by the tenants but yn the xxxv yere of Ellz [1592/3] yt was vewed bothe by Ser Thomas Dennes tenantes and the tenantes of Skyrrydon onlye for the stone or bonde called Duckeston. Marke this spessyallye that Buckefaste more ys sertenlye knowen by bandes then our maner adyunynge to ther bondes muste nedes be our londes for ther is no man else that hathe anye londes there so the prove of ther bondes dothe make serten where our londes lyethe.

The vewes

SKYRRYDON WODE ys by existimasion C akeres of londe yt lyethe in Dene Pryer. There were serten of the customary tenantes that yn truthe did use the occupasyon of the harbage as parsell of ther tenementes whiche was more then yn ryghte dyde belonge unto ther severall tenures for marke yn Kynge Richard the secondes tyme Henry the IIII and Henrye the Vth tyme the tenantes accused from curte to curte for pasturynge yn the lordes wode

fo. 80

but I suppose that after the lorde dewelled from the barten the pasture then off small valye the tenantes adyunynge by sufferans did inyoye the same, but nowe yt ys yn my one possessyon or occupasyon and was by Ser Gawyn Carewes tyme, and by this menes I did putt all the tenantes from the same. Ser Gawyn havynge a grett malles unto me and by all menes porsybell was redye to hynder me I thofte hyt but resonabell to take and inyoye that was myne and by this tytell or menes I came to tharbage of the wode that ys to saye Kynge Henry the VIII was honer of the maner of Skyrrydon and so beynge honer in the xxxiij yere of his rayne [1541/2] by his lettores patenes he did grante all the manere wythe his memberes to Ser Gawyn and to his wyfe for

The onlye menes that I have the wode

terme of ther lyves excepte the wode and serten other thynges: this excepsion myghte not hurte the interres of the tenantes that then were ynteresse but theye all that were then tenantes be nowe dedde and thos that be nowe tenantes have ther copyes from Ser Gawyn and he can grante no better interres then he hathe hym selfe whiche by menes of the excepsyon ys no thynge at all then all that was in the prynse was solde to Bassett and Bassett solde hyt to Furse and there upon Furse entered and ever sethenes he hathe inyoyede the same.

For the warde

NOTE there ys no ward betewexte the maner of Skyrrydon and Dene pryer whiche hathe bynne the occasyon of grett quareles and the bestes of bothe partes immpownded and dyveres deleveranses pleded but never no tryall but here marke well

A custom' mile

thos notes. Item in the xiiij yere of Kynge Richarde the seconde [1390/1] then ther was a customarye mylle yn Skyrrydon wode for prove there was then one Willyam Bynnemore myller accused in Skyrrydon curte for kepynge of to monye hynnes and capones at the myll and for taken of excessyve tolle and one Wyse then a customarye tenante then in the same curte suede the myller for yell gryndynge of hys corne and yn the ij yere of Henrye the IIII [1400/1] then one Voyesye myller had an accyon in Skyrrydon curte agaynste one Bonde a customarye tenante for not gryndynge of hys corne to the customarye mylle. Agayne in the seconde yere of Henrye the Vth [1414/15] one Thuscombe a custom' tenante was accused in Skyrrydon curte and ther made

Accused for fysshynge

fyne for not gryndynge of his corne to the lordes myll; and yn the iij yere of Henry the IIII [1401/2] one Tolchard was accused

in Skyrrydon curte for fysshynge in the water of Denborne yn
the xxiiij and xxv of Henrye the sexte [1445–7] then one Foxse   Pro gurgit'
presented for not paynge of his rente viz xij^d a yere pro gurgito suo
molendino and yn the xxxj of the same Henry [1452/3] the mylle
trowe was solde; note as I have bynne informed that Foxes mylle
did stonde yn Denewode for the whiche he payed xij a yere for
his were for yn the xxij yere of Henrye the VII [1506/7] ther was   *fo. 81*
one Jeferye Foxse accusede yn Skyrrydon curte *quia fregit unam*
portam super bedam molendino [sic] *et extra maner' portavit*
and yn the seconde yere of Henrye the VIII [1510/11] the pryor
of Plymton then lorde of the maner of Denepryer was accusede   Voyes were
yn Skyrrydon curte for Voyes hedde were agaynste Tynneren
mede and for the same was contynuallye amersed untyll the xxx
yere of the same Henrye [1538/9]. Yn the xiij yere of Henrye
the VIII [1521/2] one Alse Phyllyppe did by copye take one   The token
tokenmyll yn Skyrrydon wode that one Thomas Phillyppe before   mylle
helde, agayne yn the xxxvij yere of the same Henry [1545/6]
one Xper Phillyppe in Skyrrydon curte by copye did take the
reversion of the tokenmyll yn Skyrrydon wode, agayne in the
xiiij yere of Quene Ellezabethe [1571/2] one Thomas Phillyp did
in Skyrrydon curte by copye did take agayne the same myll. Item
yn the xxiij yere of the same Quene [1580/1] the same Thomas
in Skyrrydon curte was presented for that the same myll was
utterlye decayed and for the sufferans there of payed yerely one
capon at Micaellmas and allthoffe the myll ys utterlye decayed
yt the accustomed rente ys dewlye payed. By THYS yt is manyfeste   Marke then
that this CC yeres there hathe bynne a myll yn Skyrrydon wode   this
fyrste a custommarye myll, then a tokenmyll but nowe a decayed
mylle and that alwayes frelye wythe owte anye maner of charge
for were water or water curse to the lordes of Denepryer and that
the lordes of Skyrrydon was onlye lorde and m^r of Denborne, for
prove Foxse payed rente *pro gurgito*, Jeferye Foxse accused *pro*
portam &c, the pryer hym selfe accused for Voyes hedde were, and
Tolcharde accused for fysshynge and the prynse hathe granted to
Bassette by lettores patenes yn as ampell a maner as the marcus
hadde the same and Furse hathe all that Bassett hadde. FOR THE   For the warde
WARDE note that yn truthe the londes on bothe sydes the Rever
of Denborne was all wodes and the pasture of small valye and by
that menes no warde mentayned on nether syde to the knowlege
of anye person nowe levynge but yt ys reported that Deneparkes

was in tyme a dereparke for at this daye yt is knowen by the name of Deneparke and grett decayede hagges do ther appere, agayne note that Kynge Henrye the VIII was honer of the maners of Denepryer and Skyrrydon and all at one tyme but fyrste lord of Skyrrydon and the maner of Denepryer was solde to Gyles xij yeres before the maner of Skyrrydon was solde to Bassett. So then yf hyt were ons a dereparke then no dowte the honer of the parke mentayned the warde but yf there were no ward serten then Gyles beynge the fyrste purchaser no dowte was bownd to warde agaynste the prynse so ons chargeabell styll chargeabell but Gyles sayethe that ther was a ward of late yeres mentayned upon Skyrrydon by all the Ryver of Denneborne. True hyt is that nere xviij yeres paste Bassett then lorde of Skyrrydon wode solde the wode to one Awsten and bownd Awsten havynge no interres in the soyel for Ser Gawyn was then levynge that Awsten and his assynes sholde for the preservasyon of the copes make a suffyciante warde accordynge to the forme of the statute and Austen and his assynes for the only preservasion of the copes and to avoyed the penaltye of the statute havynge no interres in the soyell to that yende made the warde and not a warde to devyde the soyell but only for the preservasyon of the copes and after when the tyme of the preservasyon of the coppes was expyred then Furse toke awaye the same to his one use as lawfull was for hym to do.

AND AGAYNE yf Gyles will have Furse mentayne all the warde then hyt muste be serten yn what plase the warde sholde be for the rayeles were dyveres tymes altered for yn some plases the raye[l]s adyuned to the ryver and in som plases farre from the rever and yn som plases no reles att all for that that was don was by strongeres and that onlye for the preservasion of the copes and not to devyde the londes for theye hadde no interres nor ryght to the londes but to the wode onlye and therefore no dowte the acte donne by one that ys a myre stronger and that hathe anye interres yn the londes shall never charge the free holte of anye person by anye lawe or reson or good consyenes and agayne marke well yf the water be ours as by the foresed proves and resones yt is manyfeste then hit ys no reson nor equyte for Furse to awarde owte his one commodytye to preferre a stronger.

HORRATON ys a tenemente[110] and persell of the maner of *fo. 83*
Skyrrydon yt lyethe yn Denepryer yt is nowe in the tenure of
Water Tokerman he payethe yerelye for rente xij^s and sute to
the curte and to the curte of Lydforde and payethe yerely for
vendevile rente [ ] and for fyftyedole [ ]^d and this devyded viz,
note they paye ther beste beste for a herrett: [*blank*] one garden
and one curtelage one quarter of one aker, the Willeparke iij
akeres, the Sondeparke v akeres, the Barne parke too akeres, the
myddell parke iij akeres, the Wodeparke ij akeres and halfe, the
marell parke ij akeres and halfe.

Sm^a to. xviij akers one q^r.

HORRATON DOWNE ys also a tenemente and persell of the maner
of Skyrrydon yt lyethe in Denepryer yt is nowe yn the tenure of
John Parnyll for the yerelye rente of x^s and sute to our curte and
to the curte of Lydforde theye paye ther best beste for a herrett
and vendvyle rent [ ] and for fyftyedole [ ]^d. [*blank*] This devyded
[*blank*] one close called [*blank*].

Sm^a to x. akeres.

DENECOME[111] ys also a tenemente and ys persell of the maner *fo. 84*
of Skyrrydon yt lyethe in Denepryer and ys nowe yn the tenure
of Pasco Perye for xxvj^s viij^d rente and sute to ou^r curte and to
the curte of Lyddeforde he payethe yerelye for vendevyle rent
[ ] and for fyftydole [ ]^d and his beste beste for a herrett and
this hyt ys devyded viz [*blank*]. The howses curtelage and too
gardenes halfe one akere, the Norrawaye vij akeres, the Wester
ende v akeres, the pese iij akeres, the myddell parke vj akeres, the
Bakehowse parke vj akeres, and the medes too akeres.

Sm^a to. xxix akeres and halfe.

DENECOME one other tenemente and yt is persell of the foresede *fo. 85*
maner of Skyrrydon yt is nowe in the tenure of Edwarde Prowse
for the yerelye rente of v^s and at Micaellmas in lewe of v dewe
dayes x^d and sute to our curte and to the curte of Lydeforde he
payeth for vendevyle rente [ ] and for fyftyedole vj^d and v^s for a
herrett and hit is this devyded, one meddowe one aker, one close
ij akeres, the howses curtelage and garden quarter of one aker.

Sm^a to. iij akers one qr^a.

110. Horraton, parcel of Skyrrydon, in Dean Prior: not traced.
111. Denecombe, Deancombe: Deancombe is an extant settlement. 1 and 2 Combe
  Cottages, Grade II listed, was one house in the late sixteenth century. Dean Mill
  and Miller's House are Grade II listed, as *c.* seventeenth century (SX 723644).

DENECOME ys also one other tenemente and yt is persell of the maner of Skyrrydon and ys nowe yn the tenure of Gellen Sperke for the rente of v^s and at Micaellmas in lewe of v dewe dayes x^d and sute to our curte and to the curte of Lydford and payethe yerelye for vendevyle rente [ ] and vi^d for fyftyedole and v^s for a herrett and this hyt is devyded that is to saye the howse gardenes and curtelage and one meddowe thre quarteres of one aker, the Hyer Close ij akeres and halfe, the lower Close too akeres and halfe.

Sm^a to. v akeres three q^{rs}.

fo. 86   DENECOME ys also one other tenemente yt lyethe yn Denepryer and hit is persell of the foresede maner of Skyrrydon yt is now in the tenure of Johan Norrawaye for the yerelye rente of v^s and at Micaellmas in lewe of v dewe dayes x^d and sute to our curte and curte of Lyddeforde. She payethe for a herrett v^s and for vendevyle rente [ ] and for fyftyedole vj^d and hit is this devyded, the howses curtelage gardenes and the Close too akeres, the meddowe one aker.

Sm^a to. iij akeres.

DENECOME ys also an other tenemente in the tenure of the same Johan and ys persell of Skyrrydon maner her rente ys iiij^s her herrett iiij^s and at Micaellmas in lewe of iij dewe dayes viij^d sute to our curte & to Lydforde curt. She payethe for vendevyle rente [ ] and for fyftyedole vj^d and hyt is this devyded, viz. the howses curtelage garden and one close of londes ij akeres and halfe.

Sm^a to. ij akeres and halfe.

fo.87   DENECOME ys also one other tenemente and persell of the foresede maner of Skyrrydon and ys nowe yn the tenure of Margerett Philyppe for vj^s rente and at Micaellmas in lewe of iij dewe dayes vj^d the herrett vj^s sute to the curte and to Lydforde curte she payethe for venvyle rente [ ] and for fyftyedole vj^d and this hit is devyded, the howse curtelage and gardenes wythe the meddowe one aker, the Reckeparke and the Wodeparke iiij akeres, note the myll ys upon her copye but there ys no londes belongen to the mill theye have but a myll onlye in Skyrrydon Wode but yt the Phillypes did cleme ner halfe one aker.

Sm^a to. v akeres and halfe.

DENECOME ys also an other tenement and persell of the maner of Skyrrydon yt is nowe in the tenure of Andro Foxse for one penye rente but after Andero the rente muste be v^s and at Micaelmas for v dewe dayes x^d & sute to our curte & at Lydford & v^s for the herrett he payethe for vendevyle rente [ ] and for fyftyedole vj^d and this devyded, viz. the howse gardenes and one close of londes of ij akeres and halfe.

Sm^a to. too akeres and halfe.

[*There is no fo. 88.*]

DENECOME there ys also one other tenemente ther that of late *fo. 89* was persell of one Andero Foxes tenemen yt is but a howse and a lytell garden ther rente is iiij^s and sute to the curte and hit is nowe in the tenure of Willyam Tolcharde.

DENECOME there ys also one other tenemente persele of the maner and was a decayed howse of late persell of Andro Foxes tenemente yt is nowe yn the tenure of Richard Cornyshe for ij^s rente, yt is but a howse and a garden.

HETHEFYLDE[112] lyethe in Denepryer yt ys persell of the maner *fo. 90* of Skyrrydon yt is nowe yn the tenure of Mathewe Torner for iiij^s rente & iiij^s herrett & sute to our curte and to the curte of Lyddeforde he payethe for vendevyle rente [ ] and for fyftyedole [ ]^d yt is devyded ynto v perseles the hole nere xx akeres of londes. I suppose this in tyme was a free tenemente for the olde rente but ij^s & c.

Sm^a to. xx akeres.

TYNNEREN mede ys also persell of the maner of Skyrrydon yt lyethe yn Denepryer yt is nowe yn the tenure of John Foxse for iiij^s rente & iiij^s for a herrett and sute to our curte and to the curte of Lydforde he payethe for vendevyle rente [ ] and for fyftyedole [ ]^d, yt is but one meddowe of one aker and one quarter. Note that in consederasyon of the grante of this meddo and Andro Foxses tenemente Furse ys to have for one penye a hundrede suffyciante marell for hym selfe and for all his tenantes in Foxes quarye adyunynge to Prowses mede durynge John Foxes terme.

Sm^a to. one aker q^r.

112. Hethefylde in Dean Prior; not traced.

SHUTTACLEFE[113] ys persell of our maner of Skyrrydon Mr Richard Voyell ys our free tenante his heye rente ys iij^d in monye and one pownde of waxse and to do sute to our curte at [*for* and] to Lydford curte he payethe for vendevyle rente yerelye [ ] and for fyftyedole [ ]^d what his tenure ys I am unserten for in som olde recordes I fynde his serves Knyghte serves and yn som other socage tenure his releve unserten and therfor make som furder inquerye yt is too closes of londes and hit ys adyunynge to Horraton Downe.

fo. 91

REDECLEFFE[114] ys also persell of the maner of ~~Denepryer~~ Skyrrydon yt lyethe in Denepryer John Edwardes of Holberton[115] is nowe lord he is our free tenante he dothe paye yerely for heye rent vj^s and sute to our curte and curte of Lyddeforde he payethe for vendevyle rente [ ] and for fyftydole [ ]^d. I fynde in some of the olde recordes that hit is holden by knyghte serves and som other plase by socage the releve sholde seme to be vj^s.

Note thys Simon

Ric'

Knight

vj^d recogn'

In the lordes hondes

BUT HERE note that one Symon Redeclefe was honer off Redeclefe yn the seconde yere of Kynge Richard the Seconde [1378/9] he hade issue Richarde and yn an^o the vj of the same Richarde [1382/3] ther was a strayer presented that came to Redeclefe in the custody of Thom' Knyght; Richard Redeclefe amersed for his sute in an^o xiij of Ric' the seconde [1389/90] and yn the xiiij yere of the same Richard Redeclefe did his fealtye and payde vj^d *pro recognisione*. Yn Henry the sexte tyme ther was bothe John Redeclefe the yelder and John the younger for John the yelder yn Skyrrydon curte was accused for drevynge a dystresse from Redeclefe owte of the lybertye this was donne in the xxiiij of the same Henrye [1445/6]. Then yn the xxv^{ti} John the younger one Hayeman of Plymebrydege and Alse his wyfe all accusede in Skyrrydon curte for taken a waye of serten catell. Note at iiij severall curtes holden at Skyrrydon yn the foresede xxiiij and xxv yeres of Henry the VI [1445–7] dyveres persones and one Redeclefe amonge otheres were ponyshed for the occupyenge of the lordes pasture at Redeclefe and one Richard Moresehed

---

113. Shuttaclefe, untraced, parish unknown.
114. Redecleffe, in Dean Prior. It was extant in the tithe award as Redicleave, owned by the Yarde Bullers; Reddacleave on the modern map, at SX700639.
115. John Edwards of 'Holberton'. It is not clear if this is Halberton, Holbeton, or even Harberton. The Harbourne River runs through Dean Prior. In the 1581 subsidy a John Edwards heads the Dean Prior taxpayers (Stoate, *Devon Taxes 1581–1660*, p. 49).

accusede for taken of serten streke at Redeclefe, note also that John Redeclefe the yelder John Redeclefe the younger and one Thomas Knyghte in the viij yere of Kynge Henrye the fythe [1420/1] were all indyted of fellonye.

Felonye

NOTE FARDER that the heye rente of Redeclefe yn the fyrste seconde thyrde fowerthe fythe and sexte yeres of Kynge Edward the fowerthe [1461–7] and before was but xx^d a yere but yn the xiiij yere [1474/5] one Browne payed then vj^s a yere and hathe contynewed ever sethenes vi^s a yere for the heye rente of Redeclefe. Agayne in the xvij yere of Kynge Henrye the VIII [1525/6] the dethe of Johan Foxse in Skyrrydon curte was presented that she dyede sesede but of the one moytye of tenemente in Redeclefe and fownd Johan Rowe the wyfe of Richarde Rowe to be her onlye dofter and here the releve iij^s and the rente iij^s. Yn all our recordes yt dothe not appere by what tytell Browne came to the londes nor howe ys his here nor when he dyed nor wher he hade the fee sympell or tenante by lese but yn the x yere of Henry the seventhe untyll Quene Maryes tyme [1494–*c*.1558] one Thomas Furse and John Furse did all wayes paye the rente sute and serves for the londes of Redeclefe.

By thys hit dothe appere that one Redeclefe was honer of the londes called Redeclefe but where this londes have paste by dyssente or alynated I do not lerne hyt by anye recorde but I do marvayll by what tytell the lorde of the maner of Skyrrydon sholde have the same for yt ys serten that the lorde hadde hit wher by eschete or garden or other wyse I am not serten and agayne do marvayle whye the rente and releve sholde be incresed and where as all the reste of the free tenantes do paye ther rente only at Micaelmas the tenante of Redeclefe do nowe paye ther rente quarterly as the customary tenantes do; agayne I do not understonde why Johan Rowe sholde have the hole londes the tenantes fonde her here but for the one halfe and John Furse one of the homage. Agayne yf hit were all one manes londes whye sholde Hayeman his wyfe and Redeclefe make ther tytell all at one tyme and longe before that one Knyght and Redeclefe dewellede at Redeclefe and bothe did sutte to our curte. Note that ther ys a lytell persell of londes adyunynge to Skyrrydon yate and yt was called Furses londes whiche londes as I do suppose was persell of the lordes wastes and upon the inclosyer there of the rente myghte be incresede.

Marginal notes:
- The heye rente altered
- The dethe of Johan Foxse
- Johan Rowe tenante for medietatu'
- The some of all
- *fo. 92*

Ther tytell

BUT WILL YOU here ther tytell theye saye that Steven Browne in Ed. the IIII tyme made a lese of the londes in Redeclefe to one Marten and otheres and that one John Foxse and Johan his wyfe mad a lese of the londes in Redeclefe in Kynge Henrye the VII tyme to one Thomas Furse and others farder that Johan Rowe in Kynge Henrye the VIII tyme did by fethemente geve all her londes in Redeclefe to one John Edwardes & his heres, they saye that everyeche of the foresede Marten and Furse by forse of ther severall leses did inyoye the hole of the londes called Redeclefe and Edwards and his predyssessores have bynne alwayes accepte sole lordes of the londes in Redeclefe and have reseved the issues and profytes there of holy to ther one use and therefore the londes muste nedes be theres.

Roberte overtaken

ADMYTT that they made leses resevede rente and a fethemente was made, this myghte theye do yf theye hadde but a porsyon of the londes by the name of all ther londes. But here note that longe before Roberte Furse was honer of the maner of Skyrrydon yt was his unhappye locke to be retorned upon John Edwardes offes fownd before the escheator and upon the othe of one sympell man the jurye fownde the londes to be holden by fealtye onlye nowe when Furse came to be lorde of the maner he fownde by his recordes that the londes to be holden by knyghte serves and

but note this

John Edwardes hym selfe yn the xxvj yere of Quene Ellezabet [1583/4] in the open curte did fealtye to Furse then lorde of the maner of Skyrrydon for serten londes that he helde of the lord by knyghte serves: he holdethe no other londes but Redeclefe, upon all those cawses take good cunsell yf you do dele wythe them.

fo. 93
The tenure

STANCOMBE[116] ys a member of the maner of Skyrrydon yt lyethe wythe yn the parryshe of Ilsyngeton and maner of Ingesdon this londes was holden by knyghte serves of one Hewe Pomeroye lorde of the maner of Ingesdon the heye rente iiij^s ij^d and sute to the curte but nowe we do holde the londes of our Soverante ladye the Quene in capite as yt is a fore sayed but the heye rente only ys payed but no other sute nor serves. This londes was one

The succession and change of men

Skyrrynes and from Skyrrynes yt came to one Stancombe and from Stancome to one Taverner and he solde hit to one Cocke he hadde issue one Mycaell he solde the same to one Loker and

116. Stancombe, a member of Skyrrydon, but in the parish of Ilsington and the manor of Ingesdon (*PNDevon* II, p. 478; SX804735). The tithe award gives Higher, Middle and Lower Stancombes, but apparently only one homestead, at no. 456.

Kyngesforde and they solde hit to Ser Hewe Curteneaye he hade issue one son whiche dyede wythe owte issue and by that menes hit came to the Errell of Devon and so to the Marcus of Exon' and by his attendor yt came to the prynse and from the prynse to Bassett and from Bassett to Furse.

THERE HATHE bynne some questyon and dowte wher Stancombe Hocon Lytell Kynedon Churcheber and Fostardes Parkes do passe to Bassett and Cholmeleye yn ther lettores patenes becose theye be not ther resyted by pertyculer names but the maner onlye wythe his memberes: to awnser thys Stancombe Hocon Lytell Kynedon Churchebere and Fostardes Parkes can not be conseled as theye pretende, for the lettorse patenes be clere on our syde, for no dowte at the tyme of the grante and ever sethenes the laste yere of Kynge Henrye the sexte [1483] yt hathe bynne unyeted and accepted for a member of the manere of Skyrrydon for all the perseles of londes were then granted by copye yn Skyrrydon curte and ther did ther sute fealty and serves and in Skyrrydon curte presented for all contempts and thynges donne contrarye to the custom, there dethes herretts decaye of howses hagges strayeres sensores ale wyghtes assawtes presented yn Skyrrydon curte and there theye made all ther surrenderes yn the marcus tyme and befor and yn the tyme hyt was the kynges one possessyon and ever sethenes.

The dowte of our letores patenes

To awnser this note

AND farder here note that we cleme hit from the prynses grante and not from my lorde marcus or from anye of his awnsettores and agayne marke that yn the lettores patenes the maner of Skyrrydon and Sowthe Allyngeton ys valyed in xxv^{li} x^s. I am sure that Allyngeton the rente ys but xij^{li} x^d and all the londe of the maner of Skyrrydon yn Denepryer ys but viij^{li} xj^d one pownde of waxse so wytheowte the foresed memberes thes too maneres can not be of the clere yerely valy of xxv^{li} x^s ther will lacke iij^{li} xix^s ij^d besyde fees and other charges. NOWE then yf theye wyll thes memberes or severall quyllets aforesede to be conseled londes yn dede as by dyveres I have bynne myghtylye thretened then no dowte theye muste prove the same londes to be no parte nor persell or member of Skyrrydon maner nor so usede accepted or taken at the tyme of the grant or before but that theye are thynges serten of them selves or a member or som parte of som other maner and so usede tyme owte of mynde. I am sure yt was

Not of the valye

Marke well this

no abbye londes nor churche londes nor that the prynse was ever yn anye possessyon or toke anye of the issues or profyttes there of but only by the attendor of the marcus of Exon' as lorde of the maner of Skyrrydon, agayne what althoffe som parte of thes memberes before hyt came to the prynse were holden of other men and dyd lye in severall maneres there was none of them hadde anye uses or profytes there of but only for ther sute heye rentes and servyses; the lorde of Skyrrydon only as a member did take all the issues & profytes to his one use this CC yeres.

fo. 94

The fulle
conclusion

WHAT better or plener prove can ther be to prove thos foresede perseles or quylletes of londes to be memberes annyxsede yn dede to the maner of Skyrrydon then the tenantes this monye yeres to holde the same bye cope of curte roll taken in Skyrrydon curte and that accordynge to the custom of the same maner and ther theye have payed alwayes ther rentes to the balyefes of the maner of Skyrrydon and yn Skyrrydon curte theye have made surrenderes fealtye and amersed for not doynge of there sute and serves and this hathe contynewed this too hundred yeres. Agayne the too maneres be not of the valy of xxv^{li} x^{s} there will lacke iiij^{li} xix^{s} ij^{d} yf thes memberes sholde not be persell. The grante yn the lettores patenes ys as well by spessyall wordes the memberes wythe ther appurtynanses generall as the maner and all messuages londes tenementes of what kynde so ever they be or where so ever they lye wythe yn the Cowntye of Devon or at anye tyme before the date there of usede occupyed or inyoyed as parte persell or member of the maner or of hys memberes yn so ampell and large a maner as the marcus of Exon' hadde the same or anye other by reson of anye lawfull prescrypsyon tytell use or custom at any tyme before thes lettores patenes granted to Basset and Cholmeleye hadde or usede. So this hathe bynne alwayes usede and inyoyed by the marcus before by the prynse by Ser Gawyn Carewe and ever sethenes as parte persell and a member of the maner of Skyrrydon and so I do hope yt shall stylle contynewe.

fo. 95

Stancome Curteneye

STANKECOMBE ys nowe dyvers tetementes and devyded ynto dyveres menes tenures as his shall here after appere, the gretes porsyon ys nowe in the tenure of Marye Dyggen wyddo for the yerelye rente of xxxiˢ and sute to the curte of Skyrrydon she muste paye her beste beste for a herrett. All Stancombe tennantes have comones upon Hethefylde and thys her parte ys devyded viz:

THE mede iij akeres, the grove ij akeres, hellynge parke v akeres, the lytell mede and the allers one aker and halfe, the flowerynge perke too akeres, too other perseles iij akeres, the lame perke ij akeres, the lytell parke grove and garden iij akeres, the hyll x akeres and halfe, the Bromeparke iij akeres, the Bryggelonde iij akeres, ther ys a how[s]e newly erected.

Smᵃ to. [ ]
The fyftydole for this porsyon ys vjᵈ.

STANKECOM ys an other persell of the foresede premisses yt is also one other tenemente nowe yn the tenure of Richard Hellynges for the yerely rente of xiijˢ and sute to the curte of Skyrrydon and this hit is devyded viz:

the howse the too gardenes and curtelage halfe one aker, the too meddowes one aker, the towneplase one aker, the furse hyll one aker and halfe, the gratten one aker, the marell parke one aker, the longe parke iij akeres, the balle one aker, the Rowe grasse iiij akeres, the torres iij akeres, the wodehedde too akeres, the wode and the wymbesstowe too akeres.

Smᵃ to. [ ]
The fyftydole for this porsyon iiijᵈ.

STANKECOME ys one other quyllett or persell of londes persell of *fo. 96* the foresede premysses yt is nowe yn the tenure of Richarde Furse for the yerely rente of vijˢ and sute to the curte of Skyrrydon and this hyt ys devydede viz:
   one meddowe iij akeres
   one close of londes ij akeres
   on other close ij akeres.

STANKECOME yt is one other quyllett or persell of the foresede premysses yt is nowe yn the tenure of John Frowde for vijˢ rente and sute to the curte of Skyrrydon and this hit ys devyded viz:
   one medowe iij akeres
   one close of londes wythe the boyshes iiij akeres.

fo. 97 STANCOMBE ys also persell of the foresede maner of Skyrrydon and an other quyllett of the foresede premyses, yt ys nowe yn the tenure of Hewe Smerdon for iij^s rente and sute to our curte of Skyrrydon, yt is but one close of londes of iij akeres.

STANCOME this is also one other quyllett or persell of the foresed premysses yt ys nowe yn the tenure of Thomas Rewallen for the yerelye rente of iij^s iiij^d and sute to the curte of Skyrrydon his herrett ys iij^s iiij^d and this hyt is devyded viz:

the meddo one aker, the brode mede ij akeres, the stroberye parke one aker, the boyshes too akeres, the lytell parke one aker, the innseparke one aker.

Sm^a to. [ ]

This payethe for fyftyedole [ ] and for oxilyon rente ij^d.

fo. 98 CHURCHEBERE alias Chettesbere[117] this ys also a member of Skyrrydon and was one Churcheberes londes and for wante of issue yt dyssendede to his syster whiche marryed one Hole and one Hole did sell the same to Ser Hewe Curteneye then he annexsede the same to the maner and ever sethenes used as Stankeham hathe bynne and by dyssente hyt came to the marcus of Exon and by his attendor to the prynse so to Bassett and from hym to Furse. This londes was in trobell one Storgion made tytell but Ser Hewe hadde the same quyett and so ever sethenes yt hathe contynued. This Churchebere lyethe wythe yn the parrysshe off Ilsyngeton yt is a tenemente and serten londes nowe yn the tenure of Pasco Stancombe yn the ryght of his wyfe for the yerely rente of xxviij^s viij^d and sute to the curte of Skyrrydon and a beste beste for a herrett and this devyded viz:

The howse orchard curtelage and waste halfe one aker, Churchebere downe xx akeres, the mede iij akeres and halfe, the too marel parke iiij akeres, the Burche parke iiij akeres, the Brodaparke iij akeres, the bere one aker.

Sm^a to. xxxvj akeres

Note this tenemente hath also commones in the Hethefylde. I suppose this iiij^s ij^d that we paye to the lorde of Ingesdon was the hye rent of Stankecom and Churchebere for more Bemonte that was lorde of Ingestdon never hadde of Curteneye when he hadde bothe Stancombe and Churchebere but Mr Hewe Pomerye

117. Churchebere or Chettesbere in Ilsington parish is lost.

reseved of Manfylde ij[s] a yere for the comones whiche ys more then he ofte to have for Mr Pomerye hathe but commones there hym selfe the soyll of the Hethefylde ys the lordes of the maner of Ilsyngeton and all the strayer and theye do dreve the same and not Mr Pomerye, agayne in the olde copyes it is granted Churchebere lyenge in Stankecom.

FOSTARDES PARKES[118] ys also a tenemente and a member of the foresede maner of Skyrrydon as ys aforesayede yt lyeth yn Weste Oggewyll parrysshe yt is nowe yn the tenure of one John Wotton for the yerelye rente of x[s] and sute to the curte of Skyrrydon and yt ys devyded nowe ynto dyveres closes viz:
   [blank]

fo. 99
The tenure

THERE was yn the xxxj yere of Quene Ellezabethe [1588/9] one Thomas Renell lorde of Weste Oggewyll maner and a justes of pease made an enterye upon Fostardes parkes and did thynke by strenthe and connynge surelye to have hadde the londes and that wytheowte anye grett coste. Fyrste he made a lese of the same to one Forde for v yeres. Forde presentlye brofte hys accyon Wotton was arrested and juned issue at Hyllyre terme, ther he lette hyt remayne the Lente assyses & lekekewyse at Lamas syses but at the nexte terme after the issue juned he served Furse wythe a suppena; Furse by commyssyon did awnser the same then he exhibited a byll in to the Starre Chamber agaynste Furse and upon Furses awnser in the Chancerye there yt rested and yn dede had proses owte of the Starre Chamber for Furse and made grett showes but he dyd never serve the proses and Furse wytheowte proses wolde not appere nor dydde not, then at laste there happened syckenes the plage ynto Dene perryshe[119] then he procurede one Andro Foxse, a common lyer at the alehowse, to saye that there was a close of londes in Denecome called Fostardes parke. Upon this report at the nexte assyses beynge at Barnestabell he sued forth hys nysyprius hopynge Furse by menes of the syckenes sholde not come to the assyses and wytheall he procured a commyssyon from the juges to have Andro Foxse examyned before the mayre of Tottenes & one Richarde Werren

In lawe with Renales

His polisye

Note Fordes lese will ende the 26 of Maye 1594

Andro Foxse

---

118. Fostardes Park in West Ogwell is Fosters Park in the tithe award where it is no. 68, a house and curtilage in the west of the parish and now part of Metley.

119. Assizes may have been held in Barnstaple in 1590 because of plague; they certainly were in March 1591 (Lamplugh, *Barnstaple*, p. 46; Gray, *Lost Chronicle of Barnstaple*, p. 68).

Werrynge
Aysheleye
sweren

and Richard Aysheleye men of leke credett, but when Foxse in the presenes of the mayre and hys bretheren had tolde them a longe tale he wythe owte anye swerynge departed the towne; then the too other were examyned but they cowde saye no thynge but what they hadde harde Foxse saye, so for that tyme there was no person sweren. Then Mr Renalles by forse compelled thes

wythe owte
commysion

iij dyscryte men to com to Mr George Carye of Cockyngeton and ther the were wythe owte anye commyssyon sweren, but what the swere I do not understond nor I care not for hit, for hit is of no forse, but god be praysed the syckenes sessed at Dene som xij wekes before the syses. Furse procured a sufficiante testymonyall of the same and that he nor anye of his howse was sycke nor non in halfe a myle a nere his howse and by thes menes Furse came to the syses and iiij wyttenes wythe hym whiche was costelye for everye mele was xij^d and there loggynge dere. Furse dyde retayne a sargente and too counseleres the recorde yn curte he dyd thynke verylye that the same wolde have prosyded but all this was donne but yn hope to have Furse to have submytted his cawse to awarde. Mr Richard Sparrowe a justes and Furses

Disseved of his
hope

verye good frynde procured Furse what he myghte to submytte the cose to an awarde but Furse wolde never ylde to that, then when he had spen all the syses and he myght not optayne his purpose he towcke owte the record & so departed and ever senes quyett.

fo. 100
Your one tytell

MARKE well thos spessyall notes for the defense of your tytell fyrste Furse by spessyall wordes upon all his assurans and lycens of alynas[ion] hathe Fostardes parkes the fyne paste in an° xij of Ellez' [1569/70] and Renales made hys enterye but in xxxj of Ellez' [1588/9] and so the v yeres paste wythe owte cleme. Agayne

The lycke

all your awnsyente accowntes from the laste yere of Henry the sexte [1460/1] untyll the x Henrye the VII [1494/5] do prove that all the bayelefes of the maner of Skyrrydon reseved the rente of Fostardes parkes and payde the same at everye awdytt as a persell in charge of the maner of Skyrrydon and yn the xiiij yere of Henry the VIII [1522/3] the dethe of Stanckecom the tenante of Fostardes parke was fownde yn Skyrrydon curte and yn the same yere in the curte of Skyrrydon for iiij^{li} fyne by copye of curteroll accordynge to the custom of the maner sett to too of the Wottones and theye by forse of that copye have inyoyed the same lxx yeres durynge whiche tyme theye were for the same premisses fyrste tenante to the marcus and for the same dyd fealtye in Skyrrydon curte in the xvij of Henry the VIII [1525/6] then nexte the kynges tenantes and did hym fealtye in the xxx yere of his rayne [1538/9], theye were Ser Gawynes tenantes and dyd hym fealtye and sute to the curte; of Skyrrydon, theye were Furses tenant I mene the survyvor and dyd hym feal[t]ye and sute to hys curte; you have suffyciant recordes to prove all thys and durynge the contynuans of this copye theye have styll payd all the rente to the balyefes of Skyrrydon and ther don there sute and serves.

But here beware as the yelder Wotton was tenant for Fostardes parkes to the lorde of Skyrrydon so he was tenante to the lordes of Weste Oggewill for a persell of londes adyunynge to Fostardes parkes called Weste Oggewyll more and for the same payd his rente sute and serves to the lorde of Weste Oggewyll as hys custom[ary] tennant and yf Fostardes parkes hadde benne persell of the maner of Weste Oggewill Wotton nede not com vj myles to Skyrrydon curte. Agayne note Stancomb dewellynge at Matteleye yn Oggewyll curte was accused for an incrochemente upon Fostardes Parkes: you shall understonde in the weste parte of Fostardes parkes there was a waye which Stancom stopped and converted the hole waye to Matteleye grownd and that was the cose he was accused for he cowde not incroche our londes for we make all the hegges rownd. Marke this

AGAYNE note this spessyallye the maners of Oggewill & Skydon were bothe the prynses. Bassett bofte Skyrrydon & the Erell of Beddeford & one Brygges bofte Oggewill, the Erell & Brygges solde hit to one Baker and Coles of London, Coles solde his moyete to Richard Renales and Baker solde his to Ser Ric' Sackefylde after Ser Richard his son my lord Buckehushe solde the other parte to Renell. Durynge all this tyme Wotton occupyed the londes not yn anye of ther ryghtes nor as ther tenantes but the tenante to the lord of Skyrrydon and for the same to them payed his rente sute and serves for Fostardes parkes; here Wotton no dowte was a dyssesor to all the lordes of Oggewyll and they all wythe owte anye enterye upon Fostardes parkes do allenate the londes, yn this case yf Fostardes parke were ther londes in dede there ys no thynge consernynge Fostardes parkes passeth The only menes to barre them by forse of the alynasyon for wante of ther enterye and for them now to enter yt is to late for the dyenge of Bassett and the fynes

A good note

will barre there enterye. Note Oggewyll ys but a Curte baron & no lete for ther sensors and strayers go to the hundred. Oggewyll ys a myxte maner for Wotton ys in Denberye and there payethe a heye rente.

fo. 101

What Renales can allege

NOTE farder theye will showe a curte rolle that one Stancombe in Weste Oggewyll curte by copye did take Fostardes parkes in an° iiij° Henry VIII [1512/13]. Theye do showe also that Fostardes Parke was sett by dede &c. for viij^s rent and that one John Wotton nowe tenante was accused for a waye in Weste Oggewyll curte. Theye do showe also a paper where yn Fostardes parke in a rentall of the maner of Weste Oggewyll ys charged as persell of the maner of Weste Oggewyll; Mr Renales sayethe that there is a Fostardes parkes in Denecome and by that name sett yn Skyrrydon curte yn an° 38 H VI [1459/60]. To awnser the fyrst conseder wythe your selfe that in an° iiij of Henry the VIII [1512/13] the lorde then of

But this will awnser hym

Skyrrydon and Westeoggewyll was but one man and he myght sette his londes where he lyste. I am sure the dethe of Stancombe was fownd yn Skyrrydon curte and ther by copye the londes was granted and the tenantes styll inyoyed the same and payed contynally all there rente sute and serves as persell and member off Skyrrydon as is afore sayed so the settynge of londes in the curte dothe not make the londes persell of the maner but the longe contynuans and payemente of there rentes sute and serves.

To the settynge by dede yt is not materyall becose one man then and longe before and after was lorde of bothe maneres as is aforesede. Yt is not leke to be this Fostardes parkes becose the rente was but viij^s, yt maye be som other londes of that name for our Fostardes parkes longe before and ever sethenes have contynually payed x^s for the rente and yt dothe. For that Wotton was accused yt is not materyall for then these too maneres did belonge to too dyveres lordes so then the soyell maye be in one and the lete or maner in an other man[or] and yf hit be but a curte baron then ther presentement of no forse and so lekewyse yf hit be not presented by a full jurye of xij men yt ys serten that the custommarye tenantes of Oggewill was not then abowve vj or vij: inquer for that. For the rental yn paper yf hyt bere date sethenes an° primo Edward IIII° [1461/2] all your awnsyente accownts will discredyt the same. Item for sertentye there ys no Fostardes parkes in Denecome nor yt in Dene paryshe sett by dede or copye beynge parte parsell or member of Skyrrydon but our Fostardes parkes ys as hit dothe appere by Wottones copye ys Fostardes Parkes juxta Weste Oggewill so the copye yt selfe nameth where our Fostardes Parkes lyethe.

But will you here what Andro Foxse reported he sayed that there was Fostardes parke in Denecome that now ys called Bennets parke and for prove he sayed that in xxxv yere of Henry the VIII [1543/4] one Fostard did dewell yn Denecome under one Bennett Sybleye and this Fostard helde Bennets Close and by that menes called Fostardes parke whiche yn dede was moste false and untrewe. But yt was trewe yn dede that one Fostard a very pore tynner did dewell under Benett he never helde any close there for he never kepte cowe nor yt shepe nor scase a pygge and he contynewed there but a lytell tyme and yn the yende fledde the cunterye he never helde close in his lyfe and this was the grett mater that Foxse was sweren and Werynge and Ayssheley sweren but what they harde Foxse saye, a myghty cose no dowte & of no small credet.

Andro Foxes deposysyon

Good stuffe

Hocon otherwyse called Hoconye[120] ys also a member of Skyrrydon maner as yt is a foresede yt is devyded yn to dyveres tenementes yt lyethe wythe yn the parrysshe of Northe Bovye and wythe yn the hundred of Tyngebrudege, yt is also vyndyvyle and dothe paye for vendevyle rente yerely [ ] and sute to Lydford. I do suppose that this Hocon in tyme was a maner of hit selfe but not sethenes Richard the secondes tyme for yt is juned wythe Skyrrydon in charge for payemente of the fyftye dole. Yt did of olde tyme ever before Quene Maryes tyme wache at Skyrrydon becon, yt was Boyvyles londes and so was Westeoggell maner, this londes also ys holden in capite as aforesede. Remember what I have sayed consernyng Stancom to prove the same a member of Skyrrydon and no consyled londes by the same reson you maye prove Hocon and lytell Kynedone to be lekewyse memberes and persell of the maner of Skyrrydon, note farder from tyme to tyme

fo. 102

The tenure

---

120. Hocon, now Hookney (*PNDevon*, II, p. 470). Lower Hookney farmhouse is grade II listed as probably sixteenth century, although no features earlier than the seventeenth are evident and it was much altered in the twentieth century. Lower Hookner is at SX715824.

the strayeres sensors alewyghtes and all other thynges belongen
to the lete have contynualy bynne presented at Skyrrydon
curte, the tenant of Hocon accused for suynge one of the lordes
tenantes owte of Skyrrydon curte. There ys a grett persell of
londes that ys not yt inclosed called Kynedon; the bandes there

of ys FROM Lansacome as the water there runethe to longestone
alz the brodestone from that stone to one wother stone called the
Shodestone and from thens to Blackeavenhedde and so alonge
the water throffe Grymespownde and from thens contynuyng
the water curse to Cholacome hegge corner and from thens
northe wardes a longe the bocherynge waye untyll you come
to Flowerenlyde yate and from Flowerlyde yate by the Rewe as
hyt lyethe there unto Gollaparke Corner and from thens to the
furderparte or corner of the hagge of the same Gollaparke and
so throffe Wydeslade as the water there runnethe unto Cruston
& c.

Item the xvij daye of September in an° xxxiiij of Ellezb^t [1592]
upon som quarell by the condysente of Ser John Clyfton and
Roberte Furse there was a vewe of the bondes at the whiche
vewe there was presente dyveres customarye tenantes of bothe
maneres and serten strongeres that is to saye Andro Averye,
then reve, John Stocke, John Hele jun', John Hyllynges, Edward
Noseworthye, John Noseworthye, Pole Noseworthye, Willm
Maye, Gregorye Pethebryge, Andro Tomlyn, Falentyne Graye,
Nycolas Leman, Gregorye Lyer, Edward Noseworthye the son
of Peter Noseworthye, Thomas Masye, Crystopher Osseborne,
Thomas Couter, Pankeres Couter, Sylfester Man and Peter
Noseworthye at whyche tyme and plase bothe the partes dyd
agree upon the fyrste three bondes but Mr Clyftones tenantes
wolde not allowe Blackeavenhedde for a bond but assyned
an other plase not far dystante called the Rownd Rynke but
Grymespownd and all the reste of the foresed bondes theye all on
bothe partes did agree to be the trewe bondes, note at the same
tyme and in all there herynge the foresed Nycolas Leman a man
of grett yeres and one of Ser John Clyftones tenantes did confese
that the tenantes of Hokenye did usuallye cutt torves and there
more wode on the syde of Blackeavene lake and the tenantes of
Chollacom on the other syde and the lyke wordes then and there
did one Willyam Maye an olde man boren at Hocon reporte yn

the presens of them all agayne, we have olde recordes to prove strongers accused in Skyrrydon curte for cuttynge of venne in Hokenye waste yn an° 16 of H. VIII [1524/5].

Note farder that yn kynge Henrye the VIII tyme then one Richard Hayedon then chefe stuarde of Skyrrydon curte yn open curte sett downe this order for the occupasyon of Hokeneye waste whiche hathe eversethenes bynne observed viz: *fo. 103* The rate allowed

Grete Kynedon ys porsyoned to have Cxx shepe xvj bollockes iiij horses.

Andro Tomlyn he is to have the lyke viz Cxx shepe xvj bollockes iiij beastes.

Lytell Kenedon to have xxx shepe iiij bollockes one horse.

Mayes bargayne and Noseworthyes whiche of late was but one thynge and nowe devyded ys to have lx shepe viij bollockes too horses.

Pethebrygge ys to have lx shepe viij bollockes too horses or bestes.

HOCON ys one tenement nowe in the tenure of Andero Tomlyn for the yerely rente of x[s] and sute to Skyrrydon curte and to Lydforde he only holdethe by dede and this hit is devyded viz: *fo. 104*
the howses curtelage and one meddo called the longe mede one aker, the haye londe mede one aker, the holamede too akeres, the loyer hollamede iiij akeres, the Splat halfe one aker, the Lammaparke ij akeres and halfe, Hollamede parke too akeres and halfe, the Gratten too akeres and halfe, the Cleve too akeres and halfe, the Newe Parke too akeres and halfe, iiij closes called the Sowthe downe x akeres, Whyttawalles iij akeres, iij closes callede the Charta parkes vij akeres and halfe, iiij other closes called the Hedde londes [ ] akeres, the Crustena iij akeres, the Hyll parke too akeres, halfe the Mowre lyenge under Hollamede vj akeres, besydes all the wastes.

Sm[a] to. [ ]

Note he payethe for fyftyedole xx[d] and his beste beste for a herrett.

HOCON ys also another tenemente nowe yn the tenure of one Gregorye Pethebrygge for the yerelye rente of fyve shellynges and sute to Skyrrydon curte and to Lydeford, he payethe his beste beast for a herret and x[d] for fyftydole, he ys a copyeholder and this devyded:

The Fowtelonde one aker and halfe, the Northeyn towne too akeres, one other lytell close one aker, the Wyllredden Close one aker and halfe, the Grett Close ij akeres, there be too other closes iiij akeres, the Hyll ij akeres and halfe, the Willredden mede halfe on akere, the lower more iiij akeres, the other more too akeres, the home mede half one aker.

Sm^a to. [ ]

fo. 105 Hocon yt is an other tenemente nowe yn the tenure of Willyam Maye and Edwarde Noseworthye but theye have devyded the same and this ys Mayes parte folloynge viz:

The Slade to akeres, the Corner Parke one aker, the Downeparke iij akeres, the Hullonde one aker and halfe, the Mede one aker and halfe, the Mowre iiij akeres.

Sm^a to. [ ]

Maye holdethe hit by copye his rente is [ ] and sute to Skyrrydon curte he payethe for fyftyedole [ ] and a best best for a herret.

Hocon the other moyete nowe yn the tenure of Edwarde Noseworthe for the yerely rente of [ ] and sute to the curte of Skyrrydon & Lydforde he payethe for fyftydole [ ] and thys hyt is devyded viz:

The hylle too akeres halfe, the Brodaparke too akeres halfe, the longelonde one aker halfe, the Warrehaye too akeres, the home mede one aker, the more iiij akeres.

Sm^a to. [ ]

fo. 106 Lytell Kynedon[121] ys a persell of Hocon yt is nowe yn the tenure of the foresed Willyam Maye and Edward Noseworthye for the rente of [ ] and sute to the curte of Skyrrydon and Lyddeforde and this yt is devyded that is to saye:

for Mayes parte, the Lower Kynedon too akeres halfe, the myddell Kynedon too akeres and halfe, the furse parke too akeres halfe, halfe the Stroll.

Noseworthes parte, the hyer Kyndedon too akeres halfe, the Kynedon nexte to the Brodaparke too akeres halfe, the lower furse parke too akeres halfe, the more aker mede too akeres.

Sm^a to. of the hole of Lytell Kynedon [ ]

121. Lytell Kynedon, Grette Kynedon: now Kendon in North Bovey (SX716818), a farmhouse Grade II listed, with surviving features of the seventeenth century and a datestone of 1675, but the fabric possibly earlier.

Note that this Lytell Kynedon was in grett trobell for the parson
of Northebovye did cleme hitt to be belongen to his churche but
the Mayes ever sethenes the xxj yere of Kynge Henry the VIIth
[1505/6] have inyoyed Lytell Kynedon by copye, so our fynes
alynasyones and dyenge sesed and the foresed prescrypsyon do
clerely frustrate all ther tytell.

GRETTE Kynedon was a free tenemente holden of the maner of
Skyrrydon by the yerely rente of one pownde of waxse and sute
to our curte ther resyenses strayeres sensores and all thynge
belongen to the lette was styll presented at Skyrrydon curte but
here note this was the abbes londes of Buckefaste and by that
menes hit came to the Kynge, the Kynge solde the same to M[r]
Sowthecote and he never payed rente sute nor serves but trulye I
do thynke the strayers and thynges belongen to the lete do stylle
belonge to Skyrrydon for M[r] Sowthecote hathe grante but as the
abbett hadde the same. This londes dothe june to the londes of
Hocon and lyethe wythe yn the parryshe of Northe Bovye and
theye paye xx[d] for fyftyedole wythe Hoconye tenantes.

MOREWYLL[122] ys also a tenemente yt lyethe wythe yn the maner *fo. 107*
of Skyrrydon the lorde of Skyrrydon hadde alwayes the strayeres
and all other thynges belongen to the lete theye paye xii[d] for
fyftydole wythe Skyrrydon they paye vendevyle rente and as one
of Skyrrydon maner be vendevyle & do sute to Lyddeford, the
tenement ys xl akeres of londes and the vycars of Dene do cleme
the same and have tyme owte of mynd inyoyed the same for the
whiche they sayed mase wykely at Skyrrydon Chapell they did
paye no other rente, but the vycares for not doynge of there sute
were dyveres tymes amersed viz. in an° 18 Henr' the VII [1502/3]
and in an° 21 and 22 Henry the VIII [1529–31]. This londes
was presented for conseled londes yt was one John de la Pynnes
londes; I was putt yn good hope by my lerned cownsell that the
londes was myne by forse of my lettores patenes and I putt hit yn
lawe and hadd a spessyall convayens for the same from Bassett
but all in vayne for we can have the maner but as the Marcus
of Exon' hadde the same, the Marcus hadde not the londe but
the thynges belongen to the lete and vewe of franckeplegges and
more we can not have. Surelye for wante of this word Chanteryes

---

122. Morewyll, in Dean Prior, has not been identified.

in our lettores patenes we loste hyt but no dowte hit is no parte of the maner of Denepryer nor yt comprysed upon the vycares composysyon but here marke they have upon the composysyon one farthynge and halfe of Sentorye and the londes of the rente off iiij^s by the yere this londes called Morewyll muste be that londes of iiij^s rente but that can not be for the pryer when this compos'n was had no londes yn Skyrrydon maner nor yt the shefe of Skyrrydon maner for the vycar hadde that shefe and Morewill for for [sic] sayenge ye fore[se]de wykelye mas. But I do thynke verylye this londes of iiij^s rente muste nedes be the lytell close by Dene churche for the Sentorye ys better then a farthynge and halfe besydes that lytell close but Gyles quaryled wythe the vycar and pretended to expulse hym so the vycar not abell to resyste hym by composision gave hym Morewyll for the terme of his lyfe and the shefe the vicare gave over his interres but I do thynke verylye that nether Gyles nor his vycare hathe anye ryght to Morewyll nor to the shefe of Skyrrydon but the ryght ys no dowte yn the prynse.

THERE WAS also one other close of londes of the yerely rente of vij^s that was parsell of the maner of Skyrrydon lyenge in Denburye but sethenes one Thomas Croppen balyefe in Kynge Edward the IIII tyme the rente was never payed; yt is thofte that this close of londes ys nowe usede as parsell of the maner of Westeoggewyll called Bryxsehammore for that close yn dede dothe lye in the perryshe of Denberye.

[FURSE'S OTHER PURCHASES]

OVERDENE lyethe wythe yn the maner of Denepryer yt ys a howse and a curtelage there called the Churche howse for the whyche ys payed iiij^d yerely at Micaellmas for all rentes sutes and serves; the pryor of Plymton was lorde of the maner of Denepryer and yn the fythe yere of Henrye the VIII [1513/14] by fethemente the pryer did geve to John Moreshed and to dyveres otheres a lytell quyllett of londes in Overdene to them and to there heres for ever to the intente the parrysheneres of Denepryer sholde bulde upon the same londes one newe erected howse and calle hyt the Churche howse to the use of the fraternytye and store of Sente George in the parryshe churche of Denepryer.[123] This dede was executede and John Moreshed survyved all the reste the howse was also buldede and yn truthe the paryshe payde the rente and usede the howse to there one comodite. FARDER this John Moresehede yn an° i et ij° Phi' et Marie [1554/5] by an other fethement did grante to Roberte Furse and to dyveres otheres the fore sede Churchehowse to them and to there heres for ever to the use of the reperrasyon and mentenans of the perryshe churche of Denepryer; this fethemente was executede.

Item in an° 3° et 4° Phi' and Marye [1556/7], Moreshede beynge dede, an offes was fownd upon his dethe at Tottenes before John Peter Esquyre beynge escheator and one Xpofer Phyllyppe boren

---

123. On the Vigil of St Mary Magdalene 5 Henry VIII (21 July 1513) the prior and convent granted to Richard Cote, John Morshead and others, a piece of land lying in Overdean 80 foot in length and 30 feet in breadth between the church stile to the north, the road on the south, the churchyard on the east and common land and the way on the west, to build a church house, at a rent of 4d to the prior (*Charities* II, p. 126). The plot of land is still recognisable but there is no building.

at Denepryer and then dewellynge at Denepryer and one of the customarye tenantes of the maner of Denepryer fownd that John Moreshede dyed sesed of londes in Overdene. Item in iiij° et v° Phi' and Marye [1557/8] John Gyles lorde then of the maner of Denepryer reseved homage fealty and a releve of Roberte Furse for londes in Moreshede Nuston and Overdene.

BY THYS yt is manyfeste that Moresede was yn actuall possession and the survyvor, and the londes geven to the feffes absolutelye that strongeres sholde bulde a howse, and then to a use of a thynge that never was, for there was never anye fraternyte or store nor yt ys anye shuche store there, agayne note that the later fethemente or grante made to Roberte Furse and otheres by John Moreshed ys by forse of the statute made yn the xxiij yere of Kynge Henrye the VIII [1531/2][124] utterlye voyed for that the use was for the reparasyon of the churche and by that menes no dowte but John Moresehed dyede sesede of londes in Overdene for he was never in possessyon of anye other londes in Overdene. Mr Gyles resevethe the rente and fealtye homage and releve of Roberte Furse for londes yn Overdene. So yf Moresehede were ons in possessyon the free holte muste stylle be yn hym and his heres untyll by a lawfull acte theye be dissesed, and for that the parrysshe and powre peopell have hadde the use by the order of the parryshe Furse beynge on he is not dyssesed, for there can be no dissesenynge but by a bodye corporate or parsonell: agayne note in kynge Richarde the Secondes tyme Symon Morsehed hadde londes in Overdene, Richard Moresede in an° ix of Ed. the IIII [1469/70] did amonge other thynges grante to John his sonne londes yn Overdene, yt dothe appere by three severall offyses that Roberte Moresehede and John and John Moreshed all three dyed sesede of londes in Overdene. The perryshe nor no man else to my knowlege can showe anye conayans for the Churche howse yt is all yn my hondes; but here note, I do not revelle this to anye intent that you shall converte this howse to your one use becose our fryndes in truthe hadde hyt but yn truste, and so yt is my will and requeste that yt hit be don yn dede, but the cose I have sayed this ys that you shall defende the perryshe tytell agaynste the lorde of the maner whiche dothe cleme the same to be his, for yf there be no tenant then in ryght it muste be his for the paryshe

---

124. Act for the feoffment and assurance of lands and tenements made to the use of any parish church, chapel or such like: 23 Hen. VIII c.8.

ys no corporasyon and therefore no bodye corporate, but becose
Gyles hathe accepted the rente fealty homage & relefe we muste
be his tenantes.

NOTE that Gyles lorde of Denepryer som x or xij yeres paste *fo. 109*
dyd serve me wythe a suppena and exhibitede a byll yn the
Chancerye[125] onlye for vexasyon and to the intente to have sene
the wrytynge of the Churche howse for in his byll he did allege
that I had made dyveres enteres in the maner of Denepryer and
that I hadde dyveres wrytynges of his to whiche bylle I made
awnser that I hade dyveres parseles of londes wythe yn the
maner of Denepryer in fee sympell or fee tayell and that I hadd
dyvers dedes and wrytynges consernynge the same londes and
so justyfyede the kepynge of bothe londes and wrytynges and
truysshede his false allegasyones and ever sethenes I have bynne
yn reste.

Item he hathe of longetyme for the moste parte kepte his curte
in the Churche howse but the pryer never helde curte there,
the pryor allwayes kepte the curte at Denetowne yn a chamber
there over the yate commynge yn to curte howse then called the
pryores Chamber and there lekewyse the shrefetorne by all the
pryeres tyme was usually kepte.

DERTYNGTON we have there one close of londes[126] of one aker and *fo. 110*
halfe yt lyethe wytheyn the parryshe of Dertyngeton and maner
of Northe forde yt is socage tenure and holden of Mr Gawyn
Champernon by the yerelye rente of xx^d and sute to the curte yt
is nowe in the occupasyon of Geferye Babbe for the rente of xv^s
yerelye.

NOTE that this was one Willyam Foxses londes of Denepryer
this Willm hadde issue Andro and Andero hadde issue Willyam
Richard & Edward, Willyam the yelder by will convayed the
londes to Andero for the terme of his lyfe the remender to
Willyam the younger in fee tayle and so to Richard and Edward;
this will was never proved but that is not materiall: Andro Foxse

---

125. John Gyles Esq of Bowden brought a case (undated) in Chancery about lands
    called Overdene, purchased of Edmund Verney Esq, also the barton of Stancombe
    Prior, the inheritance of the plaintiff. The defendants were John Bradford and
    Henry Strick, who he claims entered unlawfully. There is no mention of Furse.
    The document is damaged (TNA C2/ELIZ/G10/8).
126. Dertyngton: this close of land in Dartington cannot be identified.

the xxix daye of Desember in the xx^{ti} yere of Quene Ellezabethe [1577] by the consente of Willyam his sonne solde the londe to Roberte Furse for v^{li} and becose Willyam was not then of fulle yage the same Willyam the xxiiij daye of Auguste yn the yere of our lorde god 1580 by his suffyciant dede and relese paste all the foresede londes to Roberte Furse and his heres for ever. Note farder that Robert Furse in the xxvij yere of Quene Ellezabethe [1584/5] by dede did grante this londes and serten other londes in Denepryer and Sowthebrynte to one Phillyp Whyte and leverye seson and atturnamente paste, then Whyte by hys suffyciante dede reassured the same premysses to Furse and his heres and so paste a fyne upon the same but wythe yn som too or iij yeres after this fyne levelde Willyam the younger was hanged for stelynge of a horse.

This Andero Foxse did morgage this londes to one Thomas Marten of Dertyngeton: I at all adventures procured a relese of the same from Marten. This Andero Foxse before he solde the londes made fyrste a lese of the same to one Thomas Tolcharde for lxxxx yeres to hym & to his assynes for one penye for yerely rente and Foxse bownde to paye the hey rente and for the sute. Item I did lekewyse conclude wythe Thomas Tolchard for his hole terme for the whyche I payed hym vij^{li} x^s, note that one Toller of the grante of Willm Foxse the yelder had a lese for xxxvj yeres, for the fyrste xx yeres but a penye a yere & for the reste xv^s a yere. Tolchard reseved x^d for x yeres and after I bofte Tolchardes lese I reseved dyveres yeres for my xij^{li} x^s but one penye a yere for the whiche penye I payd yerelye to the lorde for rente and sute ij^s ij^d.

fo. 111

CUTEWYLL[127] was a sympell howse and vij akeres of good londes yt dothe lye in Uggebur, this londes I bofte of Phillyppe Whyte in the xx yere of Quene Ellezab^t [1577/8] for xviij^{li} one cowe I payd xvij^d to the lorde off Langefordelester & sute to the curte, one Pasco Tomlyn then tenante his yerelye rente was x^s a yere.

Item yn the xxvij of Ellezab^t [1584/5] when I bofte the londes in Moresed of Andero then for xl^{li} I solde hym Cuttewyll and paste to hym & to his wyfe by dede and relese but he kepte hyt

---

127. Cuttewyll, a house and seven acres in Ugborough, is now Cuttwellwalls (*PNDevon* I, p. 287; SX702580).

not one quarter of a yere but he and his wyfe solde the londes in Cuttewyll to me and my heres for xl^li and theye paste hyt to me by fyne then yn the xxix of Quene Ellezab^t [1586/7] I solde agayne all the foresede londes called Cuttewyll for fyftye powndes to one Thomas Byckforde and to his heres for ever.

ILSYNGETON Roberte Furse yn the xxxij^ti yere of Quene Ellezab^t [1589/90] bofte one anuytye of iij^li to hym & his heres for ever of one Henrye Harte in full satysfaccyon of viiiC tynn beynge a despered dette this anuytye one Willyam Harte did grante to the foresede Henrye and for not payemente of the rente to distrayne Cockes londes and Hyer Syggaforde lyenge yn Ilsyngeton then Willyam Hartes one londes.

Note when this anuytye was granted one George Bowdon hadde a lese in som parte of Cockes londes a tenement so called but the parseles of Cockes londes dyd then remayne yn Willyam Hartes one occupasion that ys to saye one close of londes called the Crosse Parke and the Northe parte of Beffehele one meddo one grove adyunynge to the mede and a lytell Rolle adyunynge to the grove. Hyer Syggeforde ys a tenemente of hyt selfe then yn Willyam Hartes one tenure adyunynge to Cockes londe. Note that wytheyn a verye shorte tyme that this anuytye was granted to Henry Harte; Willyam solde the londes to Peter Wodeleye.

NOTE theye saye this anuyte ys of no forse becose in Henrye Hartes dede from Willyam there is a provyso that yf serten tynne be payd at a tyme and plase accordynge to the tenure of one oblygasyon there of hadde & made or otherwyse alwayes do exonerate acquytte and defende the same Henrye &c. then the dede of no forse. Note that howe so ever will have the benefytt of a condysion he muste prove the condysion performed yn dede whiche theye can not do by no menes for the tynne at the daye was not payed but the bonde forfyted and hit was a quarter of one yere after that the tynne sholde be delevered befor anye agremente and then in the yende Henrye Harte bownde for the payemente of viii C of the tynne. Howe is Henrye here dyscharged for durynge that quarter he was not exonerated acquytted nor defended when he of forse muste paye the tynne. So hit is clere the condysion was never performed and by my lerned cunsell I am resoned the dede made to Henrye ys good then his assurans to me can not be badde.

fo. 112 Theye stonde gretely upon this for that the fyrste oblygasyon ys delevered and scanceled and an other oblygasion hadde for the payement of the same tynne. Yn truthe yf the oblygasyon hadde be scanceled before the tyme of the delevery of the tynne and the second obligasyon then seled that then no dowte the condysyon parformed but what so ever ys donne after the bonde forfyted ys no helpe nor prove that the condysyon ys performed and therefore the dede good in lawe and consyens, and what so ever was donne by me before I did bye the annuyte can not hutte our tytell for then I was a stronger and no partye.

fo. 113 NYMETTRASY[128] there ys one gardynge and a lytell parsell of londes adyunynge to the same yt lyethe wythe yn the burrowe and yt is holden of the lorde of the burrowe for the rente of vj[d], for this londes Roberte Furse payed to one George Davye the some of fortye shellynges for the fee sympell but the londes ys convayed to all Edmond Rolondes cooheres. Item this londes was reportede to be one Rayssheles[129] londes, this George Davye procured a convayens from Rayssheleye and we have hyt from Davye, but here note that Rayssheleye was not in possessyon nor inyoyed anye of the issues or profyttes there of not att anye tyme that anye levynge creature can reporte nor Davye never inyoyede the same but Rolonde and his heres and assynes.

FARDER NOTE that this londes yn dede dothe adyune to the londs of M[r] Bere on the weste syde and the londes of Rolonde on the este syde and theye saye that Rolond was M[r] Beres tenant for the Inne or grett howse, and by that menes as a persell of the same grett howse Rolonde did inyoye the same persell of londes, and yn truthe the foresede Davye by the procurement of some of our one fryndes he beynge M[r] Beres tenante did cose M[r] Bere to passe in Daves lese this garden and persell of londes by the name of the Bunehaye, so by this you maye perseve that George Davye was wyllynge to do Rolondes heres good and to have the londes, but for sertentye he never hadde anye profytt or occupasyon there of and agayne the garden and lytell persell of londes dothe

---

128. Nymet Tracey garden and parcel of lands cannot be identified.
129. Mr Rayssheleye is possibly Roger Raslegh, who was vicar of Nymet Episcopi in 1536 (Oliver, *Ecclesiastical Antiquities* II, p. 171).

not june to the Inne or grette howse but to one other tenement of Mr Beres nowe in the tenure of one Selake by the over syde of the waye.

To AWNSER thys that Edmond Rolonde in tyme was Mr Beres tenant yn dede for the Inne or grette howse but not yn mony yeres befor he dyed, for when he dyed he helde no londes of Bere nor in longe tyme before his dethe but yt is serten that he was in actuall possessyon of the gardene & lytell persell of londes monye yeres yn his lyfe tyme and there of dyed sesed, and after hym his wyfe as persell of his londes geven unto her by his laste wyll yn lewe of her junter she and her assynes have inyoyed the same xxxiij yeres and Mr John Hoyell ever sethenes; yf Mr Beres tytell good then whye shold Davye bye Mr Raysseleyes but what tytell so ever Rolonde hadde, he no dowte dyed there of sesed and thoffe he were but a dessesor the relese wythe the warrantyse dothe barre Davye and his heres and Rayssheleye ys barred by perscrypsion and Bere muste brynge his forme downe and prove dyrectely that Rolonde did inyoye the same as his tenant by the name of the Bunehaye.

[*Fos. 114-116 are blank.*]

[ROWLAND FAMILY AND THEIR PROPERTIES]

fo. 117

The juste lyne or petygrewe of Edmond Rolonde

WYLLYAM ROWLAND and Margerye his wyfe hadde issue Edmonde and too dofters, this Willyam and his wyfe bothe of them dyed in a plage tyme[130] there chylderen verye younge, then on Edmonde Rowlande beynge unkell to the chylderen then dewellynge in the ynne at Bowe a verye ryche man and a man of good consyens havynge no chylderen of his one he then toke in charge his dystressed brotheres chylderen so then he did brynge uppe this younge Edmonde in lernynge and grette experyens in his lyfe tyme and when he dyed he and Johan Rowlande his wyfe hadde shuche confydens and love to this younge Edmond that he was there fulle and hole executor but this Johan survyved her hussebonde monye yeres but she was contynuallye mentayened by Edmond her cosen as dutyfullye as anye son sholde mentayne his one mother. The foresede too dofters were lekewyse well trayned uppe and well marryed the one to one Toser of Bowe the other to one Halse of Hycheleye parryshe and bothe them systeres hadde dyvers issues. This younge Edmonde Rowlande [c. 1500–1560] fyrste marryed one Margerett and Edmond and Margerett hadde issue Roberte Rolonde and Johan Rowlande then Margerett dyede. After her dyssesse thys Edmond marryed one Johan Alforde the dofter of John Alforde of Ockyngeton gentyllman and Grase his wyfe, what John Alforde was I mynd here after to resyte. This Edmonde Rowelande and Johan his wyffe hadde issue Edmond Rowlande, Marye Rowland, Willemott

---

130. Edmund Rowland adopted children in a plague time. See p. 62, note 80.

Rowelande and Ellezabethe Rowlande. The foresed Roberte Rolande was a very talle younge man and beynge plased yn London for lernynge there he dyede unmarryed: Edmonde dyede an infante, Ellezab[t] beynge but younge moste unhappylye dyed by mysfortune of scallynge, then Johan Rowlande his dofter marryed on Robarte Alford his wyves brother and Robarte and Johan had issue Johan Alforde, then she dyed and Roberte Alford marryed one Tomsen Davye and by her hadde issue John and Samuell. Johan Robart Alfordes dofter marryed one John Hoyell and they hadde no issue. Marye Rowlande marryed John Honychurche of Awtongyfford gentylleman and theye have issue Henrye Antonye John and vj dofteres. Willemett marryed Roberte Furse and they hadde issue John Furse and otheres as is aforesede. THYS Edmonde Rowlande was sesede of dyveres messuages londes londes and tenementes but all of his one provydynge. What the londes ys and of whom the londes was bofte yt shall here after appere.[131] This Edmond at his dyenge daye havynge no here male he by his laste will convayed all his londes to his foresede three cooheres in fee tayell wythe a condysion that yf anye of them did discontynew or frustrate the intente of the will the too other to inyoye that porsyon, but by the same he gave almoste all his londes to Johan his wyfe for term of her lyfe, and farder by his laste wylle he did geve for ever to the pow[r]e yerelye xx[s] that is to the powre of Nymettrasye vj[s] viij[d] to the powre of Northe tawton vj[s] viij[d] and to the powre of Selemonecorum vj[s] viij[d]; he gave dyveres legasyes to churches and others whiche I do omytte, he made his wyfe his executryxse.

Thys Edmonde Roland farre excyded all his fore fatheres or proyenytores for welthe wysedom and credyt, he was an *fo. 118* excellent awdytor a grett surveor and curte holder, the onlye man to make wrytynges, he commonly kepte iij clarke for that purpose and yt he hymselfe toke grett paynes; yn the commosyon tyme yn Kynge Edward the Sextes tyme [1549] he was then undershryfe of Devon and was by that menes in grett donger of his lyfe and all his goodes. He ever dewelled at Bowe towne and there kepte the ynne but after Roberte Alforde marryed his dofter he removed to a newe howse of his one buldynge and Alforde hadde the yenne and furnyture. He myche delyted merye companye and for his recreasyon wolde passe his tyme to cardes

131. See below, pp. 139–49.

tabelles & bowles he was an excelent good archarde and dyd grettelye delyte shottynge. He kepte an excellente good howse as well for the powre as the ryche and did gretelye releve his nyghtebores as well wythe mete drynke & monye as wythe good cownsell; what shall I saye he was in dede estemed as a father to his cu[n]terye, the gentyllemen generallye vij myles from hym wolde yerely vysett hym for they loved hym and so dyd all his nyghtebores, he dyd good to all men and wrong to no man; he was a myghtye man of welthe, he was no covetus man but a man that fered god. He hade a lese of a close of londes parsell of the berton of Bowe for 99 yeres, he procured a lese of one Dekeres bargayne for yeres determenabell upon iij lyves he also hadde the fee ferme of the one moyete of a fyne maner in Somerset shere called Exforde, he hadde good fees of dyveres men off honor and worshyppe, he had dyveres copyholte londes and other leses for the terme of his lyfe. There were three severall men that at the tyme of his dethe hadde londes leaye yn morgage to hym that was one Grybbell Collomperse and Knappeman but after his desesse all was redemed. He leved lx yeres he dyed the xviij daye of Marche in the second yere of Quene Ellezabthe [1560] and ys buryed at Bowe churche and there covered wyth a blewe stone and more I can not saye of Edmond Rolonde but god sende hym a joyefull daye in his resurrecsyon.

fo. 119 JOHAN ROLANDE leved xxxiij[ti] yeres after her husebonde Edmond Rolondes dyssesse and nere vj monthes, this Johan to her uter decaye and increse of her grett sorrowe and myserye wythe yn one yere nexte after her husebondes dyssesse moste unhappylye was marryed to one Edwarde Drewe of Sente Seres Newton Esquyre and becose she hadde but too dofters, the one marryed to Roberte Furse, and by promyse betewexte her and Drewe her dofter Marye sholde marrye wythe one John Drewe the sonne and here of Edward Drewe, she lefte to hym monye jules plate dettes spessyaltes chatell leses goodes londes leses and all that ever she hade upon hope of the preferremente of her dofter, whiche I am sure was then better than too towsante marke, but wythe yn a shorte tyme that he was marryed and was sure he hadde home and yn his one custodye all that ever she hadde, he beynge wyckedelye bente havyng grett delyte in omenes and that hadde the rule of his howse, he quarreled wythe her and forsoke her companye for the company of his olde mates and was by procurement extremely bente agaynst her and often mysusede her and putt her in gre[t] donger of her lyfe and yn the yende he cowde not abyde the syghte of her and by polysye and flatterye procured her to lye wythe one Mr Sneddall, but when she was gonne she thynken to retorne agayne lefte her apparrell for the moste parte there, but after she was gon she came to the howse but there she muste not come yn nor ette nor drynke there but gladde to seke loggynge among the nyghtebores, then by menes of her fryndes complente was made to the bysshoppe and by that menes she hadde some parte of her one levynges for her mentenans but never no pate of her goodes, and yn his lyfetyme solde all her leses for yeres and altered the properte of all her goodes and dyd as myche as in hym leye to barr her junture & dower. His son John by good happe dyed in London, this unhappe marrage did contynewe abowe xix yeres durynge all whiche tyme this Johan commytt her care to god; she leved a good and a godly lyfe and spent her tyme som tymes yn Exeter som tymes at Ockyngeton som tymes wythe Mr Honychurche and som tymes at Denepryer wythe Furse. Then after Mr Drewes dyssesse by menes of her fryndes she hadde x^li a yere owte of his levynge duryng her lyfe whiche contynewed xiiij yeres and one quarter. This Johan was a wyse woman and decente in her apparrell, an excellente good hussewyfe and carefull, a parfytte woman to doo anye thynge wythe her nele to knytt to make bonelase. She was a fyne coke and well estemed of all peopell, she was myche bente to faste praye and geve almese to the powre, she was a plesante woman in company and was ever of honeste lyfe and good conversasyon, nevere charged or suspected wythe anye evyll, she was a fryndely woman and lyberall to all her brotheres but spessyally to John Richarde & Roberte; she levede lxxv yeres, she dyed at Awtongyfford & there buryed in the chantery yele, she gave to everyche of her dofteres chylderen xx^s, she gave to Cxx pore persones iiij^d a pese and penye dole, dyvers other legasyes she made but she made her too dofters her executores. She dyed the xiiij daye of Auguste yn the xxxv of Quene Ellezb^t [1593] and more I canne not saye of Johan Drewe but god sende to her a joyefull daye in her resurrecsyon and joye everlastynge. She did grelye lamente the hynderans of her dofters but yt at laste they had C^li to everyche of them.

fo. 120 ## The petygrewe of John Alforde

Symon Whyddon marryede one Mr Wykes dofter of Cockecatree and theye hadde issue John and too dofters, thes too dofters the one was marryed to one Mr Byddewyll the wother to one John Alforde; the foresede John Whyddon hadde issu John Whyddon, this John the younger in Quene Marye tyme was then Lorde Chefe Justes of the Quenes Bynche and by that menes a knyght, he hade issue Willyam Edwarde and dyveres other sonnes and dofteres and the foresede John Alforde hadde issue John; this John the younger was lerned, he dewelled at Moreton, his exercyse was kepynge of curtes; this John fyrste marryed Grase one Sowthemedes dofter of Moreton and theye hadde issue the foresede Johan, maryed to Edmond Rowlande. This Sowthemed was a good freholder and hadde issue but one son and the foresed dofter but that sonne had issue John and Edmonde and bothe them have dyveres issues, sonnes and dofteres, then after Grases dessesse John Alforde marryed one Mycaeles dofter of Ockyngeton and by her he hadde issue John Richard Roberte Edmonde Willyam and one dofter called Johan. After his seconde marrage he contynually dewelled at Ockyngeton, he was a myghty lymed man & of grette stature, a man of grett welthe, all his delyte was in good hospitalite; he dyede his chylderen but younge and putt to myche tryste to his wyfe for in shorte tyme after her husebondes dyssesse she dyd marrye wythe one Gaverycke of Newton whiche wythe Alfordes goods purchased abby londes and his wyfe by happe in shorte tyme dyede so her chyderen never had ther fatheres legasye but glade to shufte for them selves, but by good happe the chylderen were plased wythe a nere cosen of theres then sufferegan of Exon' and he kepte them all to lernynge.

John the yeldeste provyde a verye wyse man of more lernynge credytt and existymasion then ever anye of the Alfordes were, he farre excyded his father in howse kepynge, he purchased dyveres parselle of londes, newe bulded all his howse and furnyshed the same rechelye, he was a sweren attorneye monye yeres but fyrst Mr Whydons clerke and rode wythe hym in syrkytt monye yeres beynge a jugge of a serkytt and from thens he contynewed at Lyones Ynne.[132] He was a tall man; he fyrste marryed one Jane

---

132. Lyons Inn was one of the several Inns of Chancery which originated as collegiate houses for study before entering one of the four Inns of Court. During the sixteenth century they became the province of attorneys.

Bowdon Mr Gyles Rysedones dofter a verye good gentyllewoman but theye hadde no issue, then after her he marryed one Willemett Calmade one Mr Fynsen Calmades wyfe and by her he hade iij dofteres. Richarde Alforde hadde issue John Alford & dyveres other sonnes and dofters. Roberte Alforde dewelled at Bowe, by his fyrste wyfe he hadde issue Johan and by his other wyfe John and Samuell as is aforesed: this Robertes exersyse was kepynge of curtes, he kepte a good howse and had manye good thynges for the terme of hys lyfe & all of his one gettynge, he was a thowsante pownde the worse for surtyshyppe and sutes of lawe. Edmond dewelled at Honychurch and had issue sones and dofters. Willyam deweled at Brode Nymet and hadde no issue, a man of grett welthe. Johan marryed wythe Willyam Reddeway of Sampeford and hadd issue sones and dofters.

Rowlandes londes

fo. 121

HETHE[133] ys a tenement yt lyethe wytheyn the parrysshe of Spreaton yt ys nowe yn the tenure of John Burges, yt is holden of the lordes of Sprayeton in free socage, we paye yerelye ij^s for rente and sute to ther curte, yt ys worthe abowve all repryses xix^s vj^d.

NOTE Rowlande hadde but the one moyetye of Hethe and before yt came to hym the londes was devyded by the tenantes and so ever sethenes contynued. Thys londes was one Hethes londes, from Hethe yt came to one Henrye Howe; Henry Howe hade issue Alexander Howe, Alexander Howe the viij daye of Desember in an^o primo Ellezab^t [1558] solde the same to Edmond Rowland by the name of all his londes in Hethe; note here I do suppose the hole tenement sholde be ours in ryght yf our one slackenes or neclygens have not barred us for this ys the truthe of the cose, Henrye Howe was sesed of all the hole and so dyed sesede. This Alexander wythe yn yage one Richard Howe his unkell was his gardener and he solde the other moytye to one Mr Hayche a lawyer; Hayche dyed sesed, his here solde hyt to Mr Estecote by fyne and the v yeres paste wythe owte anye enterye; well we maye have releve in the Chancerye but I thynge the Common lawe agaynst us, but yt inquere for Richard Howe hadde no thynge in the londe that solde hit.

133. Hethe, in Spreyton, is now Heath (*PNDevon* II, p. 447), SS694974.

This tenemente was this devyded, for our parte we have all the howses curtelage and harbegarden and one close of londes called the Hose parke [ ] akeres, one other close called the Myddelhyll [ ] akeres, the North Cleve [ ] akeres, the Come [ ] aker, and too akeres in the lower yende of the Fursehyle.

The other parte ys the Whette parke vj akeres, the mede and orcharde ij akeres, the Brodaparke xiiij akeres, the Furse parke x akeres.

NOTE this for a generall Rule that I in the ryghte of Wyllemott my wyfe have but only the thyrde parte of all Edmonde Rolondes parte or porsyones of londes where so ever hyt dothe lye yf the reste of the cooheres have issue, but yf anye of them dye wythe owte issue then we have the one half of Rolondes parte; loke his testemente muste & will derecte you; agayne loke yf anye do allenate or dyscontynewe the tayell you are to enter and inyoye your porsyon of the same.

fo. 122
Sould
[Later hand]

OCKE[134] is a justement yt lyethe yn Bysshopes Nymet yt is holden of Ser John Chechester in fre socage by the yerelye rente of [ ] and sute to his curte; yt is nowe yn the tenure of one John Thomas for the yerelye rente of xij[s] abowe all reprises. NOTE Rowlande hadde but only the thyrde parte of this londes called Ocke, the churche of Molton the one halfe and the foresed John Thomas the sexte parte; the one moytye of this londes was one Cotterelles londes, this Cotterell hadde issue iij dofters, the one marryed one Lakyngeton and had issue Thomas, the other maryed one Copleston & hadde issue George, the thyrde maryed one Flechere and hade issue one dofter whiche marryed one Morreleye. Lakyngeton and Coplestone solde ther parte to one Thomas Drewe and Drewe solde the same to Edmond Rolonde. Morley solde his parte to one Roger Walron and Walron solde hyt to John Thomas.

ITEM when Rolonde dyed he lefte no dowte all his wrytynges in a cofer, his wyfe delevered the same to one of her nyghtebores to be kepte safe faste loken and she havynge the keye, but not so donne but Drewe by dyssettefull persones was made prevy, he then wythe all spede wythe owte makynge his wyfe or anye of her fryndes or heres prevye moste falsely and unyustelye carryed

---

134. Ocke is Oak in Bishops Nympton (*PNDevon* II, pp. 384–5). This mentions only Little Oak, but the tithe award has Great and Little Oak.

the cofer to his motheres howse and ther repte the loke and toke owte what he lyste, but Rolond byenge myche of his londes of one Thomas Drewe Edwarde Drewes cosen he was sure to take a waye all the bondes and what else I do not understond, but there the cofer remayned comon to everye parson in the howse a longe tyme and for wante of the loke the myse in truthe did gretely spoyle the wrytynge so when we sholde have our wrytynges there was no thynge perfytt, som eten som loste, yt was grett happe that we had anye. All the conterpanes of all the tenantes leses excepte iij or iiij were all spoyled and for wante of them the tenantes did use the londes at there plesure and abated ther rente and payd what the lyste; here you maye lerne what hit is to leve your evyden to wemen, he was not content to spoyle the mother of all, but her heres also as farr as in hym was.

Note for wante of our evydens Lakyngetones here begane to quarel wythe us for Ocke so to be quyett Rolondes cooheres payde hym xx^{li} and for that we hadde a relese wythe warrantyse in an^o xxiij of Ellezb^r [1580/1] from Lakyngeton for all his parte of Ocke made to all the cooheres and farder a lese of all Moreles parte for one thowsante yeres; this lese for yeres was made to Edward Lakyngeton & a bonde for the performans by one Moreleye but we have but Lackyngetones assynement, no bonde from hym but onlye the bond that Moreleye seled.

ROCKE and Este Cadeworthye[135] be too severall thynges but theye june bothe together and so longe yn one manes occupasion that I can not justelye devyde them; Rocke ys holden of the lorde of Certon in fre socage and payemente of [ ] and sute to the curte and Este Cadeworthy holden of the lorde of the maner of Possebye in free socage for the yerely rent of [ ]: yt is nowe in the tenure of Roberte Gollocke and ys worthe by the yere abowve all charges wythe Venecomes rente viij^s. I do accownte Venecomes rente iij^s for a howse there lately made.

fo. 123
Sould

NOTE that Rowelonde hadde but the one halfe of this londes, the other halfe was one Gyffordes londes whiche hade issue one dofter[136] that marryed Mr George Carye of Cockyngeton and M^r

135. Rocke and Este Cadeworthy are Rock and Caddiford (*PNDevon* II, p. 407; SX779965 and 771959).
136. John Gifford of Yeo had a daughter, Wilmot, who was divorced from John Bury and married Sir George Cary.

Carye and Rolondes cooheres made partysyon of all the londes in Rocke and Este Caddeworthye the vij daye of November an° xxviij of Ellezb[r] [1586] and beynge equallye devyded by men of the contereye then lots and by lote this was our parte, that ys to saye the halhowse, the shyppen, and halfe the barne beynge the sowthe parte, the sowthe curtelage wythe all the wayes adyunynge to the mede, the sowthe parte of the mede wythe the gardynge, the bunehaye, the Westehaye, the Ruggeparke, the Ruggemede, the Berehaye all excepte one halfe aker adyunynge to goodwill garden, the bere halsewyll, scutes parke, menes parke, the brodaparke, the este gratten, the este parte of the more, the este parte of the downe; the reste of all the howses gardenes and londes Mr Carye hadde by lote.

NOTE EDMOND Venecombe was tenante to all the hole londes and before the partysyon this hyt was devyeded in severall closes, that ys to saye the downe xx akeres, the horseparke three quarters of one aker, the lytell haye one aker, the Whetehaye als the Weste haye one aker, the bunehaye halfe one aker, the mede ij akeres, the Splott and the towneplase one aker, goodwill garden and the orchard a quarter of an aker, the Ruggeparke too akeres and halfe, the Ruggemede one aker, the Wethelonde iij akeres, the bromehalsewyll iiij akeres, menes parke too akeres and halfe, the too grattenes xiij akeres, the bere one aker, the berehayes iij akeres, the lytell horse parke one aker, the lytell halsewill iij akeres, the berehalsewyll iij akeres, Soutteshyll vj akeres, the Furseparke vj akeres, the more viij akeres, the brodaparke iiij akeres, and iiij severall howses.
     Sm[a] to. [ ]

OUR PA[R]TE of Rocke and Este Caddeworthye in tyme was all one Cleffehangeres londes, he solde hit to one Thomas; John Thomas iij die January in an° ij° Edward VI [1549] solde this and other londes for xx[li] to Edmonde Rolonde. After the foresede partysyon Richard Venecombe fyrse erected his howse and there of hathe a lese.

HELLERESDONE[137] is a tenemente yt lyethe in Nymettrasye *fo. 124*
parrysshe yt is holden of Richard Preddes as of his maner of Sould
Ewtone for the yerelye [rent] of [ ] and sute to the curte, yt is
nowe yn the tenure of Richarde Rolonde for the yerelye rente of
vj[s] and hit is devyde as folloyethe viz:
[*blank*]

NOTE that Edmond Rolonde hadde but the thyrde parte of this
londes in comon with M[r] Edwarde Whyddon and one John
Hyll of Taynton; this londes in Hylleresdone was sometymes
one Bluntes londes and he hadde iij dofteres and theye all were
marryed: one Hyll marryed one and that parte John Hyll bofte,
M[r] Sampeforde bofte an other parte & he hadde issue one dofter
whiche marryed Markes Slader and Slader solde his parte to M[r]
Whydones father, the thyrde parte came to John Thomas wher
by dyssente or purchase I do not understond and John Thomas
sold his parte to Edmonde Rolonde wythe Rocke as is aforesede.

HARMESETONE[138] ys a lytell maner of hytt selfe yt lyethe in *fo. 125*
Nymettrasye and Selemonecorum yt is devyded ynto dyveres Sould
tenementes yt is holden of the Erell of Bathe by knyghte serves,
our parte by the vj parte of a knyghtes fee, we paye for heye rent
[ ] and for sute to the curte [ ], howe hit is devyded & what the
rentes is yt shall her after appere.

NOTE this maner was holye one Cotterelles londes whiche hadde
issue iij dofteres as is aforesede. Water Davye bofte the fee
sympell of Lakengetones parte and Moreles parte and after he
hadde hit he solde som parte to one and som to an other and

---

137. Hellersedon is now Hillerton (SX723981; *PNDevon* II, pp. 360–1). None of the
forms given has an 's' in it, but there is a variant with 's' in an inquisition post
mortem on Richard Prideaux 1605. This shows that he was seised in demesne of
the manor of Yew in Crediton, and held the manor of Hyllerdon or Huddesdon
in Nymet Tracy of the earl of Bath as of the manor of Nymet Bow. He held
Thewborough of William Courtenay. The original document is damaged but
refers also to Harpford, held of Vennytedborne, Chedyngbroke held of Richard
Pollard as of his manor of Posbury, messuage and lands in Scoryhill or Scoreland,
held of George Prestwood, and lands in Hembere in Tetborne St Mary held
of Hugh Acland (WSL IPM transcripts). Most occur also in his father Hugh's
inquisition of 1550.
138. Harmesetone, a manor in Nymet Tracey and Zeal Monachorum, is now
Hampson (*PNDevon* II, p. 360; SX710014), and appears as Little Hampson in
the tithe award.

so he dyed sesed yn fee sympell of no thynge. Hayes hadde his parte of Gayesham, Mr Copleston hade all his parte of all the londes yn his one hondes and yn Rowes hond and som parte of Ewenes and the free tenantes rent; Mortymer had Barones and Alford hadde Jenynges and Ewenes one thyrd parte of his howses. Serten londes Thomas Drewe did bye of Coplestone one of Cotterelles cooheres, and of his father yn lawe Gryffytt the other thyrde parte of Harmeston maner. Thomas Drewe solde the same for 96^{li} to Edmonde Roland the xxiij daye of June an^o iiij^o & v^o Phi' & Mar' [1558], by this convayens also paste to Rolond then the thyrde parte of the londes yn Ocke.

Note that in an^o iij Edward the VI [1549/50] Thomas Gryffett Margaret his wyfe and George Copleston her son paste all her londes to John Copleston & Willyam Sommaster by fethemente and fyne to serten uses. George Copleston did selle all the foresed londes with dyveres other londes to Thomas Drewe in i^o and ij^o Phi' & Mar' [1554/5] by dede inrolled yn the Banke and by fyne. More ther is an olde fethemente made by Coterell to one Fokerye and otheres consernynge this and other londes berynge date an^o iij^o Henr' the VII [1487/8]. Note that all these laste iij resyted convayenes do nowe remayne with Mr Sargent Drewe the sonne and here of Thomas Drewe.

fo. 126
Sould

Harmeseton berton ys devyded that is Water Davye held Copleston parte by lese that is the thyrde parte of one tenement or orchard and mede called Harmeston mede xiij akeres, one close called the Longe hame xij akeres, the Ryxseham x akeres, the lytell close iij akeres, the butteparke vj akeres, the hyer parte of the mede x akeres, harmestondowne xxx akeres; ther ys dewe to Rolondes cooheres for the londes in Davyes tenure yerely xxxj^s x^d and sute to Harmeston curte and iij^s iiij^d herrett.

Sould

Johan Genynge holdethe one howse and serten londes adyunynge wythe yn the burrowe of Bowe persell of the maner of Harmeston her rent ys xij^d and sute to Harmeston curte. Rolondes cooheres have but the iij parte.

fo. 127
Sould

Harmeston one other parsell of the maner and berton nowe yn the tenure of Richarde Rowe for the yerelye rente of ix^s viij^d and this yt is devyded viz. the downe xviij akeres, the lytell bromeparke too akeres and halfe, the weste bromeparke iij akeres, the lytell parke one aker, the medes iij akeres and halfe, and one howse there newlye erected. Note of all this we have but the thyrd parte of the londes.

 Sm^a to. [ ]

HARMESTON Gayesham parsell of the berton of late in the tenure   Sould
of Edmonde Gaye for ix^s viij^d rente yt is but one close contenynge xviij akeres of good pasture; we have but the iij parte of the londes.

 Sm^a to. xviij

HARMESTON an other persell of the maner in the tenure of Thomas   *fo. 128*
Ewenes yt is one tenemente wythe yn the burrowe of Bowwe and   Sould
one close called the Crosseparke iij akeres and one close called the bromeparke I thynke parsell of the berten vj akeres; we have but the iij parte of all this londes, our rente is v^s j^d and sute to our curte.

John Baron hadde in his tenure one howse wythe serten londes   Sould
adyunynge wythe yn the burrowe persell of the maner of Harmeston halfe one aker, iiij lytell closes persell of the berten vj akeres, and too medes to akeres; of all this we have but the thyrd parte of the londes.

 Sm^a to. [ ]
 His rente home ix^s ij^d.

Folehaye and Callehaye[139] are too free tenementes nowe in the tenure of one George Roddeforde, yt is holden by knyght serves and for our parte his rente is xvj^d and sute to our curte.

Chanterye Londes   *fo. 129*

THYS londes did belonge to one Cotterell and he havynge no chylde fyrste erectede the chanterye of Ayshebrynton[140] and he to the mentenans of the same chanterye by dede in Kynge Henrye the Seventhe tyme did geve all thes severall quylletes and monye more; what the londe ys yt shall followe by curse and where hit

---

139. Folehay is now Foldhay, in Zeal Monachorum (*PNDevon* II, p. 376; SX714045), and features in Ann Adams's history of the parish. Callehaye has not been traced.
140. Ashprington chantry, founded by Thomas Coterell, had lands in Nymet Tracy, Cheriton Bishop and North Tawton, according to the chantry certificate of 1546 (Oliver, *Monasticon*, p. 478). Furse corroborates this. 'The burrowe' is Bow, the more usual name for the main part of Nymet Tracey, but Furse's references to tenements and plots are too vague for easy definition.

lyethe and the juste rente, note that all chanterye londes was geven by statute to Kynge Edwarde the Sexte,[141] the prynse solde hit to one Westehorne and Balyeffe to be holden of the prynse in free socage of the maner of Sowthe Syddemowthe. Westehorne and Balyeffe solde the same to the foresede Thomas Drewe. Thomas Drewe yn an° iiij ~~Ellezebeth~~ Edward VI [1550/1] for 75ᵗⁱ solde all the chanterye londes of Ayshebrynton in Nymmettrasy Cheryton Bysshoppe and Northe Tawton to Edmond Rolond and his heres for ever. I suppose Rolonde solde the londes yn Northe Tawton to one Bocher.

NOTE WE do paye for our chanterye londes to my lorde of Bathe for the londes in Bowe for heye rente [ ] and sute to the curte and bownd to do serten offyses the wᶜʰ I do suppose ys clerelye dyscharged becose the prynse hathe created a newe tenure and we do lekewyse paye to Mʳ Bemonte the olde heye rente for Cobbadowne the whyche yf one be dyscharged all ys dyscharged: peruse the statute at large and use good cownsell or you do begynne.

fo. 130 One close of londes called the Wester bruggeparke ij akeres nowe in the tenure of John Hoyell for the rente of [ ], this lyethe within the burrowe for the whiche my lorde hathe for heye rente [ ].

Too other closes of londes callede the Brygge parkes adyunynge iij akeres and wythe yn the burrowe, the heye rente iijˢ, oure rente xxxˢ. Note that all thos iij bryggeparkes amonge other thynge are granted to Willyam Godfraye & others &c.

The Dower hayes to closes.

Sould
[later hand]

Richarde Bonde one tenemente one curtelage and one garden halfe one aker the mede one aker the iij closes vj akeres the hame ij akeres my lordes rente vjˢ viijᵈ our rente home xxˢ.

fo. 131
Sould
The
Bromeparke

Willyam Godfreye hathe one close of londes wythe yn the burrow called the Bromeparke, he payethe to my lorde iijˢ and for ower rente iijˢ iiijᵈ.

Sould all the
lands in Bow

Item the same Willyam hathe one howse and serten londes adiunynge and serten other londes called the Chanter hayes, his rent to my lorde xijᵈ our rente vjˢ viijᵈ.

141. 1 Edward VI, c.14 (1547): an Act whereby certain chantries, colleges, free chapels and the possessions of the same be given to the King's Majesty.

Edmonde Monder one howse one garden & serten londes adyunyng ner halfe one aker, the heye rente vj^d, our rente viij^s.

Hammonte one howse and serten londs, the heye rente vj^d, our rent x^s.

Reve one howse and serton londes, the heye rent vj^d, our rente xij^s: note Hamonts howse & Reves was but one howse.

Item we hadde yerely vj^d for one lytell parsell of londes of Willyam Bonde then tenant to the churche of Bysshopes Nymet and also iij^d for restynge of three resters upon our walle, this rente hathe not bynne payd the x yeres loke to hit yn tyme.

Willyall Wilston one howse and serten londes adyunynge for the *fo. 132* which he payethe to the lorde vj^d and our rente vj^s viij^d.

Falentyne Rowe one tenemente one garden and to closes of londes the hole iij akeres, he payethe home xvj^s vj^d and to the lorde iij^s vj^d.

Gregorye ys one tenemente and serten londes adyunynge for the whyche he payethe home vj^s viij^d & vj^d to the lorde. Note Edmond Roland hadde a lytell parsell of londes adyunynge to Gegoryes howse the whiche he hade of Markes Slader and that londes I do not thynke verylye ys nowe used as parsell of Gregores howse, that lytell quyllett was no Chanterye londes.

COBBADOWNE was also parsell of the Chanterye londes, yt is but one close of londes of [ ] akeres, yt lyethe in Cheryton Bysshoppe. We holde hit of the prynse as is aforesede but yt our tenant dothe paye a hye rente to Mr Beamont, this londes is nowe in the tenure of one Olyver Bennett for the rente of iiij^s the heye rente [ ].

[Other purchases by Rowland]

NYMETTRASYE yt is a tenemente nowe yn the tenure of John *fo. 133* Alford, our rente is xx^s abowve all charges, yt is holden of the lorde of Bowe in socage tenure, our parte of the heye rente ys xvj^d and sute to the curte and this hit is devyded, that ys to saye the howse garden and the haye halfe one aker, the Spettell parke [ ] akeres, the mede, the brome close, one other mede and sarten lanscor londes yn Langeforde londes, the lake parke, the Crosse parke, the Whytte haye, Smythe close, Godfraye close.

NOTE that this londes was one Rowes londes, he solde the same londes to one Buller of Exeter and Buller then presentelye solde the same to Edmode Rolonde in an° i et ij Phi' and Marye [1554/5] for xiij^{li} xiij^s iiij^d.

But here note Edmonde Rolande never hadde but the thyrde parte of this tenemente, the towne of Ockyngeton hathe an other thyrde parte and Mr George Escotte hadde the other thyrde parte, he bofte hyt of Roberte Lanseforde.

fo. 134 NYMETTRASY one Drewe was sesede of iij tenementes in Bowe, he solde hyt to Mr Colse, Colse solde hyt to John Alforde, John Alforde for xx^{li} yn an° i° Mar' [1553/4] solde the same to Edmonde Rolonde, yt is holden of the lorde of Bowe in socage tenure, we paye for heye rente ij^s ix^d and sute to the curte and this devyded, that is to saye the howse curtelage and serten londes adyunynge nowe in the tenure of John Hoyell for the yerely rente of [ ].

One other howse and lytell persell of londes adyunynge nowe in the tenure of Alse Renell for iiij^s ix^d rente yerelye. The thyrde tenemente yn the tenure of Wyllyam Duke, his rent home is vj^s viij^d and this devyded one howse one garden one close called the [blank] the other close [blank].

fo. 135 NYMETTRASYE yt is a tenemente and a lytell garden the howse fell downe then the olde Willyam Godfraye did newe bulde the same and one Thomas Tuckefylde there dewelles, the rente to the lorde but one penye and our rente xiij^s iiij^d, yt is socage tenure. This londes Edmond Rolande bofte the fee sympell for iij^{li} vj^s viij^d in an° ij° Ed. VI [1548/9] of one John Wychehalse and Johan his wyfe.

Note Edmond Rolonde for xx^s in an° ij° iij° Phi' Mar' [1555/6] did by the fee sympell of the lytell parsell of londes that now ys parsell of Gregoryes bargayn.

fo. 136 OCKYNGETON alz Ockehamtone ther we have parsell of too tenementes this londes ys holden of the lordes of Ockyngeton in free socage and the yerely rente of [ ] and sute to the curte, the one tenemente nowe in the tenure of John Cornyshe, yt is a howse and serten londes adyunynge and one persell of londes called Portemanmede [ ] akeres and one other parsell called Trendelbere one aker, his rente home ys but vj^s viij^d a yere.

The other tenemente ys in the tenure of one [*blank*] Canne for the rente of one [ ].

Note that thys londes was one Clubbes londes and he had issue iij dofteres, the one marryed one Monkeleye, he solde his parte to Mr Rolse, the second marryed one Taylder, he solde that parte lekewyse to one Hoper and Hoper solde hyt to Mr Rolses. The thyrde syster marryed one Walwynge and he for iiij^{li} yn an^o xxvj of Henry the VIII [1534/5] solde all his parte to Edmonde Rolonde and to his heres for so we are tenantes yn common wythe Mr Rolles, he hathe too partes devyded yn iij and we have but onlye the iij parte.

Note of Portemannamede Mr Roles & Rolond hadde but the one halfe and one Horewill hath the other parte.

[*This is the end of Robert Furse's work. Fo. 137 is blank, and what follows is in a later, seventeenth-century, hand, that of a son of John Furse and Welthian Snelling.*]

[CHADDLEWOOD, ACQUIRED BY JOHN FURSE THROUGH MARRIAGE]

A Particular of my Landes in Chaddlewood wch came by my Mother   *fo. 138*

[Superscript figures in this section indicate the ages of the tenants]

	li	s	d
Florence Davies ^{44} holds one tenement in Plympton Morris for yeares determinable upon her death paying yearly rent vj^d per annum	01	15	00
Phillip Avent holds att an annuall rent the Landscore in wood	00	13	04
Robert May holds the eight parte of one tenement in Plympton St Mary called Yellond containinge 20 Acres for the lives of John Woolcome ^{38} & Henry Woolcome ^{35} under the yearly rent iij^s 4^d value per annum	03	00	00
William Algar holds one tenement in Plympton Morris & payeth yearly for the same	08	00	00
Thomas Snellinge holds one tenement in Rudgway for terme of his life under the yearly rent of two pounds value per annum	04	00	00
Thomas Rose holds one tenement in Plympton Morris for the life of Elizabeth Collings ^{66} under the yearly rent of two pounds & tenn shillings value per annum	06	00	00
Thomas Rose ^{70} holds for terme of his life & John Rose ^{45} one close called Butsheadparke containeinge one acre and three quarters lyinge in Plympton St Mary under the yearly rent of vj^s viij^d value per annum	04	00	00

Phillip Edwardes [35] for his owne life & the life of Agnes Edwardes [28]
the eight parte of certaine message & tenement called Haywood
& Bromeparkes containing thirty acres under the yearly rent of
twenty pence value per annum   02   10   00

Nicholas Andrewes [63] holds for terme of his owne life & John [35]
his sonne the eight parte of one tenement in Plympton St Mary
containinge fowre acrees under the yearly rent of xij[d] value
per annum   01   00   00

[*Fo. 139 is blank.*]

A particular of the names of they persons that held the Barton of   *fo. 140*
Chaddlewood how many acrees each field measureth togeather
with the price as it was sett by the acree.

		a r p	£ s d per acre
Chapple	Little brambell parke	07 – 01 – 03	01 – 13 – 07
Molton	Turrudge meadow	05 – 02 – 02	02 – 13 – 06
Fosterd	Westerhill Turrudge	10 – 01 – 02	01 – 07 – 01
Hanaford	Heagles Crosparke	13 – 02 – 03	02 – 00 – 01
Winston	Old Parke	07 – 01 – 32	02 – 04 – 01
Winston	Craggs Turrudge	10 – 00 – 25	02 – 04 – 01
Bridwood	Middle stone parke	10 – 01 – 08	01 – 12 – 03
Warren	Broomparke	08 – 01 – 35	01 – 12 – 03
Warren	Homer meadow	04 – 00 – 35	03 – 00 – 09
Bishope	Middle meadow	03 – 02 – 00	03 – 00 – 09
	Steerparke	13 – 03 – 28	01 – 15 – 01
Oates	Great Brambleparke	10 – 02 – 24	01 – 14 – 03
Oates	Bowdens Turrudge	11 – 00 – 24	01 – 10 – 02
Bennet	Little Stoneparke	04 – 02 – 03	01 – 10 – 09
Winston	North Stoneparke	09 – 01 – 26	01 – 11- -03
Craft	Middle Downe	09 – 03 – 15	01 – 05 – 10
Winston	Slade	06 – 02 – 32	01 – 01 – 08
Reepe	Wilparke	10 – 01 – 05	01 – 01 – 01
Reepe	Eastdowne	11 – 01 – 07	01 – 08 – 01
Ryder	Warren	07 – 03 – 34	01 – 15 – 06
Oates	Easter Leaparke	09 – 02 – 10	01 – 05 – 01
Ryder	Lower Leaparke	09 – 01 – 20	01 – 05 – 07
Hanaford	Horsemeadow	02 – 00 – 16:	03 – 00 – 10
Pearse	Dysell parke	10 – 03 – 29:	01 – 00 – 06

Snellinge	Tomes Marsh	10 – 00 – 33	
Stert	Great Hill Turrudge	13 – 00 – 00	01 – 03 – 09
	The wood	18 – 01 – 09	
Stert	Long Turrudge	06 – 02 – 35	
	Aishgrove	00 – 03 – 02	
	The howses gardens &		
	Towne place	06 – 00 – 23	

[*Foliation ceases. The next page is blank.*]

Chadlewood Landes devided into six partes

		£	s	d
1	Florence Davis	024 – 04 – 00		
	The Landscore in wood	013 - 00 – 00		
	Robert May	032 – 06 – 08		
	William Algar	160 – 00 – 00		
	Thomas Snellinge	060 – 00 – 00		
	Thomas Rose	099 – 00 – 00		
	Thomas Rose	043 – 06 – 08		
	Peter Treby	024 – 06 – 08		
	Phillip Edwards	025 – 13 – 04		
	Nicholas Andrewes	010 – 17 - 00		

Sould

		£	s	d
2	Joseph Baker	130 – 00 – 00		
	Symon Hele	155 – 03 – 04		
	John Jessome	090 – 00 – 00		
	Richard Varemouth	051 – 04 – 00		
	Edward Marchant	045 – 00 – 00		
	Druncken Bridge	021 – 00 – 00		
	Christopher Hake	001 – 07 – 06		
	The eight parte of a ten^t neer Hentor			

		£	s	d
3	John Avent	199 – 06 – 08		
	Willm Woolcombe	145 – 05 – 08		
	Christopher Martyn	051 – 07 – 08		
	Balwin Watts	024 – 00 – 00		
	Mary Sumpter	027 – 00 – 02		
	John Walter	010 – 00 – 00		
	8 part of Leemill tenement	022 – 10 – 00		
	Nicholas Huntidon	014 – 08 – 00		

4	Timothy Pearse	242 – 06 – 08
	Morgan Cobridge	045 – 00 – 00
	Richard Lavers	124 – 06 – 08
	Willes tenement	024 – 00 – 00
	Mary Batton	027 – 00 – 00
	Nicholas Edwards	013 – 15 – 00
	Phillip Burne	017 – 00 – 00
5	The Mill Tenement	360 – 00 – 00
	Eight parte of the Mills	054 – 00 – 00
	Richard Turpin	016 – 06 – 03
	William Oates	003 – 14 – 00
	Ralph Harvey	038 – 00 – 00
	John Fluite	021 – 00 – 00
6	Henry Pike	380 – 00 – 00
	Phillip Edwards	061 – 07 – 04
	John Tozer	032 – 00 – 00
	parte of Blaxton meadow	020 – 00 – 00

The Barton of Chadlewood devyded into six partes

	li s		£ s d	
1	13.5	Steereparke	19 – 00 – 00	The Brewhowse pare
	06.0	Willparke	10 – 00 – 00	garden the wester end of
	08.6	Eastdowne	12 – 00 – 00	the new Barne ye hearb
		Westerhorsemead	03 – 10 – 00	garden to the easter end
		Long Terride	04 – 10 – 00	of the new barne the
				therd part of the timber
				in the Towne place & the
				Towne place in common,
				ye north side of the
				Stabell Orchard soe farre
				as the brooke, I
				exchanged these things
				heer above written for
				Long Turridg
2		The warren	10 – 00 – 00	The kitchinge & 4
		Middle Downe	10 – 10 – 00	chambers over it & one
		Easter Leyparke	08 – 10 – 00	study, little howse under
		Homer Meadow	09 – 00 – 00	ye stars, ye workemens
		Longe Turridge	04 – 10 – 00	hall & ye chambers over

	Easter horsemeadow and nursery	01 - 00 - 00	itt, ye butterie & chambers over itt, ye kitchinge Court & ye houses within it, ye easter orchard & hearbgarden in itt, the old barne the poultery Court & Pheasant Court
3	Broomparke	09 – 00 – 00	The hall & Parlour, three
	Middle Meadow	08 – 00 – 00	Chambers over, ye entry
	Dishelparke	09 – 00 – 00	& howses below ye entry,
	Wester Ley parke	10 – 10 – 00	the wester end of ye new
	Slade	06 – 10 – 00	barne, the wester orchard & hopgarden, ye stabell, & woodhowse ye hearbgarden joynynge to Broomparke, ye therd parte of the timber in the Towneplace, & ye Towneplace in common.
4	Great Stoneparke	13 – 00 – 00	
	Little Stoneparke	05 – 10 – 00	
	Olde parke	11 – 00 – 00	
	parte of Turridg meadow	07 – 00 – 00	
	parte of Craggs Turridge	12 – 10 – 00	
5	Parte of Craggs Turridg	02 – 10 – 00	
	North Stoneparke	09 – 00 – 00	
	Great Bramblepark	14 – 10 – 00	
	The Wester hill Turridg	09 – 00 – 00	
	Vincent Tomes marsh	06 – 00 – 00	
	Little Brambleparke	08 – 00 – 00	
6	Heagles Crossparke	19 – 00 – 00	
	Bowdens Turridge	14 – 00 – 00	
	parte Turridge meadow	06 – 00 – 00	
	The Easter hilly Turridge	10 – 00 – 00	

[*4 unused leaves*]

The Bounds and Lymytes of Deane Parrish [heading only]

... my Bulhayes var 2 ...... releases for their fortunes given by my father   [*Loose*
John Worth who dyed November 1689   *fragment*]

Also other Releases from divers people of great consequence

APPENDIX I
FURSE'S LEGAL CASES

Furse mentions cases in local and national courts but few can be corroborated from those court records. Quarter sessions records for Devon, for example, survive only from 1593, the year of his death.

As for the courts at Westminster, the finding aids at the National Archives are not easy to use. Often they depend on knowing the date, and that is precisely what Furse usually fails to supply.

For example, it would be interesting to find William Moreshead's pardon for murder.[1] Pardons were enrolled in the Patent Rolls, but there is no complete index, or county arrangement, and without a date it is not possible to find this pardon. John Moreshead was imprisoned, albeit sympathetically, for two years, and then released by gaol delivery.[2] Gaol delivery records at the National Archives are JUST1 and JUST3, but such finding aids as exist are useless without a given date. Again, the case against Reynell for Fostardes Park cannot be traced in Chancery or Star Chamber because of the shortcomings of the finding aids.[3]

Two cases certainly can be amplified from the public records at The National Archives. They concern the tenement Furse, and the manor of Skyrrydon, now Skerraton.

1. p. 60.
2. p. 64.
3. p. 117.

Furse

A suit in Chancery, Requests and Common Pleas. This case can be traced as REQ 2/248/12, Roger Olden, weaver, and Alice his wife, versus Robert Furse (misleadingly indexed as 'messuage in Dean Prior'). The names Hockway, Olding and Furse do not show up in the index to C2, Chancery Proceedings, nor CP 25/2, feet of fines.[4] Roger Olden, delightfully described as of 'Cherryton fflippen', which must reflect both local pronunciation and a clerk or scrivener's mishearing of it, complains that about four years before Robert Furse of Dean Prior was lawfully seised in a messuage or tenement called Furse in Cheriton, and for a sum of money demised and granted it to one Richard Hookewaye deceased and Alice Langham for three lives. Hookway died a year and a half ago, Olden entered by right of Alice now his wife, and held the premises quietly until now, when one William Hooper offered Furse a large sum of money for it. According to the plaintiff, Furse made out that he had entered by force, and 'so pluckt him out of possession thereof' and gave it to Hooper. Olden took the case to the quarter sesssions to no avail, and now complains that Furse has brought suits against him at the common law. Olden asks for the case to be referred to named justices of the peace in Devon. Letters were directed to these justices 28 November 1584. They reported to the Council that in 21 January the defendant refused to produce any witness to be examined, and said he had of late answered the matter in Chancery. The complainant produced witnesses, who had already made depositions by virtue of a commission out of Chancery on a suit between Hookwaye, since deceased, and Furse. They said Hookway, about Roodmas before his death, demised the tenancy to John Pierce, weaver, of Cruwys Morchard, and then died about Lammas next. Alice Cade, one of the complainants, desired Pierce to give up the premises, which he did, and she occupied quietly until removed by the sheriff or his officers. John Pierce deposed 'that uppon motion made unto the said deff as well by the said Alice as also by this depon[t] at and in the castell of Exon' for the havinge of an ende tochynge the premysses he the said deff aunswered theyme that there shoulde never be an ende in yt as longe as he lyved, but woulde rather spende fyve hundreth powndes in the matter . . .' The conclusion is not clear

4. p. 26.

from the court documents, but Furse avers that his tenant is Hooper and so must have prevailed. It is enlightening to have another's account of his ruthless bombast.

Skyrrydon (Skerraton)

Skyrrydon manor meant a great deal to Furse and he relates at length (pp. 94–102) the legal difficulties he had in securing its purchase from the feckless young Philip Bassett. The manor was mentioned in Domesday Book,[5] and was held by David de Scyredun in 1212. 'Roger Mirabel held his land of Sciredon, and the manors of Kingdon and Hokeneton by the serjeanty of three arrows when the King hunted in the Forest of Dartmoor. Mirabel was outlawed, and his land forfeited, and the King gave the land to Master Walter Medicus, and Master John Boyvile and Dionysia his wife, the daughter and heir of the said Walter, now holdeth.'[6] Walter Medicus was also known as de Sciredon, and as le Devenys, the Devon-man, which Furse spells Debenys. The manor is mentioned in the inquisitions post mortem of John Boyvile or Bonvile 1367, and William Bonvile 1461.[7] Heiress Cecily Bonvile married Thomas Grey, Marquess of Dorset, who died in 1501.

In 1541/2 it was granted in survivorship to Gawin Carewe and his wife Mary for life.[8] On 28 September 1553 Mary granted it to Edward Courteney, Earl of Devon, who was later exiled.[9]

On 2 November 1557 it was sold to James Bassett, with Ranolf Cholmeley as trustee.[10] James was the third son of Sir John Bassett (1463–1528) of Tehidy and Umberleigh. When James Bassett died, 21 November 1558, he held the reversion of Skyrrydon and South Allington from the Crown, as of the manor of East Greenwich, not in chief. He also held Colerudge and Colump John. His son and heir Philip was then aged 1 year 8 months.[11] Sir Peter Carewe had the child's wardship, but this was debatable because Ranolf Cholmeley was still living. James

5. Thorn, *Domesday Book: Devon*, 52:45.
6. Moore, *Forest of Dartmoor*, p. 8, citing the Hundred Rolls 1275.
7. *Calendar of Inquisitions Post Mortem*, Edward III, vol. XIII, no. 211; Record Commissioners, *Calendarium Inquisitionum Post Mortem*, vol. IV.
8. *Calendar of State Papers*, Henry VIII, vol. XVI.
9. *Calendar of Patent Rolls*, Philip and Mary, vol. I.
10. *Calendar of Patent Rolls*, Philip and Mary, vol. IV.
11. TNA C142/122/30.

died over £4000 in debt. Philip also had land in Kent, and was described as 'of Kent' when he was admitted to Lincolns Inn 8 October 1572. His contemporaries at Lincolns Inn included John Savage of Cheshire (7 November 1571) and Hugh Cholmeley of Cheshire (6 March 1572), nephew of Ranolf, two young men who played a part in the subsequent events related by Furse.[12] Ranolf Cholmeley, who was Recorder of London, died in 1565 while Philip Bassett was still a minor, but he had met with Mr Henry Roper, Bassett's maternal grandfather, and Thomas, Roger, and Edward Roper, his uncles, with a view to discharging James Bassett's debts. By feoffment and fine Cholmeley passed to Thomas and Edward Roper Colerudge, Burchhhayes, Columb John, Ponsford, Paddebrok, Skyrrydon and South Allington as feoffees for the life of the widow Mary Bassett (who died 1572), with remainder to Philip and by default his younger brother Charles. Cholmeley had licence to make this alienation 6 May 1562.[13] In exchange Cholmeley received Heanton and Muddaven. A grant to James Bassett 21 May 1557 had included Heanton Punchardon and Heanton Forinseca.[14] 'Muddaven' appears to be Muddiford, in Marwood. Heanton was also included in a grant to Arthur Bassett 8 March 1565.[15] Arthur was the son of James's elder brother John, and must have been party to the exchange. Heanton had in fact been in the Bassett family since Sir John Bassett inherited it from his aunt, who was sister of Philip Beaumont who died in 1473.[16]

When Philip Bassett came of age he began to sell off his lands. On 1 March 1580 he was given licence to alienate the manor of Skerraton and other lands, named, in Dean Prior, Hookney, Kendon, North Bovey, Churchbere, Stanckham, Ilsington and West Ogwill, to Robert Furse.[17] That Easter term, by final concord, he sold to Furse, for a consideration of £12 (not the true price), the manor of Skyridon and 60 messuages, three tofts, one watermill, 60 gardens, 1000 acres of land, 300 acres of meadow, 100 acres of pasture, 100 acres of wood, and 1000 acres of heath and furze, 6s rent and rent of 1lb of wax, in Dean

12. Lincolns Inn, *Admissions.*
13. *Calendar of Patent Rolls,* Elizabeth I, vol. III, 1563–66, pp. 202–3.
14. *Calendar of Patent Rolls,* Philip and Mary, vol. III, p. 403.
15. *Calendar of Patent Rolls,* Elizabeth I, vol. III, 1563–66, pp. 202–3.
16. Lysons, *Magna Britannia: Devon,* p. cxxxiii.
17. *Calendar of Patent Rolls,* Elizabeth I, vol. VIII, 1578–80, p. 238.

Prior, Houckney, Little Kynedon, Northbovye, Churchebere, Stanckeham, Ilsington and Westoggewelle.[18] There were two difficulties. One was the grant to Gawin Carewe, which in the end was resolved as a tenancy to Furse. Carewe died in 1583. The other was the entail to Charles Bassett, but this was resolved by a further conveyance from him. It was probably easy to put pressure on him as he was a Roman Catholic, who eventually left England and died as a friar or monk abroad.

In 1582 Philip Bassett made further sales, including Coleridge and lands in Zeal Monachorum to John Dunscombe. Dunscombe was a London usurer, to whom Furse also mortgaged More, Chiddingbroke, and his Crediton properties on 6 May 1580, to be repaid 27 November following, which he asserts he did, in the presence of Philip Bassett, Humfrey Prideaux and John Hoayell.[19] This seems to have been part and parcel of his sale to Richard Prideaux.[20] Bassett also sold Columb John and lands in Broadclyst to John Chichester and John Melford and the heirs of Chichester.[21] On 28 April 1582 Bassett granted and let to John Acland the manor of Columb John in the parish of Broadclyst for 99 years on the lives of Acland, John Mallett and John Acland, son of Hugh.[22] Philip's difficulties were not resolved. When the sheriff of Devon made a return to the Council on 24 October 1585, he wrote: 'Answers of the recusants within that county. James Courtney has left for London, and Philip Bassett is not to be found, but he is probably in the Fleet at London.[23] Philip tried, with a £1000 bribe, to persuade Sir Hugh Cholmeley to frustrate the assurance to Furse, and also to return Heanton and Mudaven, which he had 'sold' to Dunscombe, but Sir Hugh refused. As well as Dunscombe, Acland and Russewyll were dissatisfied customers, claiming Columb John, Ponsford and Paddebroke. Whatever the sale to Chichester represents, possibly a short-term mortgage, Risdon says that Bassett sold Columb John to William Rowswell Esq, and he alienated it to Sir John Acland.[24]

18. TNA CP25/2/110/1355/22ELIZ1EASTER
19. p. 40.
20. pp. xvi, 42.
21. *Calendar of Patent Rolls*, Elizabeth I, vol. IX, 1580–83, pp. 161, 267.
22. Referred to in Devon RO 1148M add 2/L 15/275.
23. *State Papers Domestic*, 1581–90, p. 279.
24. Risdon, *Survey of Devon*, p. 59.

Sir John Savage of Cheshire was a neighbour and friend of Cholmeley, and his son John, Bassett's contemporary at Lincoln's Inn, had been defrauded by Bassett of £600. Acland tried to bribe this young man to use his influence with his father to persuade Cholmeley to action, and Sir Hugh did indeed come to Devon and enter Heanton and Mudaven, to represent all Bassett's land, in January 1588. Acland and Russewyll, or Rowswell, made Bassett ride to Sir Hugh's with them and seal three releases, of Heanton and Mudaven to Sir Hugh, who later conveyed to Dunscombe, Columb John to Acland, and other lands to Russewyll. Sir Hugh sent a threatening letter to Furse, presumably trying to bring Skyrrydon into this equation, but Furse successfully ignored it, and felt confidently secure in his property.

APPENDIX II
SPORTS AND PASTIMES
MENTIONED BY FURSE

Furse approved of those of his ancestors who shone in manly sports, and listed their accomplishments, for example at pages 30, 31, 43, 53, 55, 56, 67, 135–6.

Joseph Strutt collected information as *The Sports and pastimes of the people of England* in the early nineteenth century, and the specialist chapters in C.T. Onions *Shakespeare's England* (1917) are instructive, as is Christina Hole's *English Sports and Pastimes*. Richard Carew's *Survey of Cornwall*, 1602, gives contemporary accounts of archery and wrestling (pp. 75–6).

Statute law struggled to encourage those sports and activities which prepared young men for war, and to ban sedentary pursuits that went with gambling and dissipation. An act for the maintenace of artillery and debarring of unlawful games, 33 Henry VIII c. 9 (1541/2) forbade bowling, coyting, coysh, cayls, half bowls, tennis, dicing, tables or carding. Sir Thomas Elyot approved of wrestling, running and swimming because they could be useful in war, and of course riding and swordplay. Hunting was an imitation of battle. He thought dice mere idleness because it was a game of chance, cards and tables at least required a little wit, and chess much more. Use of the bow was essential for war, and he grudgingly approved tennis for young men, but was against 'clash', bowls, quoits and football.[25] 'To ride cumlie: to run faire at the tilte or ring:

25. Elyot, *The Governor*, pp. 60–68, 91, 92.

to plaie at all weapones; to shote faire in bow, or surelie in gon' were the 'noble exercises' of the Tudor period, and so too were running, vaulting, wrestling, dancing and singing, and all similar employments 'conteining either some fitte exercise for warre, or some pleasant pastime for peace,' wrote Roger Ascham.[26] The Cotswold Games, held in the last quarter of the sixteenth century, included wrestling, leaping, cudgel playing, sword-and-buckler, pitching the bar, throwing the sledge(hammer), and tossing the pike.[27] Leaping, often equated with vaulting, generally meant skilled moves, somersaults, leaping through hoops and so on. Sword and buckler was a dance-like combat regulated by music.

Wrestling, or wraxelling, was held in particularly high regard in the west country as a manly art. Devon wrestling was similar to Cornish, but kicking was allowed, with specially reinforced boots.[28]

'Casting of the bar is frequently mentioned by the romance writers as one part of a hero's education, and a poet of the sixteenth century thinks it highly commendable for kings and princes, by way of exercise, to throw "the stone, the barre, or the plummet". Henry VIII, after his accession to the throne, according to Hall and Holinshed, retained "the castinge of the barre" among his favourite amusements.'[29]

'Shooting' in the sixteenth century might mean either with the bow, or a handgun. Carew uses it for archery. Roger Ascham's *Toxophilus, or the schole of shooting*, 1571, is about archery. At p. 30 Furse most probably means shooting with the bow, but at p. 136 he distinguishes archery and shooting. Despite requirements for all able-bodied man to practise with the bow it was by the later part of the century practised with less enthusiasm as new means of warfare made it less relevant. 'During the Tudor period firearms began to be used for sporting purposes, and it was these which, eventually and in different ways, hastened the decline of both falconry and fowling. The early shot-guns were very primitive engines, often quite as dangerous to their users as

26. Hole, *English Sports and Pastimes*, p. 24, quoting Ascham, *The Scholemaster*, 1571.
27. Onions, *Shakespeare's England*, p. 451.
28. Anon., 'Devonshire Wrastling and Wrastlers', *The Devonian Yearbook* 1922, pp. 60–65.
29. Strutt, *Sports and Pastimes*, p. 140.

the game; they were cumbersome and inefficient, and made but a poor substitute for the cross-bow or the hawk.'[30] By 'shooting' Furse may be distinguishing the cross-bow from the archer's long-bow. He provided a caliver for the muster, so was familiar with firearms. The caliver was the lightest portable firearm except the pistol, and was used as a fowling piece.

Hunting would be principally be of deer, also the hare, that is edible beasts. Elyot also mentions the fox.[31]

As to more domestic but active sports, tennis is well known as a favourite pastime of Henry VIII in his youth, but nevertheless, was regarded as frivolous. Tennis was a favourite pastime of John Moreshead, Furse's grandfather.[32] Bowling might be on a green, but increasingly houses were being built with bowling alleys.

The sedentary pastimes Furse mentions are dicing, which Strutt thinks probably the most ancient of sedentary games, cards, which gained in popularity in the fifteenth century with cheaper paper and woodblock printing, and tables, which was a form of backgammon.

30. Hole, *English Sports and Pastimes*, p. 20.
31. Collier, 'Sport on Dartmoor'.
32. p. 67

APPENDIX III
FURSE'S FAMILY AND PEDIGREE

The following details from parish registers and Vivian's edition of the visitations amplify the notes made by Furse and later his son at pages 76–7.

The child Robert Furse was buried 21 December 1577 at Dean Prior, but apparently not baptised there, probably dying before baptism.

Baptisms of two daughters are evident in the Dean Prior registers 1562 and later in the 1560s, but their names are lost owing to damage. They are probably Joan and Margaret. Joan married at Mary Tavy in 1581. Furse himself does not mention a Margaret, although Vivian does in *Visitations* (p. 385), and may have seen the parish register when in better condition. He gives her date of baptism as 1562, and does not mention Joan. Annes's baptism is not evident at Dean Prior, but there is damage to the register. Furse records her marriage to John Wolcomb of Plympton. Vivian records a second marriage to William Gould of Staverton in 1618.

Mary was baptised 10 March 1564/5, and her marriage was in 1591 or 1592.

Elizabeth was baptised 7 March, probably 1568, but pages are damaged.

Wilmot was baptised 14 May 1570 at Dean Prior, and married at St Thomas in 1592.

Grace was baptised 24 April 1573.

Jane was baptised 5 June 1575.

Susanna was baptised 15 April 1579 and married at Dean Prior 21 January 1604/5.

Anne was baptised 11 October 1581.

John was baptised 24 June 1584, and died 16 March 1609/10.

John's children's baptisms were: Robert 21 September 1606, Elizabeth (Plympton St Mary) 24 March 1606, Frances (Dean Prior) 14 October 1607, John 27 December 1608, and Ferdinand or Fardinando 14 January 1609.

Rolonde de Cumba alias Furse

William de la Furse (temp. Edward III, 1327–77)

Thomas

John de la Furse = Mabelye (Vicarye?)

William Furse = —— Engelysche (temp Henry V, 1413–22)

William Furse, at Cherton = (Annes?) Averye

Robert Furse, at Colebrooke (fl. temp. Edward IV, d. temp Henry VII, c.1461–1509) = Joan

John Furse I (c.1438–1508) = Annes Adler (c.1460–1540)

| John II (c.1481–1549) (1) = Mary Foxsecombe alias Trunchard (2) = Anne Remond (3) = Margaret Cuttelyffe | Bawden d.s.p. | William of Broomham |

John d.s.p. (d. 1564?) William — 3 sons, 1 dau.

dau. = Richard Man — 3 daus.

dau. = —— Harres — sons and daus.

| John III (1506–72) (1) = Joan Moreshead (c.1510–50) (2) = (1) Joan Powle (2) = John Seller | Jerome d.s.p. | Edward d.s.p. | Crysten = Robert Remonde | Joan = John Toychen | Pasco = John Marten |

| Robert (c.1535–93) = (1) Wilmot Rowland (2) = Arthur Hart | John = Cateren Lake | Edward = Margery Cowke alias Best | Steven |

| Joan (b. c.1562) = John Cake | Annes (b. c.1563) = John Wolcombe | Mary (1) = John Redeclefe | Elizabeth (b. c.1568) = Rafe Wodeleye | Wilmot (b. 1570) = John Byrdall |

Roger
Grace
Mary
John
William
Joan

7 others
died as
infants

Mary
Jane
Wilmot
William (d.)
William
Agnes

Wilmot
Sibley

(2) = John
Redeclefe

Joan
Mary
William

Rafe
Elizabeth
Innes
Annes

Mellerye (d.)
son (d.)
Elizabeth
Margaret
Wilmot

FURSE PEDIGREE, deduced from

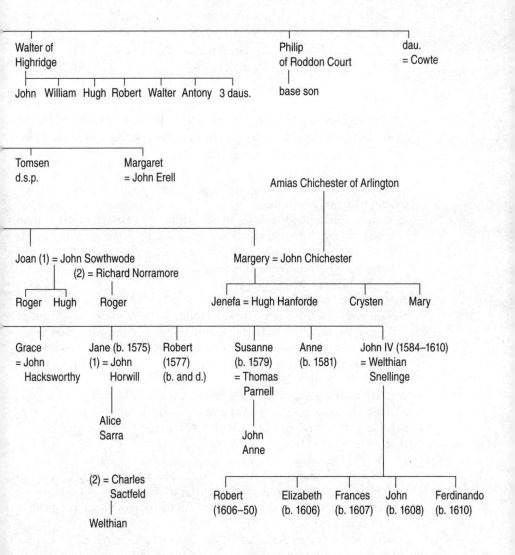

Walter of
Highridge

John   William   Hugh   Robert   Walter   Antony   3 daus.

Philip
of Roddon Court

base son

dau.
= Cowte

Tomsen
d.s.p.

Margaret
= John Erell

Amias Chichester of Arlington

Joan (1) = John Sowthwode
        (2) = Richard Norramore

Roger   Hugh   Roger

Margery = John Chichester

Jenefa = Hugh Hanforde   Crysten   Mary

Grace
= John
   Hacksworthy

Jane (b. 1575)
(1) = John
      Horwill

Alice
Sarra

(2) = Charles
      Sactfeld

Welthian

Robert
(1577)
(b. and d.)

Susanne
(b. 1579)
= Thomas
   Parnell

John
Anne

Anne
(b. 1581)

John IV (1584–1610)
= Welthian
   Snellinge

Robert
(1606–50)

Elizabeth
(b. 1606)

Frances
(b. 1607)

John
(b. 1608)

Ferdinando
(b. 1610)

the text, and latterly from parish registers

GLOSSARY

This includes both forms containing Furse's idiosyncratic or dialectical spellings and usages of ordinary words, such as 'f' for 'gh', and out-dated and unfamiliar words.

abowne, *for* above.

adyunynge, *for* adjoining.

agistment (justament); taking in of cattle or livestock to feed at so much a head; the opening of a forest for a specified time to livestock; a rate or charge on owner or occupier of pasture lands; however, Furse uses it in the sense of a property, not a right.

alewights; ale tasters.

allers; alders (p. 67).

almain rivet (p. 75): body armour similar to the corselet, *q. v.,* but in basic form only the breastplate and apron, but the latter was made up of overlapping pieces attached by rivets and sliding into slots. If there was a backplate it was known as a pair of almain rivets. It was usually worn by a billman.

amerse (amerse); amercement; a fine in a manorial court.

ancient demesne (p. 42); land belonging to the Crown in 1066.

angel; a coin, worth 6*s*. 8*d*. from 1464; later 7*s*. 6*d*., 10*s*. and 11*s*.

apses; aspens (p. 81).

arbege, *for* herbage.

assize of annoyance; annoyance, or nuisance, means any hurt done to a place by placing on it anything that might breed infection, or by encroachment; the assize is a writ requiring redress or removal of the nuisance.

attornments; the agreement of the owner of an estate in land to become the tenant of a person who has acquired the estate next in reversion or remainder, or the right to the rent or services by which the land is held.

auxilium vicecomitatis (oxylion rent); a customary aid or duty payable to the sheriff out of certain manors, for the better support of their office.
awter, awtor, *for* author.

bande, *for* bond.
Banke, *for* Court of Common Bench (p. 144).
barste, *for* burst (p. 19).
barten, berton, home farm.
beads, pair of (p. 48); a rosary.
beste beste, *for* best beast.
blinded (p. 66); uncertain, but the sense is hoodwinked.
bofte, *for* bought.
bunter; sifter of grain.

caliver; a development of the harquebus, midway between the harquebus, an early firearm about 3 feet long, and the musket.
castell tongue (p. 57); Castilian.
censarii ('sensores'); moormen, with liberty to dwell in the forest of Dartmoor although having no tenement there (Crossing 1912). In medieval Latin, a tenant paying rent, a farmer.
chattell lease; leasehold farm or holding.
clowte; cloth.
cole (p. 93); charcoal, here, from peat.
common juror (p. 75); ordinary jurors serving on a common jury as opposed to a special jury, of persons of a certain status.
common of pasture; right of pasturing cattle on the common land.
common of turbary; liberty of digging turf for fuel on another's ground, a right pertaining to a house.
Commosyon (Commotion), the; Prayer Book Rebellion 1549.
concealed lands (pp. 113, 125); land held privily from the king by a person having no title thereto, used especially of former monastic land.
copyhold; tenure protected by title written into manor court roll.
corselet, corslet; light body armour consisting of metal breastplate and backplate held together by straps, sometimes with a collar (gorget), and a metal apron to reach the upper thigh, worn by pikemen.
cose, *for* cause.
cousin, denoting much wider range of relatives than modern usage.
curte, *for* court.

daystes (p. 80); context suggests strays, or estrays.
dewell, *for* dwell.

distress; distraint, a chattell legally seized for constraining the owner to pay money owed, or satisfaction of a wrong.

dofter, *for* daughter.

drye; a drying-house.

dyssessor, *for* disseisor.

entry, make; actual taking possession of lands or tenements by entering or setting foot on.

escheat; an incident of feudal law, whereby a fief reverted to the lord when a tenant died without leaving a successor qualified to inherit under the original grant, hence lapsing of land to the Crown or lord of the manor on the death of a tenant intestate or without heirs.

escheator; an officer appointed yearly by the Lord Treasurer to take notice in the county and certify into the Exchequer.

erell, *for* earl.

estrays; animals found wandering in the manor or lordship. If not claimed in a year and a day they were forfeit to the Crown, but the lord of the manor usually had a special grant from the Crown for such.

existima, existimacyon; estimate.

excambe, *for* exchange.

farthing; a variable land measure, usually a quarter of a hide or of an acre.

fee simple; a freehold estate of inheritance, absolute and unqualified.

fee tail; entail, restriction of inheritance of land to a particular heir or class of heirs; settlement on persons in succession, none of whom can then dispose of the land.

fellon, *for* fellin (p. 80); a disease of cattle also called black-leg, black-quarter, quarter-evil, quarter-ill.

felon, felonry; felonry is the state of having forfeited lands and goods on conviction of certain offences.

felon de see; suicide.

fenne (venne) (pp. 93, 123), *for* fen or 'vain'; peat on which bog-grasses grow, but with no topsoil (Crossing 1912).

fethement *for* feoffment; the conveyance of freehold estate; the deed of conveyance.

fiftydole; fifteenth, share of subsidy paid to the Crown.

forma pauperis, in (p. 27); in the character of a pauper. Statutes of 1495 (11 Henry VII c.12) and 1532 (23 Henry VIII c15) provided that every poor person wishing to bring an action at law, with property not worth £5 save his wearing apparel and the subject of the action, was excused court fees and had an attorney and counsel assigned without payment.

fowle, *for either* fool *or* fowl.

frankpledge *see* view.

free socage; socage is land held by free suitors of the lord's court generally for services; in free socage the services are generally 'free', that is fealty and a fixed rent, as distinct from villein socage in which the services are base.

garden, gardener, *for* guardian.

gigmill, gyggemylle; mill for raising nap on cloth by teazels or wire-cards.

glade to (p. 138); the sense is, 'had to'.

grand jury; inquisition of from 12 to 23 freeholders of a county returned by the sheriff to sessions of the peace, and commissions of oyer and terminer and general gaol delivery.

gurgito, stream.

gyggehalter, probably gijoalter (Cornish dialect), part of the rigging of a ship (Wright), used by Furse for a giddy girl; compare giglet (OED).

hagged, hagges, *for* hedged, hedges.

harbage, *for* herbage; herbaceous growth; legally the natural growth or pasture as distinct from the land itself.

harquebus; an early firearm about 3 feet long.

here, *for* here *and for* heir.

herrett, *for* heriott; render to the lord on a tenant's death, usually the best live beast or dead chattel by legal custom.

heye rent, *for* high rent; chief rent, *redditus capitalis*, freeholder's rent of assize which cannot be departed from or varied.

hick, hycke, (p. 21); can be cant for a man, and in particular a rough countryman or booby.

homage; jury (manorial).

honer, *for* owner.

howe, *for* how, *and for* who.

howse, *for* house, *and for* whose.

inusyon, inyunsion, *for* injunction.

june, *for* join.

junter, junture, *for* jointure; the holding of property to the joint use of a husband and wife for life or in tail, as a provision for the latter, in the event of her widowhood.

just title; right of possession.

justament, *see* agistment.

kit, kytte (p. 21); can be a kitten, a staved vessel, a basket, an outfit or tools, a type of fish or a dancing-master's fiddle.

knight service; tenure of land under the condition of performing military service.

knight's fee; amount of land for which the services of an armed knight were due to the sovereign.

kyettusness; covetousness.

lake; stream (p. 122).

lammas; 1 August or 12 August.

lanscor, *for* landscore; a dividing line between two estates (Rose-Troup 1938, pp. 261, 263); an early form of enclosure under the common field system; a parcel of land not actually bounded by hedges or fences but marked out by land-marks only (*Charities* 1830, App. p. 32).

lese, *for* lease.

lette, *for* leet; legal court of a manor as distinct from court baron dealing with land tenure.

levynge, *for* living, *or* leaving.

livery; act of giving seisin or possession.

marcus, *for* marquess.

marell, *for* marl.

mark; a money of account, 13*s*. 4*d*. It was not a coin, but a unit recognised internationally.

mill trowe, trough; corn bin.

moaytye, *for* moiety.

mony, *for* many.

morte mayne, *for* mortmain; land held by a corporation or monastic house that cannot be alienated.

myre, *for* mere.

nele, nell, *for* needle.

newde, *for* need.

nisi prius; 'unless before': an action summoned to Westminster unless heard before a given date by justices in assize.

noble; a gold coin worth 6*s*. 8*d*.

nofty, *for* naughty.

nussery, *for* nursery.

nyghtebores, *for* neighbours.

ob., obolus; halfpenny.

ocke; oak.

ockekernes; acorns.

offes, offyse, *for* office; inquest or entitlement showing sovereign's entitlement.

ofte, *for* ought.

one, *for* one, *and for* own.

or, *for* ere, before.

outlaw, outlawry; outlawry is the being put out of the law for contempt in wilfully avoiding the execution of the process of the king's court.

oxylion rent, *see* auxilium vicecomitis.

paste howse; a building where pastry is made.

patonye in trust, *for* patentee.

per persyonalety; by personalty, personal estate or goods.

persell, *for* parcel, partly.

person, *for* parson.

pettigrew, *for* pedigree.

plestur (p. 19); plaster, dressing.

poll deed; a deed-poll is made by a single person or persons having similar interests, and is polled or cut even as opposed to a deed indented.

polle door (p. 72); uncertain, but presumably relating to a pulley.

possession; physical control with intention, both visible, or evidenced by external signs.

privilege, writ of; a process to enforce or maintain a privilege.

pro recognision'; by recognition, an acknowledgement by recognitors, such as jurors in an assize of novel disseisin.

proscrypsion, *for* prescription; a right, immunity or obligation existing by reason of a lapse of time.

pryntes, apprentice.

'pylle', verb, Isaiah; possibly for pull, pluck, or strip: the sense is cheat or misuse.

quillett; a small plot of land of no precise size.

rayeles, reles, *for* rails, railings.

redynge; ridding, cleaning

relese, *for* release; a freeholder could lease his land, usually for a year, to an occupier who had entered it by deed of grant (a release), holding for himself a future interest (a reversion) which was an incorporeal hereditament, and which could be conveyed without livery of seisin.

releve, *for* relief; a payment made to the overlord by the heir of a feudal tenant on taking up possession of the vacant estate.

rente secke; a rent reserved by deed in favour of some person, without a clause of distress in case of arrears, and so differing from a rent-charge.

resters (p. 158); apparently some kind of support beam.

resyences, *probably for* residens, a tenant bound to live on the land of his lord.

roodmas; Rood day could be the Exaltation of the Cross, 14 September, or Invention of the Cross, 3 May.

rowler, roweller, *for* roiler; one who roams idly or dissolutely.

ryal (ryeles); a coin worth 10*s.* under Edward IV and Henry VII, 15*s.* under Mary and Elizabeth.

seges; seats or benches.

sensores, *see* censarii.

Sentorye, *for* Sanctuary; glebe.

sethenes, *for* since.

sherro rent, *for* sherriff rent; *see* auxilium vicecomitatis.

shyndell, *for* shingle.

socage tenure; tenure of land by certain determinable services other than knight service. Land held by free suitors of a lord's court. The services are free, generally fealty and a fixed rent, as opposed to villein service with 'base' services.

socke rente, *see* rent secke.

soyell, *for* soil.

sm^a to., *for* summa totalis, total amount.

spessyaltyes, *for* specialty; contract under seal.

stowle, *for* stool.

strayers, *for* strays, *see* estrays.

streke; a long irregular strip of land.

stroll; space between two enclosures.

strongeres, *for* strangers; in the context of Dartmoor and venvil, a man from other parts of Devon.

stronggury, *for* stranguary; a condition of constant desire to pass water, although only a few drops can be voided, symptom of inflammation in the urinary tract (Markovitch).

supply(e) (p. 98); supplication, entreaty.

stuffed; well stored or provided.

syne (p. 49); sinew.

tabeles, *for* tables; a form of backgammon.

tales; when a jury has been summoned, if enough do not appear, either party may pray a tales, that is ask the court to make up the deficiency.

the, *for* the, *and for* thee.

ther, *for* there, *and for* their.

throffe, *for* through.

this, *for* this, *and for* thus.

tithing; a group of ten men who stood security for each other, and were bound to the king for upholding the law.

toawyes; toys (p. 22).

toft; a homestead or croft.

token, *for* tucking; fulling.

toller; inspector of tin bounds and collector of the tolls or revenues of tin mines.

towellehowse, *for* toolhouse.

towne; farmstead or any settlement.

truysshede, *probably for* trashed, in the early sense 'restrained, hindered'.

turbary, common of; right to cut turf or peat for fuel.

unynscely; unnicely.

unteasted; intestate.

venne; *see* fenne.

venvil, vendeville (p. 93, etc.); corruption of *fines villarum*, or township fines, although the payment is a rent not a fine, and peculiar to tenements with rights on Dartmoor (Moore 1890).

view of frankpledge; inspection of the tithing system at the sheriff's tourn or manor court.

waif; goods found but not claimed, akin to stray.

ward, *for* boundary, fence.

wenehouse, *for* wainhouse.

were, *for* were, *and for* weir.

where, *may be* whether.

worell, worlye, *for* world, worldly.

wraxell, *for* wrestle.

writ of privilege, *see* privilege.

wykely; weekly.

yage, *for* age.

yate, *for* gate.

yearthe, *for* earth.

yease, *for* ease (p. 78).

yee, *for* eye.

yelder, *for* elder.
yele, *for* aisle.
yell, *for* ill.
yende, *for* end.
yt, *for* it, *and for* yet.

BIBLIOGRAPHY

Manuscript sources are given in full throughout the volume, and are not listed here.

Adams, Ann, *Zeal Monachorum: a Devon rural parish* (Exeter, 2002).

Anon., 'Devonshire Wrastling and Wrastlers', *The Devonian Yearbook*, 1922, pp. 60–65.

Alexander, J. J., and Hooper, W. R., *The History of Great Torrington, North Devon* (Sutton, 1948).

Apperson, G. L. (ed.), *Gleanings after Time: chapters in social and domestic history* (London, 1907).

Apperson, G. L., *English Proverbs and Provincial Phrases: a historical dictionary* (London and New York, 1929).

Ascham, Roger, *The Scholemaster* (1570, 1571), ed. Edward Arber (London, 1870).

Baldwin, William, *A Treatise of Morall Philosophie* (1547), ed. Thomas Palfreyman (1620).

Bibles:

The Byble in Englysshe (The Great Bible) (London, 1540).

The New Testament, translated by William Tyndale, 1534 (Cambridge, 1939).

The Bible translated into Englysshe by Myles Coverdale, second edition (London, 1550).

The Bible, that is, the Holy Scriptures contained in the Old and New Testament (London, Robert Barker, 1611) ('Geneva' Bible, first in 1560).

Blake, Norman Francis, *Caxton and his World* (London, 1969).

Boorde, Alexander, *Introduction of Knowledge, 1547, Dyetary of Helth, 1542*, ed. F. J. Furnivall, Early English Text Society, E.S. 10 (1870).

Brown, Stewart, *Lower Cotterbury Farmhouse, Blackawton, Devon* (Stewart Brown Associates, 2007, available at Devon County Council Historic Environment Record).

Buhler, C. F. (ed.), *Dictes and Sayings of the Philosophers* (1939), Early English Text Society, O.S. 211 (London).

Byrne, M. St Clare (ed.), *The Elizabethan Home, discovered in two dialogues by Claudius Hollyband and Peter Erondell* (London, 1949).

Calendar of Inquisitions Post Mortem, Edward III, vol. XII (1938).

Calendar of Inquisitions Post Mortem, Henry VII, vol. II, *Years 13–20* (1915).

Calendar of Patent Rolls, Philip and Mary, vol. I (1937), vol. III (1938), vol. IV (1939).

Calendar of Patent Rolls, Elizabeth, vol. II (1948), vol. IV (1961), vol VIII (1986), vol. IX (1986).

Calendar of State Papers Domestic, Edward VI, Mary, Elizabeth and James I, vol. II, *1581–1590* (1865).

Calendar of State Papers: Ireland, Tudor Period 1571–1575, revised edition, Mary O'Dowd (ed.) (2000).

Calendar of State Papers relating to Ireland, Henry VIII, Edward VI, Mary and Elizabeth, vol. I, 1509–1573 (1860), vol. II, 1574–1585 (1867).

Cam, Helen Maud, *The Hundred and the Hundred Rolls* (London, 1930).

Campbell, Mildred, *The English Yeoman under Elizabeth and the Early Stuarts* (New Haven, 1942).

Carbonell, Barbara M. H., 'Notes on the history of the parishes of Nymet Tracey, alias Bow, with Broad Nymet', *Transactions of the Devonshire Association*, 60 (1928), pp. 299–312.

Carew, Richard, *The Survey of Cornwall* (1602), edited by John Chynoweth, Nicholas Orme and Alexandra Walsham, Devon and Cornwall Record Society, New Series, 47 (Exeter, 2004).

Carpenter, H. J., 'Furse of Moreshead. A family record of the sixteenth century', *Transactions of the Devonshire Association*, 26 (1894), pp. 168–184.

Castlehow, Revd J. A. S., 'The Duchy of Lancaster in the County of Devon', *Transactions of the Devonshire Association*, 80 (1948), pp. 193–209.

Cecil, William, Lord Burghley, *Precepts or directions for the well ordering and carriage of a man's life, through the whole course thereof: left by William, Lord Burghley, to his son at his death* (London, 1636).

Chanter, John Roberts, *Sketches of the Literary History of Barnstaple, to which is appended the diary of Philip Wyott* (Barnstaple, 1866).

Charities: *Report of the Commissioners concerning Charities containing that part which relates to the County of Devon*, 3 vols. (Exeter, 1826–30).

Chope, R. Pearse, *Dialect of Hartland* (London, 1891).

Collier, W. T., 'Sport on Dartmoor', *Transactions of the Devonshire Association*, 27 (1895), pp. 113–123.

Creighton, Charles, *A History of Epidemics in Britain*. vol. I, *From A.D. 664 to the Great Plague* (1891).

Cresswell, Beatrix, 'Chained books and libraries in Devon parish churches' (1911), *Transactions of the Exeter Diocesan Architectural Society*, series III, 3 (c.1916), pp. 91–97.

Crossing, William, *Guide to Dartmoor* (1912).

Cruden, Alexander, *A Complete Concordance to the Old and New Testaments* (London and New York, 1895).

Cruwys, M. C. S., *Cruwys Morchard Notebook* (Exeter and London, 1939).

D'Evelyn, Charlotte (ed.), *Peter Idley's Instructions to his Son* (Boston, 1935).

Devereux, E. J., 'Richard Taverner's translations of Erasmus', *The Library*, fifth series, 19 (1964), pp. 212–214.

Dunstan, G. R. (ed.), *The Register of Edmund Lacy, Bishop of Exeter, 1420–1455*, Devon and Cornwall Record Society, New Series 7, 10, 13, 16, 18 (1963–1972).

Dyboski, R. (ed.), *Richard Hill's Commonplace Book*, Early English Text Society, E.S. 101 (1907).

Elyot, Thomas, *The Book named the Governor*, ed. S. E. Lehmberg (London, 1962).

Erasmus, Desiderius, *Opera Omnia*, 10 vols. (Leyden, 1703).

Erasmus, Desiderius, *Collected Works*, ed. Craig R. Thompson et al., sundry volumes between 36 and 86 (Toronto, 1978).

Erskine, Audrey M. (ed.), *The Devonshire Lay Subsidy of 1332*, Devon and Cornwall Record Society, New Series, 14 (1969).

Finberg, H. P. R., *Tavistock Abbey* (Cambridge, 1951).

Fry, Edward Alexander (ed.), *Calendar of Wills and Administrations relating to the Counties of Devon and Cornwall proved in the Court of the Principal Registry of the Bishop of Exeter 1559–1779 and of Devon only in the Court of the Archdeaconry of Exeter* (Devonshire Association, Plymouth, 1908).

Furnivall, F. J. (ed.), *Early English Meals and Manners*, Early English Text Society, O.S., vol. 32 (1868).

Furnivall, F. J. (ed.), *Caxton's Book of Curtesye*, Early English Text Society, E.S., vol. 3 (1868).

Gover, J. E. B., Mawer, A., and Stenton, F. M., *The Place-Names of Devon*, 2 vols., English Place-Name Society, 8, 9 (Cambridge 1931, 1932).

Gray, Todd, *The Lost Chronicle of Barnstaple* (Exeter, 1998).

Halliwell, James Orchard (ed.), *The Private Diary of Dr John Dee and the Catalogue of his Library of Manuscripts*, Camden Society, vol. 19 (1842).

Hellinga, Lotte, and Trapp, J. B. (eds.), *The Cambridge History of the Book in Britain*, vol. III (Cambridge, 1999).

Hemery, Eric, *High Dartmoor* (London, 1983).

Hingeston-Randolph, F. C., *The Register of John de Grandisson, Bishop of Exeter*, vol. III (London and Exeter, 1897).

Hogg, James (ed.), *Richard Whytford*, vol. 5, *A Werke for Housholders*, Salzburg Studies in English Literature: Elizabethan and Renaissance Studies (Salzburg, 1979).

Holdsworth, W. S., *An Historical Introduction to the Land Law* (Oxford, 1927).

Hole, Christina, *English Sports and Pastimes* (London, 1949).

Hoskins, W. G., 'The estates of the Caroline gentry', in W. G. Hoskins and H. P. R. Finberg, *Devonshire Studies* (London, 1952), pp. 334–65.

Howard, A. J., and Stoate, T. L., eds., *The Devon Muster Roll for 1569* (Bristol, 1977).

Idley: see D'Evelyn.

Jowitt: *Jowitt's Dictionary of English Law by the late Hon. the Earl Jowitt and Clifford Walsh*, 2nd edition, by John Burke, 2 vols. (London, 1977).

Keene, C. J. Perry, *Herrick's Parish: Dean Prior: with stories and songs of the Dean Bourne* (Plymouth, 1926).

Kelly, *Directory of Devon*, various editions.

Keystone Historic Buildings Consultants, *Broomham, King's Nympton, Devon*, Report K443 (Exeter, June 1995).

Kingdon, Eric V., 'Tavistock Library', *Transactions of the Devonshire Association*, 78 (1946), pp. 229–238.

Lamplugh, Lois, *Barnstaple, Town on the Taw* (Chichester, 1983).

Lamplugh, Lois, *A Look at the Past of Swimbridge* (Swimbridge, 1993).

Latham, Agnes M. C. (ed.), *The Poems of Sir Walter Raleigh* (London, 1951).

Letters and Papers, Foreign and Domestic, Henry VIII, vol. XVI (1898).

Lever, Murray, *A Devonshire Word-List compiled in 1990 by Murray Lever, Recorder of Devonshire Dialect for the Devonshire Association* (WSL: MS duplicated).

Lincolns Inn: *Record of the Honourable Society of Lincolns Inn*, vol. I, *Admissions from A.D. 1420 to A.D. 1799* (London, 1896).

Lloyd, L. J., and Erskine, A. M., *The Library of Exeter Cathedral* (Exeter, 2004).

Local Population Studies, *The Plague Reconsidered: a new look at its origins and effects in sixteenth and seventeeth century England* (Matlock, 1977).

Louis, Cameron (ed.), *The Commonplace Book of Robert Reynes of Acle (Tanner MS 407)* (Ottawa, 1977).

Lysons, Daniel and Samuel, *Magna Britannia*, vol. 6, *Devon*, 2 parts (1822).

Marcovitch, Harvey (ed.), *Black's Medical Dictionary*, 41st edition (London, 2005).

Moore, Stuart A., *A Short History of the Rights of Common upon the Forest of Dartmoor*, Dartmoor Preservation Association, Publication 1 (Plymouth, 1890).

Nicholls, John Gough (ed.), *The Diary of Henry Machin, Citizen and Merchant Taylor of London from A.D. 1550 to A.D. 1563*, Camden Society, vol. 42 (1868).

Oliver, George, *Ecclesiastical Antiquities in Devon, being observations on several churches in Devonshire with some memoranda for the history of Cornwall*, 2 vols. (Exeter, 1840).

Onions, C. T. (ed.), *Shakespeare's England: an account of the life and manners of his age*, 2 vols. (Oxford, 1916).

Orme, Nicholas, *Education in the West of England 1066–1548* (Exeter, 1976).

Orme, Nicholas, 'Schools and schoolbooks', in Hellinga, Lotte, and Trapp, J. B. (ed.), *The Cambridge History of the Book in Britain*, III (Cambridge, 1999), pp. 449–469.

Ovid: Deferrari, Roy J., Barry, Sister M. Inviolata, and McGuire, Martin R. P. (eds.), *A Concordance of Ovid* (Washington, 1939).

Pennington, Robert R., *Stannary Law: a history of the mining law of Devon and Cornwall* (Newton Abbot, 1973).

Pevsner, Nikolaus, and Cherry, Bridget, *The Buildings of England: Devon*, 2nd edition (London, 1989).

Pollard, A. W., and Redgrave, G. R., *A Short-title Catalogue of Books Printed in England, Scotland and Ireland, and of English Books Printed Abroad 1475–1640*, 2nd edition, revised and enlarged by W. A. Jackson, F. S. Ferguson and Katharine F. Pantzer, 3 vols. (London, 1976–1991).

Power, Eileen, *The Goodman of Paris: a treatise on moral and domestic economy by a citizen of Paris, c.1393 (The Menagier of Paris)* (London, 1928).

Prince, John, *The Worthies of Devon* (London, 1810).

Public Records: *Index of Inquisitions Post Mortem*, vol. I, Henry VIII to Philip and Mary, Lists and Indexes vol. XXIII (1907).

Record Commissioners, *Calendarium Inquisitionum Post Mortem sive Escaetarum*, vol. 4 (1828).

Ransom, Bill, *A History of Ilsington* (Chichester, 2005).

Reichel, Revd Oswald J., 'The earlier sections of Testa de Nevill relating to Devon done into English', *Transactions of the Devonshire Association*, 37 (1905), pp. 410–456.

Reichel, Revd Oswald J., and others (eds.), *Devon Feet of Fines*, 2 vols, Devon and Cornwall Record Society (1912, 1939).

Reichel, Revd Oswald J., 'The manor and hundred of Crediton', *Transactions of the Devonshire Association*, 54 (1923), pp. 146–181.

Reynes: see Louis.

Risdon, Tristram (d. 1640), *The Chorographical Description or Survey of the County of Devon* (London, 1811).

Rose-Troup, Frances, *The Western Rebellion 1549, an account of the insurrection in Devon and Cornwall against Religious Innovation* (London, 1913).

Rose-Troup, Frances, 'The new Edgar charter and the South Hams', *Transactions of the Devonshire Association*, vol. 61 (1929), pp. 249–280.

Rose-Troup, Frances, 'Anglo-Saxon Charter of Brentford (Brampford)', *Transactions of the Devonshire Association*, 70 (1938), pp. 253–276.

Ryan, William Granger (ed.), *The Golden Legend of Jacobus de Voragine* (Princeton and Chichester, 1993).

Rylands, John Paul, *The Visitation of Cheshire in the year 1580 (with additions from 1566, 1533 and 1591)*, Publications of the Harleian Society, 18 (1882).

Rylands, John Paul, *Pedigrees made at the Visitation of Cheshire 1613* (ed. Sir George J. Armytage and J. P. Rylands), Lancashire and Cheshire Records Society, 58 (Manchester, 1909).

Shrewsbury, J. F. D., *A History of Bubonic Plague in the British Isles* (Cambridge, 1970).

Slack, Paul, *The Impact of Plague in Tudor and Stuart England* (London, Boston, Melbourne and Henley, 1985).

Statutes of the Realm, Record Commissioners (1810).

Stoate, T. L. (ed.), *Devon Lay Subsidy Rolls, 1524–7* (Bristol 1979).

Stoate, T. L. (ed.), *Devon Taxes 1581–1660* (Bristol, 1988).

Strutt, Joseph, *The Sports and Pastimes of the People of England* (London, 1898).

Taverner, Richard, *Erasmus, Desiderius: Adagia English. Proverbs*

or adages gathered out of the Chiliades and Englished. Facsimile
introduced by DeWitt T. Starnes (Delmar, New York, 1956).

Taverner, Richard, *Flores, aliquot sententarium ex variis collecti
scriptoribus: the Flowers of Sencies Englished by R. Taverner*
(1540).

Thorn, Caroline and Frank (eds.), *Domesday Book* (general ed. John
Morris), vol. 9: *Devon*, 2 vols. (Chichester, 1985).

Tilley, M. P., *Dictionary of the Proverbs in England in the Sixteenth
and Seventeenth Centuries* (Ann Arbor, 1950).

Tingey, J. C., *Calendar of Devon Deeds Enrolled in Pursuance of
the Statute 21 Henry VIII*, 4 vols. (Devon and Cornwall Record
Society, 1930, typescript, WSL and elsewhere).

Udall, Nicholas, *Apothegms first gathered by Erasmus* (1564; Boston,
1877)

Venn, Major T. W., *Crediton alias Critton alias Kirton and hereabouts*,
duplicated typescript, 2 vols (c. 1955-61) at WSL.

Vivian, Lt.Col. J. L., *The Visitations of the County of Devon
comprising the Heralds' Visitations of 1531, 1564 and 1620*,
including additions (Exeter, 1895).

Vowel, John, alias Hoker, *The Description of the Citie of Exeter*,
transcribed and ed. Walter J. Harte, J. W. Schopp, and H. Tapley-
Soper, 3 vols. (Devon and Cornwall Record Society, 1919–1947).

Westcote, Thomas, *A View of Devonshire in MDCXXXI with a
Pedigree of its Gentry*, ed. George Oliver and Pitman Jones (Exeter,
1845).

White, Beatrice, (ed.), *The Vulgaria of John Stanbridge and the
Vulgaria of Robert Whittinton*, Early English Text Society, O.S.
187 (1932).

Whytford: *see* Hogg.

Worth, R. Hansford, 'The tenants and commoners of Dartmoor',
Transactions of the Devonshire Association, 76 (1944), pp. 187–
214.

Worthy, Charles, *Ashburton and its Neighbourhood, or the Antiquities
and History of the Borough of Ashburton* (Ashburton, 1875).

Worthy, Charles, *Devonshire Parishes or the antiquities, heraldry
and family history of twenty eight parishes in the Archdeaconry of
Totnes*, 2 vols. (Exeter and London, 1887, 1889).

Wright, Thomas, *Anglo-Saxon and Old English Vocabularies* (1884).

Wright, Thomas, *Dictionary of Obsolete and Provincial English*
(London, 1857).

Wright, T. (ed.), *The Book of the Knight of La Tour-Landry*, Early
English Text Society, O.S. 33 (1868).

INDEX OF NAMES

Variant spellings are not entered separately in the index if they would appear adjacent to the modern spelling. Forenames are also generally in modern form, though left in Furse's spelling if ambiguous. Furse often gives no forename, but if it can be established by research, it is given in brackets, if not, given as a dash. Places are in Devon unless otherwise specified.

INDEX OF SUBJECTS

DEVON AND CORNWALL RECORD SOCIETY PUBLICATIONS

The following New Series titles are obtainable from the Administrator, Devon and Cornwall Record Society, 7 The Close, Exeter EX1 1EZ

Unless otherwise indicated, prices are: £15.00 UK, £20.00 overseas (surface mail). All prices include p/p.

At joining, new members are offered volumes of the preceding 4 years at current subscription prices rather than the listed price.

Fully-paid members are offered a discount on volumes older than 5 years if the remaining stock exceeds 20: please enquire.

ISSN/ISBN 978-0-901853-

New Series

Extra Series
1   *Exeter Freemen 1266–1967*, edited by Margery M Rowe and
Andrew M Jackson, 1973. *£18.00 UK, £23.00 overseas* - 18
6

Shelf list of the Society's Collections, revised June 1986. *£2.30 UK,
£3.50 overseas.*
http://www.devon.gov.uk/library/locstudy/dcrs.html.

New Series out of print:
*1 Devon Monastic Lands: Calendar of Particulars for Grants 1536-
1558*, ed. Youings, 1955; *3 The Diocese of Exeter in 1821: vol. I
Cornwall*, ed. Cook, 1958; *5 The Cartulary of St Michael's Mount*,
ed. Hull, 1962; *8 The Cartulary of Canonsleigh Abbey*, calendared
& ed. London, 1965; *9 Benjamin Donn's Map of Devon 1765.* Intro.
Ravenhill, 1965; *11 Devon Inventories of the 16th & 17th Centuries*,
ed. Cash, 1966; *14 The Devonshire Lay Subsidy of 1332*, ed. Audrey
M Erskine, 1969; *7, 10, 13, 16, 18 The Register of Edmund Lacy,
Bishop of Exeter 1420–1455* (five volumes), ed. Dunstan, 1963–1972

*Extra Series out of print: Guide to the Parish and Non-Parochial
Registers of Devon and Cornwall 1538–1837,* compiled: Peskett,
1979 & supplement 1983